SOVIET STRATEGIC INITIATIVES

▲▼ **C. G. Jacobsen** *(Carl G.)*

SOVIET STRATEGIC INITIATIVES,

Challenge and Response

PRAEGER

PRAEGER SPECIAL STUDIES • PRAEGER SCIENTIFIC

Published in 1979 by Praeger Publishers
A Division of Holt, Rinehart and Winston/CBS, Inc.
383 Madison Avenue, New York, New York 10017 U.S.A.

© 1979 by Praeger Publishers

Library of Congress Catalog Number: 79-89850

9 038 987654321

Printed in the United States of America

ACKNOWLEDGMENTS

I am grateful to all those who offered advice and aid, some accepted, some not, but all appreciated.

I am especially indebted to D. R. Jones, Director of Nova Scotia's Russian Research Center, for research help that greatly facilitated the completion of the project; to Dr. Frank Trager, for editorial advice and assistance; to Harriet Fast Scott, Dr. W. F. Scott, and Peter Vigor, Director of Sandhurst's Soviet Studies Centre, for much appreciated moral and professional support; and to those Ottawa and Washington agencies that helped cover the costs of research. On a more general level Dr. John Holmes, Director of the Canadian Institute for International Affairs, and my father, Ambassador F. H. Jacobsen deserve credit for sustaining faith, for encouragements, and suggestions. Finally, to my family, thanks!

CONTENTS

LIST OF TABLE AND FIGURES

LIST OF ABBREVIATIONS

ABM	Anti-Ballistic Missile
AIJEX	Arctic Ice Joint Experiment
ASW	Anti-Submarine Warfare
BDM	The air-droppable version of the BMP
BMD	Ballistic Missile Defense
BMP	Combat vehicle & armoured personnel carrier
C-B	Chemical-Biological
CPSU	Communist Party of the Soviet Union
FIAT	Italian multinational, producer of aircraft, automobile et al.
FNL	National Front for the Liberation of Angola
G-I-UK	Greenland-Iceland-United Kingdom
GRU	Soviet Military Intelligence
ICBM	Intercontinental Ballistic Missile
IRBM	Intermediate-Range Ballistic Missile
KGB	State Security Committee
KOP	(Naval) vessels giving fire support
KVS	*Kommunist Vooruzhennykh Sil*
MAD	Mutual Assured Destruction
MG	Machine guns
MIG	Jets made by Soviet Mikoyan design bureau
MIRV	Multiple Independently Targeted Reentry Vehicles
MPLA	Movimento Popular de Libertação de Angola (Popular Movement for the Liberation of Angola)
MRB	Motor Rifle Brigade
MRBM	Medium-Range Ballistic Missile
MS	*Morskoi Sbornik*
MSE	*Mineral Sciences and Engineering*
MZ	*Mezhdunarodnaya Zhizn'*
NATO	North Atlantic Treaty Organization
NURS	Non-guided missiles (such as the Katiusha rockets)
PLO	Palestine Liberation Organization
PNE	Peaceful Nuclear Explosion
PTURS	Anti tank guided missiles
PVO	Protivovozdushnaia Oborona Strany
RCMP	Royal Canadian Mounted Police
SALT	Strategic Arms Limitation Talks
SLBM	Submarine-Launched Ballistic Missile
SSBN	Strategic Submarine Ballistic Missile
UNITA	União das Populações de Angola (National Union for the Total Liberation of Angola)
V-IZ	*Voenno-Istoricheskii Zhurnal*
VPO	*Vestnik Protivovozdushnoi Oborony*
VTOL	Vertical Take-Off and Landing (aircraft)

INTRODUCTION:
THE SOVIET UNION'S STRATEGIC POSTURE

This book examines Soviet strategy and doctrine, relating the evolving biases of Soviet strategic literature to the evidence of emerging capabilities and to the potentials of technological trends. The prejudices, predilections, and aspirations of Soviet strategic planners today serve to define the character and diversity of the action patterns they may pursue tomorrow. Major weapon systems can require a decade or more of development and testing. Decisions of the late 1970s dictate the options of the late 1980s, and perhaps even 1990s, just as decisions dating from the late 1950s and the turn of the decade dictated the strategic options and room for maneuver of the 1960s and early 1970s.

Most Western authors on defense issues have tended to be unaware of the scope and quality of relevant Soviet writing. It is only recently that good translations have begun to appear. The continuing gaps of awareness may be seen as a residue of the natural arrogance of an earlier era of unquestioned Western superiority. Today such lack of familiarity can only lead to indulgent complacency or paranoid overreaction, both equally dangerous.

The detrimental consequences of lack of exposure to the peculiarities of Soviet thinking are compounded by the human inclination to fall back on the premises and truths of the past. In the strategic arena we fret about the dangers of a hostile "first strike." Yet, the fact is that only fixed land-based forces are really vulnerable. Sea and air-based forces alone have awesome overkill potential. Furthermore, even land-based forces are less exposed than traditionally feared, partly because a truly coordinated strike poses almost insurmountable practical problems but perhaps more because of the recently acknowledged phenomenon of fratricide (whereby the first warhead explosion is itself likely to incapacitate the follow-up companion warheads required to insure destruction of a hardened target). In any case, lingering unease could always be overcome by conversion to mobile and hence less easily targetable missiles. In a similar vein we often discuss the G-I-UK (Greenland-Iceland-United Kingdom) bottleneck into the Atlantic as the place to try to intercept Soviet submarines headed west. This discussion echoes World War II aspirations against German U-boats, and it reflects the subsequent decades' transiting requirements of Soviet submarines with limited-range missiles. But newer Soviet submarines have intercontinental-range missiles which allow them to fire from protected home waters. Soviet pioneering of the technologies that have revolutionized Arctic accessibility has at the same time provided them with a novel capacity to operate and transit to the north of the danger zone.

The point is not that traditional areas of concern have become irrelevant. Certainly Moscow has explicitly acknowledged, appreciated, and indeed trumpeted the political advantages to be gained from perceptions of power shifts in its favor. It has always been acutely aware of the fact that military power in peacetime is only useful to the extent that it can be translated into political influence. But Moscow does appear persuaded that accruing advantages as concern some of the parameters of the strategic balance, while offsetting U.S. advantages in others, nevertheless can have only marginal impact on the military reality of "Mutual Assured Destruction," or MAD (the basic tenet of the balance, that both sides retain sufficient non-vulnerable kill capacity and, in fact, overkill capacity to guarantee the destruction of an attacker even after the absorption of a hostile first strike). Moscow has sought novel ways of circumventing the restrictions of the established balance, and these will be addressed in Chapter Two. For the longer-term future, however, it may be that greater importance should be attached to the extraordinary perseverance and funding commitment of the Soviet Union's innovative search for a viable means of ballistic missile defense. This search, aimed at negating the fundamental deterrent core of MAD, is receiving a rising flow of investment (as is the more belated but determined U.S. effort in the field) and will be the subject of analysis in Chapter One.

Moving away from what might be called the apex of the strategic equilibrium, it is clear that there exists a similar discrepancy between Western concerns and Soviet aspirations in the more conventional spheres of the balance of power. Western authors focus on the changing correlation of forces in the so-called Central Balance in Europe, and to a lesser extent in the European flank constellations involving Norway and Greece/Turkey. It is clear that past NATO superiority in Europe has been severely eroded, though the claim that it has been superceded by Warsaw Pact preeminence is open to considerable doubt and debate. This will also be dealt with in Chapter Two. But, again, while there is no question that Soviet forces in Europe continue to be upgraded in a determined manner, there is evidence that expectations remain limited to perceptions of offset and marginal utility. The greater change of the 1970s lay rather in a novel Soviet theoretical emphasis on the need to be able to engage, act, and react in areas distant from the homeland. The increasing volume of Soviet theory on interventionary-type warfare, with concomitant justifications and commitments, is analyzed towards the end of Chapter Two and in Chapter Three. Chapter Four looks at the literature on the physical means and tactics that are evolving and might be employed in distant interventionary locales. Chapter Five analyzes the long-range naval and air power projection capabilities now being acquired by the Soviet Union, its ability to establish and protect distant "lines of communications." The general question of Soviet air mobility and the uniqueness of the Soviet approach to this modus operandi is discussed in the section on air projection.

The final chapters look more specifically at the flanks that have received the greater attention, in theory and investment, in Moscow. These are, as indicated, not the immediate flanks of the European balance but rather the ultimate flanks of the high Arctic and the southern hemisphere. The Canadian Arctic and Angola may appear strange bedfellows, differing geographically, climatically, ethnically, and historically. Yet, the emergence of Soviet theory relevant to both point to the common denominator of location on flanks of ever increasing importance. Angola and the Canadian Arctic are both part of flanking potentials that may decisively affect future strategic balance calculations. They are interrelated and perhaps even interdependent in the grander scheme, as are the Spitzbergen-Kola problem complex and the "Canadian Basin" in its particular northern manifestation. Of the two flanks, pan-Arctica has the more narrowly military-strategic value. Southerly latitudes, on the other hand, are primarily associated with political-military rationales, with peacetime (and early-war phase) strategies. But they are joined as the mutually complementary halves of Moscow's evident persuasion that the most propitious venues for incremental strategic change in its favor now lie beyond the traditional geographic focuses of the balance.

Chapter Six analyzes the geopolitical and military restraints and temptations that have dictated and motivated the gradual extension of Moscow's interest sphere in the north. It charts the thrust of Soviet involvement and stake, from the prewar, primary emphasis on the perceived threat to Leningrad, through the postwar buildup of Murmansk-Kola into the single most vital strategic power complex in the Soviet Union, to the establishment of a major presence in pan-Arctica right up to Canada's northern extremities. Chapter Seven then discusses the wider amalgam of Soviet scientific and economic endeavors in the Arctic, the dynamism of its Arctic ocean and ocean floor wealth extraction programs. The Soviet definition of strategy, as transcending the purely military component of power and incorporating also a consideration of the potentials of economic and other elements, serves as a unifying theme.

The final chapter discusses Soviet activities, presence, and assertions of interest in "southern flank" areas. It analyzes the extent and character of the Soviet engagement in Angola in late 1975 and early 1976, and in Ethiopia during the first half of 1978. It charts the steadily growing Soviet capacity to intervene in distant conflicts, together with the parallel increase in Moscow's willingness to commit itself to action. The Soviet perception of circumstances that warrant intervention is discussed as is the Soviet perception of constraints.

Appendix A presents an in-depth analysis of Soviet military-party relations. It is included because it addresses a thematic question that implicitly permeates much of the text, a question fundamental to the whole field of "Soviet studies." Appendix B reviews Soviet China policy. Although peripheral to the main concerns of the present endeavor, there is evidence that "the China consideration" has influenced and affected Soviet southern flank initiatives. Soviet China policy today emphasizes containment. But military-political dispositions capable of containing China from the south also have ramifications for more southerly latitudes. A Soviet-Vietnamese alliance may have the primary purpose of alerting Peking to a two-front specter. But it also serves to buttress aspirations the partners may have further south.

This book does not pretend to present a comprehensive picture of the structures and complexities of the Soviet Armed Forces or of the multifaceted elements of Soviet defense preparations. For that the reader must turn elsewhere. The two case studies of Angolan and Ethiopian events are included because these were occasions of direct, unambiguous, and extensive Soviet military involvement in distant conflicts. They are presented as yardsticks of emerging capabilities, as milestones by which to measure the direction and impetus of change. They are expanded upon not for their intrinsic interest but because they cast the cold light of experience on the question of Soviet doctrine's practical grounding and potential.

The book's sole concern is to document and chart trends of import for the future, trends of theory, procurement, and inclination. It does not seek to dissect the status quo, nor does it toy with futurology. But by focusing on documentable trends, on ascertainable change, and on the aspirations and uncertainties that underlie and shape the patterns of change, the book does attempt to construct a more realistic spectrum of likely Soviet objectives and capabilities going into the final two decades of the century. The book tries to show what Soviet strategists believe will be possible and what is unattainable. It provides evidence of targets of opportunity and aspiration but also acknowledgments of restraints, both domestic and external. If the book proves useful in narrowing the scope for extremist prognoses of future Soviet capabilities and intentions and in facilitating the identification of credible scenarios then it will have served its purpose.

SOVIET STRATEGIC INITIATIVES

1

THE SOVIET UNION'S STRATEGIC POSTURE: THE SOVIET DRIVE FOR OFFSETTING STRATEGIC POWER

The late 1960s and 1970s saw increasing talk of how the world had become multi-polar. The rising aspirations and capabilities of Japan, China, and the European Common Market were seen to dilute the predominance of the traditional poles, Washington and Moscow. There is little doubt that this perception reflected economic, political, and ideological realities, but in a strictly military sense it was illusory. Militarily, the world was effectively uni-polar until the early 1960s. Overwhelming U.S. strategic superiority was manifest. It only really became bi-polar in about 1965, and it is likely to remain bi-polar through the 1980s, and perhaps beyond.[1]

The immediate postwar balance of power between the main antagonists was decisively lopsided. The United States could obliterate the Soviet Union; the Soviet Union could not strike at the U.S. homeland. Even after the Soviet development of the atomic and hydrogen bombs, Moscow remained basically emasculated due to the lack of any sure way of delivering the bombs onto U.S. territory. Moscow could threaten London or Paris, but in the contest of a final showdown these might be presumed to have been less vital to U.S. survival than Moscow, Leningrad, and Kiev were to the survival of the Soviet Union. By the early and mid-1950s, the Soviet Union had developed some intermediate-range bombers that could reach the United States on one-way missions. However, the kamikaze spirit has rarely been associated with the Slavic soul, except perhaps in revenge. Anyway, their penetration potential against Western defenses remained dubious.

The late 1950s development of the Intercontinental Ballistic Missile (ICBM) promised release from the straightjacket of ultimate inferiority. This was an era of considerable Soviet sabrerattling and the famous Khrushchevian boast that the Soviet Union could now shoot a fly out of the sky. But it was soon realized that early expectations as to the efficacy and effect of the missiles had been naive. The basic imbalance remained.

Early Soviet missiles were primitive and "first-generational." They were encumbered by significant "degradation factors," that is, faults that degraded from efficiency prognostications. A certain number would be incapacitated through manufacturing faults, others through storage, firing preparation, command and control, take-off, or in-flight faults. Some have calculated the composite of the degradational factors associated with first generational missiles to be so high that only ten percent or so could realistically be expected to land on target. The Soviet arsenal at the end of the decade numbered in the twenties. Thus, the Kennedy campaign's rhetoric about a missile gap was clearly politically inspired and highly misleading. Even under the most optimal of conditions Moscow could only expect to strike U.S. soil with a tiny fraction of the bombs that could be dropped on Soviet cities by U.S. bombers alone. The dramatic missile procurement program of the early Kennedy Administration did not correct the imbalance; rather, it temporarily exacerbated the real imbalance in favor of the United States.

Soviet inferiority was in fact even more marked than implied by the above. On the one hand, push-button readiness was a myth. Not only were early missiles primitive, so also were early types of missile fuels. It was only later that fuels were developed that could be stored in the missiles for longer periods, finally almost indefinitely. In those days they had to be constantly drained and refilled, with the practical result that missiles were normally left unfuelled. Second, safety precautions and command and control facilities and procedures were equally primitive. We now know that caution prevailed, with the net result that the missiles of the time would in fact have taken days to get off the ground. Finally, they were deployed above ground and not in protected silos. They were hence exceedingly vulnerable to hostile action.

This is one reason why this era was the most dangerous period since World War II, why Herman Kahn once exclaimed that it was an accident that an accident did not happen. In a crisis situation, had Moscow seen war as probable, it would have known that it would have to initiate it to have any prospect of reaching her adversary. There was a great temptation factor for the Soviet Union to strike first. There was an equal temptation factor for the United States to strike first. Washington knew that if it struck first it could probably insure U.S. immunity; if it waited, New York and Chicago might well be lost. The poor intelligence of the day increased the danger. There was the famous U.S. Strategic Air Command alert when nuclear armed bombers were sent off towards the Soviet Union only to be called back in the nick of time when it was learned that the radar-identified objects approaching over Canada were flocks of Canadian geese and not Soviet bomber squadrons, as originally presumed. For each such incident that was publicized there were a large number that were not.

Through the early 1960s, Soviet efforts were focused on securing the survivability of the forces available. Reinforced silos were constructed, and there were experiments with mobile missiles. The navy, which had been thought to have become obsolete with the advent of missiles, came rather to be seen as essential for their survival; a portion of the missile force was put to sea. Primitive Ballistic Missile Defense (BMD) systems were developed. Command and control procedures were greatly improved.

By the mid-1960s, Moscow had finally succeeded in developing a secure second strike force. This is a force sufficiently invulnerable that it could with confidence be expected to survive an enemy first strike and be available for use in a retaliatory strike. The dangerous, uncertainty-based temptation syndrome was no more. The Soviets had effected true, if limited, countervailing power. The remaining 1960s and early 1970s were taken up with the effort to match the wider panoply and resultant options flexibility of the U.S. arsenal.

The program initiated in 1961 to build a strategic navy with global reach was pursued with vigor. By 1970, emerging capabilities were demonstrated in the first worldwide exercise "Okean." By the mid-1970s one saw the initial deployment of the 4-5,000 mile "Delta" submarine-launched missiles; they could be fired from coastal waters secure from what was in any case the marginal anti-submarine warfare potential of NATO (submarines previously had to proceed to areas much closer to their designated targets, areas dominated by NATO [North Atlantic Treaty Organization]). And one saw the testing of the first of a series of Soviet "mini-carriers," small but potent carriers designed for vertical and short-takeoff and landing planes. The early 1970s also witnessed the development of an intermediate-range supersonic bomber with possible intercontinental potential and a considerable increase in long-range air transport and assault potentials.

There is one peculiarity of Soviet developmental efforts during these years that must be elaborated upon before we proceed to a consideration of the Strategic Arms Limitation Talks (SALT) negotiations and "detente." The early Soviet favoring of Ballistic Missile Defense concepts reflected their profound unease with Mutual Assured Destruction.[2] This concept, termed MAD by its U.S. detractors, lay at the core of the Kennedy, Johnson, Nixon, Ford, and Carter Administrations' approach to strategic realities. It decreed that mutual vulnerability effected through agreements to desist from defensive procurements would, by guaranteeing to each the unchallenged capacity to destroy the other, in effect prove the most efficacious deterrent, the best guarantee of peace. The contrary Soviet preference for "war survival," for an indigenous defense capacity, was given early expression. Soviet efforts to research and develop a BMD clearly dated to the development of first-generation ICBMs.

A prototype experimental BMD system was deployed around Leningrad from about 1961 to 1964. The latter year saw the construction of the first truly operational system around Moscow. Later improvements focused on the Moscow locale. By the mid-1960s it appeared that Soviet BMD technology had reached a level of some potency against the then current threat. A number of scientists were becoming convinced that the relative cost of defensive versus offensive system increments, the "cost-exchange ratio," was beginning to shift in favor of defense. Moscow's refusal to contemplate BMD restrictions during their preliminary SALT soundings with the Johnson Administration reflected both their theoretical predisposition and their confidence in their developing Anti-Ballistic Missile (AMB) potential.

The situation had changed by the late 1960s when the United States succeeded in developing Multiple Independently Targeted Reentry Vehicles (MIRVs). When formal SALT negotiations finally began, during the Nixon Administration (the earlier scheduled opening of talks had been suspended following the Soviet intervention in Czechoslovakia), it was Moscow's turn to advocate BMD restrictions. Later Soviet pronouncements and Soviet strategic literature drove home the point that Moscow had not and has not been converted to MAD as anything but a temporarily unavoidable consequence of the technological parameters of the day.[3] It also appears evident that the Soviet volte-face was not due to any excessive awe of U.S. BMD prospects (with its detractors' theoretical arguments bolstered first by continuing evidence of Soviet BMD predilections and later by scientific confirmation of changing cost-exchange ratios, the U.S. Government had finally proceeded with a tentative, limited BMD deployment program). Rather, the Soviet change reflected tactical recognition of the fact that the promised effectiveness of then current Soviet ABM technology was emasculated by the saturation potential of MIRVs. Furthermore, it reflected recognition of the prospect that MIRV would remain a U.S. preserve at least until the early 1970s, and that consequential Soviet MIRV deployment would await the mid and later 1970s. In other words, while the pioneering Soviet ABM technology appeared offset by the U.S. MIRV, the developing U.S. BMD retained promise due to the continuing Soviet dependence on single-warhead missiles.

SALT I, signed in 1972, placed quantitative limits on offensive and defensive missile systems. The offensive system limitations accorded Moscow *pro forma* superiority, reflecting the discrepancy between Moscow's preference for reliance on a dyadic mix of land and sea-based missiles and the United States' contrary prejudice for a "triad" of the two missile modes and a strategic air component; the missile booster advantage granted to the Soviet Union could be seen as roughly equivalent to the potential of U.S. air-borne elements. The quantitative limits furthermore appeared above projected deployment designs and thus nonrestrictive to military establishments increasingly oriented toward the pursuit of improvements rather through qualitative measures. There was, hence, military quiescence when the respective political leaderships found it politically opportune to cement detente perceptions with the appearance of a successful arms agreement. One rationale for Soviet support has been previously outlined. U.S. support flowed from similar calculations, once it became clear that offsetting Soviet MIRV capabilities were imminent.

But Moscow's acceptance of SALT's BMD accord was more complex. In part, as indicated, it sprang from its acknowledgment that present AMB technology had been negated for the superpower context by the advent of multiple-warhead technologies. It faced a situation in which BMD deployment extensions could result only in a futile exacerbation of political tensions, in that it would not only defy U.S. strategic preferences but could and surely would be effectively countered by the now more cost-effective U.S. offensive increments that would inevitably ensue. There ended the analogy with U.S. considerations. The Soviet Union was equally if not more motivated by a different realization, namely that the limited BMD already deployed sufficed to defend against existing and foreseeable third power "ultimate threat" potentials. One might note that the defense of the Moscow heartland against the third-power threat of perceived greatest potential, namely China, was augmented by a SALT-condoned Central Asian Anti-Ballistic Missile and radar testing range (a locale of significant promise in view of the projected flight paths of future Chinese ICBMs). It was of course only in late 1975 that the PRC reportedly deployed its first primitive ICBMs (the approximately 3500-mile range of the two missiles purportedly deployed was longer than that usually associated with Medium or Intermediate-Range Ballistic Missiles, MRBMs and IRBMs but shorter than the 8000-plus mile ranges of true ICBMs, ranges needed to cover U.S. territory); there appeared scant prospect of any PRC potential to penetrate even the existing modest Moscow BMD complex before well into the 1980s, and even that prospect was dubious. Maximum protection for Moscow was the crux. The second BMD deployment complex originally permitted soon came to be seen as expendable, as its realization could never do more than redirect hostile means from one area of secondary importance to another of like importance. It was a ready candidate when the powers once again felt the need to provide symbolic proof of the benefits of detente, in 1973, when SALT was amended so as to sanction only one operational site.

Yet BMD development had not been arrested. By restricting ABM deployment, SALT served to put its status into hiatus, but in this respect also it merely sanctified existing realities. One must go back to about 1967, when

Moscow arrived at three decisions. First, since developed ABM designs held too uncertain a promise against the new threat potential, additional deployments were deferred in favor of concentration on more research. This decision, to fund continued large-scale BMD research, testified eloquently to the depth of Moscow's commitment to "war survival" strategies, to its abiding dislike of deterrence dependence or "mutual assured destruction," and, finally, to the perseverence of considerable if less imminent expectations. The persistence of Moscow's striving for strategic defense capabilities was furthermore underlined by the second decision. Announced on the first of January 1968 and elaborated upon in November of the same year, it decreed that previously voluntary paramilitary training of the civilian populace was henceforth to be obligatory and that training should be extended to schoolchildren. There were a number of reasons for these directives and this increasing militarization of the civilian population; some tied in with efforts to insure against any lowering of military preparedness following 1967's reduction of conscription periods. But it would appear that an additional rationale was found in BMD obstacles and the desire to offset these to whatever extent possible through the further improvement of civil defense potentials. It is noteworthy that the subsequent years saw a significant increase in the already formidable availability of literature on the implications of nuclear/chemical/bacteriological war environments and advising on protective measures. Finally, the third decision of this period may be identified as increased financial priority to the quantitative and qualitative upgrading of the offensive arsenal. Thus, a consideration of the research and developmental lead time required for 1974's extensive Soviet MIRV tests indicates a dating of the original diversion of significant funds to the approximate time frame of 1966-67.

By the mid-1970s evidence had accumulated showing that the ongoing Soviet BMD research endeavors were accelerating, perhaps reflecting funds released by the success of the MIRV programs. There were numerous reports that Soviet testing was severely straining the spirit if not the letter of the rather amorphous research restrictions incorporated into SALT II. There were reports of new ABM models and of novel associated radar developments. There was, furthermore, some evidence of efforts directed towards BMD concepts dispensing with ABMs, that is, BMD concepts based rather on rapidly evolving laser and particle beam technologies.

Moscow has seen MAD as an unpalatable but technologically necessitated characteristic of the superpower balance. It resigned itself to MAD as an unavoidable byproduct of technological circumstance. But Moscow did not feel compelled to accept it as a characteristic of Soviet relations with other powers. BMD research was and is pursued vigorously. As previously suggested, one presumes that the requisite funding is authorized with some expectation that a degree of immunity against third powers can be perpetuated. The ultimate hope of relief from MAD requirements vis-à-vis the United States itself is also clearly not altogether absent. Emerging Soviet MIRV capabilities have made the Soviet

Union somewhat less loath to challenge the more dormant U.S. BMD research efforts.

The ultimate potential of BMD remains a matter of contention subject to significant debate within scientific circles. Though increasingly disputed, the U.S. scientific consensus is that really effective laser and particle beam BMD concepts still belong to a more distant future.[4] One might add that a unilateral breakthrough may in any case be unlikely due to the extraordinary tentacles and interpenetration of the superpowers' intelligence services.

The SALT II Treaty, said to be ready for signing in April 1979 (as this volume went to press), encapsuled the uncertain nature of Soviet-American relations heading into the 1980s. The treaty apparently did not address itself to either BMD or to the proliferation of "grey area" weapons technologies, of systems that could serve both local and strategic purposes. The treaty did entail a lowering of Soviet missile numbers, but the missiles in question were old and arguably redundant. The favored deployments and ambitions of both sides still appeared immune from cuts or restrictions. The military relevance of SALT II appeared as dubious as that of SALT I. The ardor of its advocates reflected the treaty's political importance. It was seen as a symbolic first step towards a possible reaffirmation of detente. The ardor of U.S. SALT II opponents, their long success in delaying its conclusion and their determination to thwart its ratification similarly reflected not on its military substance, but on starkly different attitudes to detente in gentral. Clearly more ambitious arms control (SALT III) would have to be preceded by a degree of political rapprochement or tolerance that was not at hand.

The Soviet Union has become a global superpower. It has built a power base commensurate with that of the United States and with its own self-perceived role and needs. The USSR has acquired the means to act and react on distant seas and shores. Yet, while it has negated U.S. predominance, it has not superseded it. Talk of superiority on the strategic arena is fatuous as long as MAD prevails as the balance's operative characteristic. The *only* weapons innovation on the horizon that might radically alter the fundamentals of the equilibrium is this highly questionable possibility of revolutionary total BMDs, BMDs that would probably rely on high energy potentials. But, as noted above, there are few scientists who expect such to evolve within the time frame addressed here.

Having rid themselves of the raison d'être underlying their erstwhile and sometimes paranoic inferiority complex, Soviet leaders have acquired a basic confidence not previously manifest. Hence the phenomenon of increased Jackson-Vanik pressure for Jewish emigration being accompanied by a decrease in actual emigration; hence Moscow's refusal to countenance the 1974 Congressionally imposed trade bill conditions. Soviet Union cannot afford such obvious humiliations. Its self-chosen image, bolstered by increasing confidence, demands "equality."

Yet equality can have various connotations. In the central superpower context it may be seen to demand moderation, to reflect limitations and constraints on the exercise of power (examples might be sought, for example, in the cautious Soviet policy toward Allende's Chile, or revolutionary Portugal or Iran[5]). But, on the periphery, either in areas of previously disproportionate U.S. influence or in areas previously free from superpower presence or interest, it might be seen to legitimize, justify, or fuel a more assertive stance. Examples such as Angola or Ethiopia and increased Soviet activities in the Indian Ocean and Arctic expanses come to mind.

While implicit rules of the game might be evolving as concerned certain arenas of international politics, it was apparent that neither the Soviet Union nor the international community at large had yet reconciled themselves to a *modus vivendi* accommodation of sometime conflicting interests.

NOTES

1. The evolution of postwar Soviet strategic concepts and capabilities (up to 1972) is elaborated upon in this author's *Soviet Strategy-Soviet Foreign Policy*, 2nd rev. ed. Robert MacLehose, (Glasgow: The University Press, 1974). See also, "Achievement of Strategic Parity," *International Perspectives* (January 1977) pp. 12–16, and "The Strategic Balance, U.S.-U.S.S.R.," *Co-existence* (November 1977) pp. 196–204.

2. For those wishing to pursue the data presented in this section, see "Ballistic Missile Defence: A Survey of the Historical Evolution of Soviet Concepts, Research and Deployment," in *Soviet Military Review Annual 1977* (Gulf Breeze, Fl.: Academic International, 1977) pp. 164–175.

3. Ibid.

4. The rupturing of lethargy, the increasing unease, and the consequent infusion of research funding on the U.S. side is documented in *Aviation Week and Space Technology*, October 2, 9, 16, 30, and November 6, 13, 1978.

It must be acknowledged that a certain exaggeration of Soviet efforts has served the interests of U.S. advocates of new defense technologies. But such distortion appears to be one of degree rather than essence. Soviet strategic literature offers ample confirmation of their inherent interest and prejudice.

5. Soviet anti-Shah propaganda only became consequential after the 1978 "revolution" had already gathered seemingly irreversible steam. The reticence in exploiting an obvious anti-U.S. potential may have been due to unease lest fundamentalist Islamic fervor infect neighboring Central Asian republics. Caucasian dependence on Iranian energy supplies added an economic deterrent. Moscow appeared to appreciate that the ouster of U.S. influence was not a zero-sum proposition and that the immediate gain could be offset by adverse future ramifications.

2

SOVIET OBJECTIVES FOR THE 1980S

In apparent recognition of the probability that her ambitious ballistic missile defense research aspirations would not come to fruition for some time, Moscow has sought venues for more immediate, if incremental, advantage, venues of promise for the 1980s.[1] Soviet deployments and doctrinal promulgations of the early and mid-1970s identify three foci. One lies in its impressive measures to upgrade the forward war-fighting potential of its forces in Europe. The second is found in increasing evidence that it has assigned an inter-war diplomacy and arbiter "withholding" mission to its naval strategic forces, a testimony to confidence and to a recognition of surplus capabilities. Finally, there has been a steady increase in theory and ability related to distant intervention, in the potential to initiate and react, to assert interests, and to protect clients and investments also in regions far from the homeland.

The third developmental trend, establishing and cementing the USSR as a truly global superpower, is the most novel and perhaps for that very reason the one least understood. The imperatives, ambitions, and restraints of Soviet doctrine and capacity in this sphere will provide the focal core of this study. Before pursuing and elucidating the variables of Soviet interventionary potential, however, some comment must be made on the other trends of consequence. Moscow clearly perceives the import of these closer-to-home trends as the necessary guarantor for the pursuit of more distant interests.[2]

THE CENTRAL BALANCE

The central balance of theater forces in Europe has, perhaps inevitably, always drawn the primary attention of Western defense correspondents. The mid-1970s saw increasingly alarmist reporting of Soviet and Warsaw Pact strengths in this arena in the popular press, in Western strategic literature, and in the statements of NATO spokesmen.[3] It became clear that Soviet forces in Europe had been and continued to be the beneficiary of impressive and innovative modernization programs.

Where the always quantitatively powerful Soviet air capacity had suffered from severe range and payload restrictions, the now emerging aircraft challenged notions of qualitative deficiencies. Where the potential of earlier models had been restricted to interception and limited ground support aspirations, newer models promised a previously unknown capacity for longer-range interdiction of enemy reserve, supply, and communication lines and for more sustained and aggressive ground support missions.[4] At the same time, much increased Soviet helicopter and air transport capability began to supplement the already formidable enemy rear disruption potential of the paratroop formations, with the more awesome prospect of airlifted leapfrogging motor rifle batallions, troops with more armor, more firepower, more staying power.[5]

Soviet armor potential saw equally arresting change. Whereas some Western observers extrapolating from the demonstrated efficacy of anti-tank missiles during the 1973 Middle East War had forecast the demise of this iron fist of Soviet forces in Europe,[6] the disconcerting trend has been to accelerate the speed of the punch, not to diminish its lethality.[7] Having researched, tested, and developed the missiles used in 1973, the Soviets were fully cognizant of the new technologies' import. The threat was recognized, although, interestingly, it was seen as less of a danger to the tank than to their unique BMP, the new more lightly armored tank companion, troop transporter, and anti-tank missile vehicle, and to its air-droppable cousin, the BDM.[8] Yet neither suffered production contractions.[9]

Part of the answer lay in Soviet expectations that a major conflict would involve nuclear and perhaps chemical-biological (C-B) weaponry, in the fact that Soviet tanks and BMPs had designed-in protection for nuclear/C-B environments, and that such environments would not be conducive to infantry anti-tank prospects.[10] The other part of the answer became evident with the deployment of large helicopter gunships capable of sweeping forward areas, together with evidence that Soviet armor training was not being constrained by caution but rather was imbued with the need for ever faster, precipitating mobility, more aggressive flexibility.[11]

The stress was on combined arms, combined central command, leapfrogging into the enemy rear, air and helicopter sweeping, and disruption of the enemy front and rear, followed by the vigorous advance of tank and anti-tank units for punch and envelopment.[12] Marshal Tukhachevsky, the Stalin purge victim who pioneered the concept of combining (paratroop) drops into the enemy rear with panzer-type hits and sweeps, a concept first appreciated by the invaders of 1941, would have been proud.[13] His every instinct would have approved the attempted circumvention of improved defenses not through resignation but through innovative search for countering movement, unanticipated speed, and imaginative advance.

Nevertheless, the Soviet force potential in Europe is not problem-free. First of all, total Soviet and Warsaw Pact personnel strengths in Europe are not that superior to U.S./NATO strengths, even if one accepts the larger disparity presented in the latter's estimates.[14] The disparity has certainly been greater in some earlier years. The point has been made that certain Warsaw Pact contingents might also be less than committed, less than reliable, for offensive designs.[15] There is in fact evidence that their contingency role is rear and logistical rather than front line.[16] It may additionally be relevant to point to manpower restrictions within the Soviet forces themselves. There are Far Eastern requirements, actual and potential, and there is the emerging squeeze of declining population growth rates, especially and most dramatically among the ethnic Russian 50 percent.[17] The Soviet forces will become more "Asian," a source of possible if by no means necessary instability.

Second, one ought to note the political resistance to defense increments that has become evident in most NATO member governments.[18] Fear perceptions are clearly not sufficiently universal to drown out alternative allotment pleas. Some are politically confident that a prosperous and relatively disunited Europe is more useful to Moscow as a source of technology, trade, and credits than a sullen, devastated, or occupied Europe could ever be. Some point to previous occasions of unrest in Eastern Europe and the "garrisoning" requirement that this has placed on Soviet forces (a point relevant also to total numbers considerations); they point to the disruption potential of alienation and disgruntlement demonstrated in 1968, in Paris and question both Soviet ability and will to sustain continental occupation.

Finally, Soviet military strength does not negate that of the West. Soviet helicopter gunship procurement was, after all, spurred by U.S. Viet Nam demonstrations of their utility and potential; the United States still has more helicopter gunships than does Moscow.[19] The West may have been surprised by the efficacy of anti-tank missiles in the Middle East, but subsequent frenzied allied developmental efforts have now come to fruition, quantitatively and qualitatively. Fear equations are sometimes misleading: NATO tank balance figures generally include Warsaw Pact reserve tanks but exclude NATO reserves; they ignore qualitative advantages that might offset quantitative deficiencies, and they ignore anti-tank means.[20] There are many who see current NATO potentials as sufficient, if wasteful and woefully coordinated due to lack of standardization, and who suggest that the problem, if any, lies in questionable will, not questionable capability.[21]

NATO superiority has been eroded, but it has not been superseded; the possibily shifting correlation of forces has been gradual, not precipitous.[22] The new lethality and mobility of Soviet forces might well sweep all or part of Europe, if all went according to plan. But battle tends to lead plans astray. The ifs are probably too weighty to be chanced in anything but dire emergency.

WITHHOLDING STRATEGY

This venue for change in Moscow's favor also concerns that dire emergency, warfighting and war survival. One needs to go back a few years. Traditional Soviet attitudes to withholding were negative, as evinced in their scathing treatments of Admiral Jellico's reticence after the battle of Jutland, and in their castigation of the British for their "doctrine of conserving forces."[23] This attitude changed in 1972 with Admiral Gorshkov's famous *Morskoi Sbornik* series. Gorshkov praised Jellico's recognition that the battle had served his purpose, that pursuit and destruction was unnecessary, that withheld power could serve the larger strategic purpose better than wasteful engagement.[24]

Gorshkov's reevaluation of the efficacy of withholding strategies took on special significance with his treatment of the navy's war-fighting role and mission. The navy's strategic power had been seen as wedded to that of the Strategic Rocket Troops; together they formed the essence of Soviet deterrence.[25] And for peacetime deterrence purposes they have remained wedded. But Gorshkov drew a line between peacetime and wartime functions,[26] a dichotomy echoed by then Minister of Defense Grechko and by subsequent Soviet writings.[27] When talking of combat initiation and wartime roles, the Strategic Rocket Troops retain pride of place, but now followed by all the other services, with the navy listed last. There was emphatically no slighting of the navy's strategic potential. Gorshkov placed a heavy premium on the navy's ability to strike at inland targets, highlighting both the premium and the flexibility of its potential by stressing the survivability of the strategic submarine force.[28] He asserted that supportive facilities now sufficed to guarantee its immunity.

Finally, the series placed a conclusive emphasis on the military-*political* roles of the navy, shying away quite dramatically from the earlier task of combatting the enemy fleet. Part of the answer lay in recognition of the dubiousness of that aspiration. Gorshkov had in fact always been sceptical of anti-submarine warfare (ASW) potentials. As he noted in 1972, the World War II German U-boat campaign had long defied personnel odds of 100 to 1 in favor of Allied ASW efforts; he furthermore claimed that postwar technological development entailed a further favoring of the submarines; and he ended by asserting that the Soviet Union now possessed the supporting surface and air umbrella the lack of which had been the ultimate determinant of German failure.[29] A later Soviet source indicated that the maximum attrition Moscow expected to be able to inflict on Western submarine forces was 15 percent.[30] That this task had for so long been preeminent, therefore, reflected less on offensive ASW aspirations, and more on the vital need for ASW defense for strategic submarines forced by the short range of their missiles to penetrate close to hostile shores. The early-1970s advent of the Delta-class submarine-launched ballistic missile (SLBM),[31] capable of striking U.S. territory from the safety of home waters, eliminated the need for projection and obviated the dangers associated with such projection.

In spite of the supporting logic of emerging means, some Western analysts remained leery of reading any categorical doctrinal departure or innovation into Gorshkov's sometimes obscure and allegorical prose of 1972.[32] But, as suggested, later evidence has supported those less reticent. In his 1974 *Navy Day* article, Gorshkov asserted, "Our Navy has always had two main tasks—combat against the enemy fleet and operations against the shore. But . . . now . . . the main fleet mission is coming to be operations against targets on land."[33] Gorshkov's early 1976 book returned to the same themes, now shorn of ambiguity:

> The introduction of nuclear weapons into the Navies of the Great Powers has appreciably enlarged the sphere for using Naval Forces against the shore. At first carrier aviation and then ballistic missiles launched from submarines determined a Navy's potential for making attacks on enemy territory. Naval operations against the shore have (now) assumed a significance in war that is new in principle. . . .
>
> In our day a Navy operating against the shore possesses the capability not only of accomplishing tasks leading to territorial changes, but also of directly influencing the course and outcome of war. As a result, naval operations against the shore have assumed dominance in armed combat at sea, and both the technical policy for building up the Navy and the development of naval art are subordinated to them. . . . Naval combat against the enemy fleet . . . has become a secondary task.[34]

The year 1976 brought emphatic testimony by prominent Soviet regime spokesmen to the effect that Gorshkov's writings are indeed to be equated with established Soviet naval doctrine.[35]

J. M. McConnell, of the (U.S.) Center for Naval Analyses, summarizes Gorshkov's ranking of contemporary Soviet Naval missions thus:

> the very first one . . . is the capability of supporting the U.S.S.R. in its direct military-political confrontation with the West, i.e. deterrence in peace and with-holding strategy in war—both military-political missions. But the second one he lists is the peacetime Naval diplomacy, also basically a military-political mission—what the Soviets call "protecting state interests on the world ocean." And as the third and last one he lists the capability of "successfully taking up the fight with the enemy's strong navy, repelling his strikes from the ocean."[36]

As concerns withholding strategy, one might well argue that a limited version had in fact always been in effect. The Soviet Navy's strategic fleet never followed the U.S. Navy's pattern of forward deployment.[37] Thus, there had always been a time lag of substance between its mobilization and its potential engagement. It always seemed confident of its capacity for surge deployment to firing locations, whether such deployment was to be attempted subsequent upon conflict initiation or at a later stage. The confidence clearly rested in part on the Soviet expectation that "ocean communications . . . will not play any vital role, especially as the major ports and naval bases of the belligerents will most probably have been destroyed by nuclear-missile strikes."[38] The apparent lack of concern about Western ASW efforts, say, in the favored chokepoint of the Greenland-Iceland-United Kingdom (G-I-UK) "gap," was hence based not only on technological scepticism regarding ambitious ASW schemes but also on the belief in a nuclear environment that would incapacitate the support facilities necessary to such schemes. One might finally mention yet another reason for confidence: through the late 1960s, Moscow had explored and charted Arctic floors, and Arctic phenomena; by the early 1970s, there could be little doubt of its ability to circumvent the G-I-UK gap by transitting to its north.[39]

Yet the doctrinal change of the 1970s, to a withholding strategy and a primal focus on "influencing the course and outcome of war" obviously extended, and in fact put a question mark to the finite nature of the time frame between mobilization and physical engagement.[40] This was further emphasized by the decision to exlude anti-communication assignments from the now relegated task of "combatting the enemy fleet," and instead include it in the overall mission of "operations against the shore," a change explicitly attributed to the navy's "ability to fulfill strategic tasks of an offensive nature."[41] "Combatting the enemy fleet" had of course been a time-pressure mission; the focus on "strategic tasks" had become a time-luxury mission. As the 1970s progressed, talk of counterforce-type targetting and missions, with their inherent demand for urgency, became the preserve of Strategic Rocket Troops; economic complex, industrial, and communication-base targetting became the preserve of the navy.

The withholding doctrine, presumably centered on the Delta submarine and missile, was not just a function of these missiles' peculiar (long-range) characteristics. It was also a function of confidence that home waters were in fact inviolable, and that was an assurance that rested on the culmination of a number of complementary development trends.

Emergent Soviet capacity for local sea control sufficed already at the opening of the 1970s to instill doubts about NATO's ability to penetrate the Norwegian Sea.[42] Since 1971, Soviet doctrinal statements have made it quite clear that they consider unquestioned local sea control to be a necessary adjunct to withholding aspirations: "Sea control on behalf of missile submarines is not a secondary but a 'main goal' along with strategic strike itself, and is to be carried out, using surface ships, aviation and general-purpose submarines, as 'the first and main tasks' from 'the very beginning of the war.'"[43] The one early question mark of the trilogy of means, aviation, was to see rapid improvement through the early 1970s. The northern testing of the first Soviet vertical take-off and landing (VTOL) carrier pointed to evolving sea-based potential.[44] In the meantime, the early assignment of the supersonic Backfire bomber to naval aviation served to improve dramatically the range and punch of shore-based cover.[45] Apart from the acquisition of VTOL technology, naval aviation was also a prominent beneficiary of the Soviet predilection for planes able to land and take off on or from roads and unprepared airstrips.[46] In an environment of strategic threat to fixed land bases this ability could prove consequential for survivability and confidence.

Finally, the emergence of pan-Arctica as a region of disproportionate Soviet knowledge and activity will of course continue to be of vital import for Soviet withholding aspirations, even if the insurance requirement for transitting appears diminished by current technological trends.[47] Complete or partial dominance of pan-Arctica extends the defense perimeter. It secures and expands the acreage of sea control upon which withheld force elements rely.

Nevertheless, while Soviet withholding doctrine does testify both to confidence and to recognition that "surplus" means are now available, and while they may have secured a favorable environment for the effectuating of the doctrine, this does not necessarily entail decisive advantage. The same constellation of confidence and surplus would appear to apply to the other side. Although protected by more extensive reaches of favored waters, waters controlled by its own or allied navies, the United States is now also procuring the insurance SLBM range that permits protected home water stationing. Moscow has long presumed (projected?) a U.S. intention to withhold part of its strategic arsenal from any initial exchange.[48] Once again, as with the balance in Europe, success—for withholding's ambition of inter-war bargaining and diplomacy leverage—would likely depend more on a possible disparity of wills than on a disparity of demonstrable force potentials.

"INTERVENTIONARY" DOCTRINE

The early and mid-1970s saw the publication of a number of Soviet statements evincing new-found appreciation of interventionary prospects in distant areas. The point of departure may have been provided by the 1971 Party Congress and by the emphasis with which General Secretary Brezhnev then reaffirmed Moscow's "duty" to oppose imperialist aggression and support wars of national liberation.[49]

The year 1972 witnessed two noteworthy developments. First, one of the premier Soviet strategic authors of the day, V. M. Kulish (in his book *Military Force and International Relations*) suggested that one might now conceive of purely military, secular rationales for interventionary designs. This had in fact been suggested earlier, but the ideological reevaluation hinted at by the suggestion had not then been followed up, as it was now to be. The point is that interventionary wars had traditionally been defined ideologically, as imperialist-

initiated ventures undertaken to assuage the sociopolitical contradictions inherent in capitalist societies, as evidence of capitalism's desperate need for cap-
tive markets, and therefore as policy options from which socialist states were
definitially excluded. Kulish's treatment, however, implied that Soviet society,
while presumed free from societal contradictions and the need to resolve them
through conflict, might nevertheless find reason to intervene in local conflict
situations; and the intervention need not be circumscribed to the just rendering
of aid to forces of national liberation. It might take the form of a physical Soviet force initiative:

> military support must be furnished to those nations fighting for their
> freedom. . . . The Soviet Union may require mobile and well trained
> and well equipped armed forces. . . . The actual situation may re-
> quire the Soviet Union to carry out measures aimed at restraining
> the aggressive acts of imperialism . . . expanding the scale of Soviet
> military presence and military assistance furnished by other socialist
> states are being viewed today as a very important factor in interna-
> tional relations.[50]

February of the same year saw the publication of the first of Fleet Admiral
Gorshkov's eleven-article series on "Navies in Peace and War," in *Morskoi
Sbornik*. The series proved arresting reading for a number of reasons (as noted
in the preceding section), not least its pervasive focus on the military-*political*
role of the navy. The military-political strategic mission, "deterrence in peace
and with-holding strategy in war," was now ranked first, followed by "peacetime naval diplomacy." The earlier priority item of "successfully taking up the
fight with the enemy's strong navy, repelling his strikes from the ocean" was
relegated to third. As McConnell has noted,

> Gorshkov differentiates between two tasks in peacetime naval
> diplomacy—one directly involving the security of the U.S.S.R. itself
> and its maritime frontiers, and the other involving Soviet state in-
> terests in the seas and in the third world. . . . The second task
> doesn't directly involve U.S.S.R. territory or Communist interests,
> but state interests, state economic interests in the seas—merchant
> marine, fishing fleet and especially the mineral resources of the sea
> water and seabed, . . . and Soviet state economic, political and mili-
> tary interests in non-communist countries of the third world. Gorsh-
> kov speaks of protecting state interests as an "especially important"
> task.[51]

Gorshkov furthermore emphasized that the navy was not merely a stand-
by protector of state interests but was itself an active instrument of state policy.[52]

Gorshkov's arguments were especially interesting in view of then Defense
Minister Grechko's May 1974 statement in *Voprosi Istorii KPSS*:

The external function of the Soviet state and its Armed Forces and of the other socialist countries and their armies has now been enriched with new content. . . . At the present stage the historic function of the Armed Forces is not restricted merely to their function in defending our Motherland and the other socialist countries. In its foreign policy activity the Soviet state actively purposefully opposes the export of counter-revolution and the policy of oppression, supports the national liberation struggle, and resolutely resists imperialistic aggression in whatever distant region of our planet it may appear.[53]

One recalls the carefully enunciated, traditional Soviet differentiations among different categories of war and hence different commitments, investments, and propensities to risk taking. Wars directly involving the socialist motherland were always associated with the most inexorable connotations; its "holiness," "sacredness," and "inviolability" were repeatedly invoked. Categories further down the scale, however, commanded lower levels of commitment. As concerned contingencies such as discussed by Grechko the theoretical Soviet policy stance had never been in doubt. But care had always been taken not to commit the Soviet Union to follow through with action policies of substance. Therein lay the novelty of Grechko's formulation. It suggested a degree of actual commitment that went well beyond what had been conveyed previously by Soviet spokesmen.

Brezhnev followed up with the following statement at the February 1976 Party Congress: "Our Party is rendering and will render support to peoples who are fighting for their freedom—we are acting as our revolutionary conscience and our communist convictions permit us."[54]

The increasingly assertive and confident rhetoric was accompanied by and presumably reflected the emergence of significantly improved long-range force projection capabilities. The dramatic improvement of Soviet long-range air capabilities since the mid-1960s, as well as the more visible and possibly even more dramatic improvement in Soviet distant ocean naval capabilities over the same years, will be discussed later. Suffice it to note here that the evolution of the requisite theory and capability has been accompanied by corresponding action patterns.

Kulish referred to the earlier forms of more assertive Soviet Third World behavior patterns in his previously mentioned 1972 book:

In some situations the very knowledge of a Soviet military presence in an area in which a conflict situation is developing may serve to restrain the imperialists and local reaction, prevent them from dealing out violence to the local populace and eliminate a threat to overall peace and international security. It is precisely this type of role that ships of the Soviet Navy are playing in the Mediterranean Sea.[55]

Or, as Gorshkov put it, the fleet is able "to a relatively greater degree than other branches of the Armed Forces to put pressure on potential opponents without direct use of its weapons."[56] Kulish's comment appears to relate particularly to the presence and posture of the Soviet squadron in Alexandria during the June War of 1967; its commander's initiative to thwart possible Israeli designs against the Suez Canal may be described as the first instance of Soviet coercive diplomacy in areas far from the homeland, certainly the first instance backed by credible force and reserve potential.

The subsequent expansion of Soviet fleet spatial activities—they established operational patterns in the Indian Ocean and the Caribbean in 1968, off West Africa in 1970—and of available physical hardware was accompanied by other incidents of muscle flexing. A listing of some of these will serve to illustrate the trend:[57] Yemen, 1967 (ferrying South Yemen troops from Aden around the coast to staging areas from which it is assumed they crossed the border to support the Dhofar rebels); Ghana, 1969 (when the appearance of a Soviet task force off the Ghanaian coast seems to have had a salutary effect in insuring the release of Soviet fishermen charged with illegal fishing in territorial waters); Somalia, 1970 (when an unsuccessful coup announced at the time of a Soviet port visit sparked a lengthy prolongation of a stay originally scheduled for only five days, a prolongation entailing consequential symbolic and possibly actual support for the regime in power); the West African patrol, first established in 1970 (in response to a Guinean plea to protect against repetition of that year's Portuguese raid on Conakry and other Guinean base refuges of the PAIGC Bissau rebels); Egypt, 1970 (when the Soviet Navy played a significant role in the transferral and maintenance of Soviet air defense contingents dispatched during the War of Attrition); Sierra Leone and Bangladesh, 1971 (in the case of Bangladesh one thinks of the prompt northward dispatch of the Soviet Indian Ocean squadron and the follow-up dispatch of additional Pacific Fleet units from Valdivostok in response to the westward movements of the U.S. Enterprise and other elements of the U.S. 7th Fleet); the reaction to U.S. bombing of Hanoi-Haiphong, 1972 (again, through the dispatch of Pacific Fleet units); the Persian Gulf crisis of 1973 (when a Soviet naval squadron and the naval commander-in-chief himself were sent to Iraq while the crisis was still unfolding, presumably to "protect state interests"); the October Middle East War of the same year (when Moscow provided extensive military and diplomatic support to the Arab cause while the conflict was still in progress, support ranging from the ferrying and escorting of Moroccan troops to Syria before the war to the final ultimatum to Washington which succeeded in spurring the U.S. pressure required to stop Israel from proceeding with her West Bank thrust). There were also other incidents, such as provided by the Soviet stance during the Lebanese and Jordanian crisis of 1970, during the Libyan revolution, or for example, at the time of the North Korean seizure of the Pueblo.

Regular Soviet air reconnaissance of the South Atlantic, out of Conakry, had been established by 1973.[58] By the mid-1970s, the Soviet Navy had acquired access to the repair and provisioning facilities of a number of Indian Ocean ports.[59] They were constructing their second base-type complex in Somalia. And, on the other side of Africa, the rebels' success in Bissau saw what had originated as a temporary, task-oriented Soviet presence evolve into more permanent-looking patrol activity.

By 1975, in Angola, Moscow proved willing and able to render decisive financial, material, and advisory assistance to the MPLA in its struggle against its more narrowly tribal-based, but Western-backed rivals, the FNL and UNITA. And when South African intervention threatened to tip the scales against the popular movement (with at least a measure of U.S. encouragement, according to sources close to the South African government),[60] Moscow responded by sponsoring and supporting the ultimately successful Cuban counter-intervention (the sequence emerges from South African testimony that their first encounter with Cuban troops occurred towards the end of their northward coastal thrust, just south of Luanda).[61] The many facets of Soviet Angola policy are treated elsewhere.[62] But some points warrant mention in this context.

The first point relates to the uniqueness of the Angolan situation, and hence to the fact that extrapolation from these events may prove hazardous. The apparently dynamic and forceful Soviet policy in reality held scant risk. On the one hand, its purposeful support for the MPLA through the years of anti-colonialist struggle lent its continued support an air of legitimacy in the eyes of most black African commentators,[63] whereas U.S. intentions could all too easily be made to look suspect in view of past U.S. support for the colonial regime. On the other hand, the post-Vietnam/Watergate mood of the U.S. Congress appeared from the beginning to rule out the scale of U.S. interventionary assistance that would be required to secure FNL/UNITA victory. The perceived "proxy" South African intervention and the apparent U.S. quasi-alliance with the "Number One Enemy" (as Pretoria is known through most of the continent) served to reinforce and exacerbate the image conjured up by Washington's erstwhile support for the "fascist" Salazar.[64] The United States found itself in the same dilemma as the People's Republic of China, of appearing to base policy decisions solely on anti-Soviet criteria with little if any regard for African sensibilities. The dilemma was perhaps more embarrassing to Peking since the FNL, which Peking also chose to support, was not only the anti-MPLA faction with the least "national" support but was indubitably the least "progressive" of the alternative movements and the one generally recognized as the main recipient of C.I.A. aid; even the PRC's staunchest African friends, Tanzania and Mozambique, felt compelled to support the MPLA. The denouement was significant. Peking found herself obliged to withdraw from the arena, as did the State Department's foremost Africa expert, Nathaniel Davies, who resigned. Washington felt compelled to opoose the MPLA,[65] thus insuring a degree of MPLA indebtedness to Moscow that might not otherwise have ensued, yet the United States was unable to pursue the requisite policy actions. Black Africa was alienated, yet Luanda was not secured from Soviet influence; it was a neither/nor cul de sac.

Soviet policy in Angola was impressive for its determination.[66] It provided vivid testimony of a rather impressive long-range deployment capability. The Soviet Union and its allies had initiated and maintained a coordinated air and sea lift of personnel and equipment from Cuba and a motley variety of Mediterranean, Black Sea, and East European ports.[67] Nevertheless, the precedent was one of limited applicability or relevance.

The same comment must be made of Soviet aid to Ethiopia during the Ogaden War of early 1978. Here the scale of the Soviet air and sea lift and the quantity and quality of the supplied arsenal (the most modern tanks, helicopter gunships, and so on) was even more impressive—as was required by the more potent capabilities of the new adversary—and so was the crushing air-lift and tank mobility that retook Jigjiga. Yet again the intervention was protected by a fortuitous environment. Because of the OAU's sanctifying of the principle of nonviolability of established borders, overt U.S. assistance to the *pro forma* aggressor, namely Somalia, was politically impossible. Washington's countering potential was stymied by the fact that its own African allies felt compelled to condone a Soviet/Cuban intervention defined as defending Ethiopia's territorial integrity.

In coming months or years Rhodesia and southern Africa may provide similarly conducive circumstances to oil Soviet-Cuban interventionary designs. U.S. policy options are again constrained by the context's racial imperatives, by the perceived greater moral imperative ("anti-racism") of Soviet-supported causes. China's options are again squeezed between its practical inability to supplant the Soviet role and the deleterious ideological consequences of opposing it.

Moscow's willingness to repeat this type of initiative in an area with regard to which U.S. policy options appear less restricted must remain open to considerable doubt. Yet the steadfastness of trends as concern capability does allow some scope for projection.

There is one other factor of relevance; the physical involvement of Soviet allies, especially East Germany,[68] and, most dramatically in scale and impact, Cuba.[69] Cuba's prominent involvement in the above-described conflict constellations is particularly interesting, the more so since it too frequently and in too facile a fashion has been disparaged by the epitaph "proxy." While Cuban interests appear complementary to Moscow's, they are also distinct. A number of independent motives propel Havana's actions: its cultural identification with Africa, as seen in its self-perception as an Afro-Latin society, the enduring Guevarist element of its ideological commitment which compels it towards an activist participation in presumed anti-colonial anti-imperialist struggles; the ideal-preserving and discontent-averting implications of the export of surplus expertise from a society saturated by the output of dramatically-extended educational opportunities to societies suffering from continued shortages; and, finally, the long-term implications of favored access to raw materials and processing prospects, such as conjured up by Angola. Soviet-Cuban interdependencies may have been decisive for Havana's African role so far. But the consequent increase in capabilities and confidence may give increased room to particular Cuban rationales. Thus, one could envisage future Cuban interventions either as an adjunct to Soviet interests or, conceivably, as independent phenomena (for example, in Latin America).

This teaser might in certain circumstances prove as discomforting to Moscow as it promises to be to Washington, and it may be too early to postulate the success that breeds assurance. African attrition of Cuba's sons and daughters could yet cause strains within Cuban society. Soviet policy councils still appear conservative and cautious to most. Past client relationships have all too often proved all too difficult to manipulate and control. The fact remains that U.S. interventionary capacity will not soon be negated; the United States is still able to call on more allies and "proxies" in more conflict permutations than is Moscow.[70] Nevertheless, the fact of approaching similar capacity for the Soviet Union is in itself startling. The differing dynamisms of the equation may also prove more weighty than suggested by a comparison restricted to actuality. As long as it lasts, the Soviet Union has furthermore found an extraordinarily effective procedural formula for intervention: Cuban troops in the front line, with their supplies and homeland guaranteed by Moscow. Cuban prominence produces a less fearful, less hostile reaction than would Soviet prominence. One might hazard that even a successful U.S. counter-intervention against a "Cuban" initiative in certain circumstances could prove pyrrhic and self-defeating: the Goliath-David propaganda potential promises glory even to a "defeated" Cuban force.

With the 1980s approaching, the Central European front echoed earlier decades. On the strategic front, however, Moscow had gone beyond the securing of offsetting power, and proceeded with programs motivated by at least a limited hope of advantage. As concerns distant power projection, Moscow has negated earlier U.S. military impunity in this field, thereby changing the fundamental parameters of global politics. Distant Soviet commitments have proven credible; Soviet protection has been shown to be a realistic alternative. Soviet policy choices for the 1980s are no longer restricted to the defensive, reactive sphere but allow rather for initiative and assertion. Moscow's choice in calibrating continued restraints and new muscle will be a prominent determinant of both world atmospherics and world realities. The United States and NATO retain their longer-established claim to that status, but the new actor has negated their license of uniqueness and hence altered the rules of the game. Where the USSR had previously been a regional superpower, it was now emerging for the first time as a truly global power, with the flexibility of policy options such a description connotes.

NOTES

1. For Soviet BMD aspirations, see this author's "Ballistic Missile Defence: A Survey of the Historical Evolution of Soviet Concepts, Research and Deployment," in *1977 Soviet Military Review Annual* (Gulf Breeze, Fl: Academic International, 1977) pp. 164–75; and "Soviet Strategic Capabilities: The Superpower 'Balance'," in *Current History*, October 1977, p. 97–99, cont. p. 134–36; see also Chapter One.

2. Greater Soviet freedom to pursue distant interests and commitments are explicitly attributed to the "changing correlation of forces." See, for example, article by E. Rybkin in *Voenno-istoricheskii Zhurnal*, no. 1 (1977); (hereafter referred to as *VZ*); the article by Nikitin and Khalipov in *Vestnik Protivovozdushnoi Oborony*, no. 1 (1977); (hereafter referred to as *VPO*); or that by Kramar in *Morskoi Sbornik*, no. 1 (1974); (hereafter referred to as *MS*). Yet other sources are cited below.

3. NATO Conference communiques of the period abounded with alarmist rhetoric and statistics. See, for example, *Aviation Week and Space Technology* report, May 23, 1977; for scholarly analyses, see, for example, John Erickson's "Soviet Military Power," *Strategic Review*, no. 19 (1973); and Colin Gray's "Deterrence and Defence in Europe," *(RUSI) Journal of the Royal United Services Institute for Defence Studies*, December 1974.

4. See Robert P. Berman's *Soviet Air Power in Transition*, Studies in Defense Policy (Washington, D.C.: Brookings Institution, 1978); and "Soviet Aerospace Almanac 1978," *Air Force*, March 1978.

5. *Air Force*, March 1978; also Major Bramlett's "Soviet Airmobility: An Overview," and Graham Turbiville's "A Soviet View of Helicopter Assault Operations," *Military Review*, January 1977, and October 1975, respectively; for an early, trend-setting Soviet source, see Lyotov and Sagaydak's *Motostrel Kovyi Batal'on v Takticheskom Vozdushnom Desante* (Moscow: Voenizdat, 1967); for later Soviet writings, see below.

6. Colonel Atkeson, "Is The Soviet Army Obsolete?" *Army*, May 1974, is illustrative.

7. P. A. Karber, "The Soviet Anti-Tank Debate," *Military Review* (November 1976). See, also, General Bukharenko, in *VV*, November 1975, and below.

8. "Soviet Anti-tank Debate," *Voennyi Vestnik* (November 1975); see also discussion by John Erickson, "Trends in the Soviet Combined Arms Concept," *Strategic Review* (Winter 1977).

9. *The Military Balance 1977–78*, International Institute of Strategic Studies, (IISS), London, England, Fall, 1977.

10. See C. G. Jacobsen, "A Response," printed in the same *Army*, May 1974, issue that featured Atkeson's above-mentioned article; see also Savkin, in *VV* March 1974, and Pishakov and Kirpach, in *VV*, June 1975. (H. Fast Scott first alerted the author of these sources).

11. Bukharenko, in *VV*, no. 11 (1975). Note also, for example, I. Tikhomirov and A. Panasenko, *VV*, no. 2 (1975).

12. See Bramlett, "Soviet Airmobility," Turbiville, "Helicopter Assault," and Karber, "Soviet Anti-tank." See also General of the Army Kulikov, in *Kommunist*, May, 1976.

13. A. Parry, "Tukhachevski: Ahead of his Time," and H. Matson, "Tukhachevsky: Dynamic Revolutionary," in *Military Review*, March 1978, and May 1969, respectively.

14. For a review of arms negotiations pertaining to the balance in Europe, see C. G. Jacobsen, "SALT, Mutual and Balanced Force Reductions (MBFR): Soviet Perspectives on Security and Arms Negotiation," postscript to *Soviet Strategy–Soviet Foreign Policy*. Note also that the new (June 1978) Soviet proposals to the M(B)FR negotiations hinted at willingness to accept *pro forma* parity; for Western figure consensus, see annual issues of *The Military Balance*.

15. A forthcoming book by Dale Herspring of the U.S. State Department, now assigned to Moscow as military-political officer, elaborates on the considerations that underlie this argument. See also Herspring and Volgyes, "Towards a Conceptualization of Political Reliability in the East European Warsaw Pact Armies" *Armed Forces and Society.*

16. This was most definitely the pattern of the Warsaw Pact intervention into Czechoslovakia in 1968. See also Herspring and Volgyes, "Conceptualization."

17. T. Rokowska-Harmstone, "Ethnicity in the Soviet Union," *Annals of the American Academy of Political and Social Sciences*, September 1977. (Note her quote from Suslov's article in *Kommunist*, January 1972.)

18. The mid and later 1970s saw perennial U.S. pressure on its NATO partners for increased commitments. Yet, even when a concensus was procured for three percent increments, it was clear that a number of allied governments were dragging and would continue to drag their feet.

19. *The Military Balance 1977-79*, IISS, Fall 1978, p. 8.

20. Ibid; see also Jacobsen, "SALT: MBFR" (especially quotes from F. S. Wyle).

21. R. W. Komer, "Treating NATO's Self-inflicted Wound," *Foreign Policy* (Winter 1973-74); and see Canby, *Foreign Policy* (Fall 1972).

22. *The Military Balance 1977-78.*

23. Admiral Belli typified prevailing attitudes in his article in N. B. Pavlovich, ed., *Flot v Pervoi Mirovoi Voine* (Moscow: Voenizdat, 1974), pp. 118-20. The author is indebted to J. M. McConnell of the U.S. Naval Analyses Center, for first drawing his attention to much of the evidence upon which this section is based.

24. Admiral Gorshkov, *MS*, no. 5, 1972.

25. This was first confirmed by Marshal Sokolovsky in the third, 1968, edition of his famed *Voennaia Strategia* [Soviet Military Strategy] (see p. 235 of Harriet Fast Scott's excellent 1971 Stanford Research Institute (SRI) translation).

26. See analysis by J. M. McConnell, in MccGwire and McDonnell, *Soviet Naval Influence* (New York: Praeger, 1977), pp. 577-78, 585-92.

27. Marshal Grechko, *Krasnaia Zvezda*, December 17, 1972; see also V. Tolubko, in *Sel'skaia Zhizn'*, February 23, 1973.

28. Admiral Gorshkov, *MS*, nos. 5, (especially p. 17) 9, 10, 11 (especially p. 26), 1972, and no. 2, 1973.

29. Ibid.

30. O. Shulman, *MS*, no. 8, 1976, indicates that "oslablenie," the chosen term in this case, entails the expectation of a 10-15 percent success rate. Note also G. A. Trofimenko's article in *S.Sh.A.*, no. 10, 1970 in which he asserted submarines to be "virtually invulnerable" (p. 26).

31. *The Military Balance 1972-73* and subsequent issues to 1977-78, trace the development.

32. Professor M. MccGwire, Dalhousie University, has been perhaps the foremost sceptic.

33. Admiral Gorshkov, *Pravda*, July 28, 1974. Note that Gorshkov here, as in later articles, such as his much-discussed December 1974 *Morskoi Sbornik* contribution, may talk of the need for "readiness," the ability to take the "initiative" and to engage in a sudden strike aimed at the attainment of "such a strategic objective as the destruction of the military-economic potential of the enemy," but he still studiously avoids discussion of time urgency in relation to the general outbreak of hostilities. Thus, the quotations relate to theoretical capability, "naval art," and not to current "doctrine," which dictates applicability; see also discussion in J. M. McConnell's "Military-Political Tasks of the Soviet Navy in War and Peace," *Soviet Oceans Development*, October 1976 (especially footnote 57).

34. S. G. Gorshkov, *Morskaya Moshch' Gosudarstva*, (Moscow: Voenizdat, 1976), p. 360. See also, for example, B. Makeev, *Morskoi Sbornik*, no. 2, 1977, especially p. 19.

35. Dr. Bogdanov, Deputy Director of the Academy of Sciences' Institute for the U.S.A. and Canada, is one such spokesman.

36. J. M. McConnell, "Soviet Coercive Naval Diplomacy, the Rules of the Game," (Talk given at Carleton University, Ottawa, April 5, 1976). The quotation is taken from this author's notes from the oral presentation.

37. See Norman Polmar's article in *Air Force*, March 1978; and Colin Gray, "Soviet Rocket Forces: Military Capability, Political Utility," ibid.

38. Translated by McConnell, in *Strategy and Missions of the Soviet Navy in the Year 2000*, Center for Naval Analyses Professional Paper no. 206, Center for Naval Analyses, Arlington, Virginia, November 1977. For the original, as well as other supporting quotes, see Filionov, Kharlamov, and Gorshkov, in *Morskoi Sbornik*, no. 3, 1965, pp. 39–41; no. 1, 1966, pp. 35–36, and no. 2, 1967, p. 18; Sokolovsky, *Voennaia Strategia*, p. 308; and *Istoriya Voennomorskogo Iskusstva*, (Moscow: Voenizdat, 1969), p. 540.

39. *Soviet Strategic Interests and Canada's Northern Sovereignty*, (Canadian) Department of National Defence ORAE Extra-Mural Paper no. 4, Ottawa, 1978.

40. Gorshkov, *Morskaya Moshch'*; McConnell, *Strategy and Missions*, traces the antecedents to today's doctrine. Note also A. Mikhailovsky, "The Tactical Aspect of Secrecy," *Strategic Review* (Winter 1975): 95: "In modern warfare success will be determined largely by surprise, unexpectedness of actions, and the conserving of one's forces until the attack is delivered." Note also increasingly frequent references, when talking of the navy, to "radical qualitative change" (L. I. Korzun, *Na Strazhe Mira i Sotsialisma* [Moscow: Znanie, 1978], p. 57); "new missions" (S. Gorshkov, *V-1Z*, no. 10, 1977); "new tasks" (A. Folkin, *MS*, no. 3, 1977); and "strategic missions that directly influence the course and outcome of a war" (B. Makeev, *MS*, no. 2, 1977).

41. Gorshkov, *Morskaya Moshch'*, pp. 360–61.

42. See *New York Times*, November 1, 1971.

43. McConnell, *Strategy and Missions*; his sources: Gorshkov, *Morskaya Moshch'* pp. 352–54, 374, 377, 380; and articles by Sokha, Kostev, Vlasov, and V'yunenko, in *MS*, no. 9, 1974, p. 28; no. 3, 1973, p. 40; no. 3, 1974, pp. 22, 27; no. 10, 1975, p. 22, respectively.

44. Polmar, *Air Force*, March 1978.

45. Ibid.

46. Ibid.

47. *Soviet Strategic Interests and Canada's Northern Sovereignty*.

48. See articles by Aleshkin and Erofeev, in *MS*, no. 1, 1972, (especially pp. 22, 89). The fact that Washington has chosen to put its developing long-range Trident missile aboard a submarine (also "Trident") designed for prolonged distant and deep deployment, while considered redundant by the many critics of the submarine, does at least testify to the extent of presumed immunity from Soviet ASW efficacy.

49. See the Novosti translation of Brezhnev's *Report to the Congress*, Pamphlet, Moscow: Novosti Press.

50. V. M. Kulish, *Military Force in International Relations* (Moscow: Mezhdunarodnie Otnoshenie, 1972), JPRS translation 58947, May 1973, p. 103.

51. McConnell, "Soviet Coercive Naval Diplomacy."

52. T. A. Neely, Jr., *S. G. Gorshkov, Red Star Rising at Sea* (U.S. Naval Institute, 1974), p. 120.

53. FBIS, 30 May 1974, emphasis added, as per W. F. Scott, in *Air Force Magazine*, March 1978.

54. See the Novosti title of Brezhnev's *Report to the Congress*, p. 12.

55. V. M. Kulish, *Military Force*, p. 103.

56. Translation by McConnell, in "Soviet Coercive Naval Diplomacy."

57. Oleg Smolansky, presented an admirable synopsis of some of these at the 1973 Maritime Seminar at Dalhousie University. See also Jacobsen, "Deterrence or Warfighting: The Soviet Military Posture and its Relevance to Soviet Concepts of Strategy," *Canadian-American Slavic Studies* (Spring 1975); or, for example, McConnell's above-cited exposition.

58. *New York Times*, December 6, 1973.

59. See P. F. Nugent, *The Soviet Navy in the Indian Ocean* (Master's thesis, School of International Affairs, Carleton University, 1976). The thesis's preparation was supervised by this author.

60. Reuter Report from Johannesburg citing S. A. Senator Denis Worrall (to the effect that Washington had given "certain assurances" to Pretoria before the South African government committed troops to Angola); *Ottawa Citizen*, February 19, 1976.

61. Sometime during the latter half of October; the original, more limited South African intervention, to "protect the Cunene Dam," had taken place by August 1975. See M. Marder's *Times-Post News Service* analysis, in the *Ottawa Citizen*, January 7, 1976; more recent British sources date the South African intervention to July 1975.

62. C. G. Jacobsen, "The Evolution of Soviet Theory and Capability Re-Intervention in Distant Areas," *Soviet Armed Forces Review Annual II* (Academic International, 1978, p. 351-363).

63. See, for example, *New York Times*, January 4, 1976, for detailed report on the attitudes of African states and African organizations.

64. Ibid.

65. Deputy Secretary of Defense R. Ellsworth presented a succinct summary of the relevant strategic perceptions in his February 3, 1976, U.S., Senate, Foreign Relations Committee, Subcommittee on Africa; or see, for example, Secretary of State Kissinger's January 29, 1976 testimony to the same subcommittee.

66. See, for example, *Pravda*, February 1, 1976, or *Tass*, February 7, 1976.

67. As regards the quantity and quality of weaponry supplied, see "Massive Soviet Shipments to Angola," *International Defence Review* 9, no. 1 (February 1976): 19-20.

68. Compare "Moscow's Helping Hands," *Time*, February 20, 1978, and "The Africa Korps," *Newsweek*, June 19, 1968, with *Pravda*, May 31, 1968.

69. "Africa/Cover Stories," *Time*, June 5, 1978, pp. 20-30.

70. Ibid., p. 21 (for map differentiating between "non-aligned," "Western influence," "French influence" and military presence, and "Soviet and Cuban influence" and military presence). Note also Iranian, Saudi, and Egyptian aid to Somalia during the Ogaden War. See also *Komsomol'skaya Pravda*, January 27, 1978; *New Times* (Moscow), February 2, 1978; *Pravda*, February 4, 1978; and *APN* (Soviet English-language News Agency) ('commentary'), April 19, 1978.

3

SOVIET INTERVENTION: WHY?

It has been established that the early 1970s saw the emergence and evolution of what can only be called a Soviet "doctrine of intervention."[1] By the mid-1970s, there was already a considerable body of Soviet literature on the topic. Also by the mid-1970s it was becoming clear that distant power projection capabilities, the wherewithal to implement doctrine, had developed apace; in Angola and Ethiopia the world had witnessed the first concrete expressions of the import and implications of emergent trends. The Soviet Union had acquired and was exercising the will and means to make its presence felt in areas where Western dominance previously had not been challenged.

The following analysis will draw on the most recent Soviet literature, mostly from the later 1970s, tracing the concepts and capabilities that are receiving primary attention in Moscow as the 1980s approach. The aim will be to present a comprehensive checklist of strengths and weaknesses, potentials and restraints, as perceived by Soviet authors in an effort to establish a more realistic understanding of the parameters that will affect Soviet action patterns in the 1980s. One cannot aspire to predict with certainty, yet an understanding of the dynamism of advantage and constraint is a contextual prerequisite to a properly calibrated response.

The analysis will first address the questions of motivation. Why does Moscow now consider certain interventionary designs possible, minimum-risk, when they had previously been considered too risky? Why does Moscow purportedly see certain interventionary designs as not only possible, but necessary and unavoidable? Why does it see no contradiction between these, on the one hand, and the aspirations of detente and "international relaxation of tensions" on the other? In Chapter Four the focus will then shift to recent writings on means, physical capabilities, and the tactics for their utilization.

At the heart of the Soviet world view lies the Leninist (and, to a degree, Clausewitzian)[2] tenet that

> the nature of the epoch, its contradictions and peculiarities . . . conditions the definite type and form of war and consequently, the character of each war and its essence will in one way or another express the characteristics of that epoch in which it broke out, was fought and terminated.[3]

Thus, in the epoch of imperialism wars were fought for material gain. In today's epoch, however, while imperialist aspirations remain, their license and impunity have been negated by the changing "correlation of forces" in the world, by the now countervailing power of the "socialist commonwealth." That power, and the correcting pendulum-swing dynamism of "national liberation," which it and it alone makes possible, are the differentiating factors of the present epoch. It is because the international "balance of forces has changed at the base in favour of socialism, to the detriment of capitalism" that we witness "successes in the class struggle . . . (and the) developing activity demonstrated by the progressive forces, growing out of the national-liberation movement."[4]

"Political realism" is said to be forcing "imperialist" leaders to desist from Cold War ventures.[5] Still, there remain inevitable contradictions between the opposing social systems, and imperialists have not foresworn their own aspirations.[6]

> Although the possibilities for aggressive actions by imperialism are limited, its nature remains as before . . . (in fact) recently the aggressive circles leading the capitalist states have significantly reactivated their militaristic subversive activity and tried to return the world to the days of the "cold war."[7]
>
> Western "forces of war and aggression . . . whip up the armaments race, (and) oppose the liquidation of fundamental international crises, by crudely interfering in the internal affairs of other lands, attempting to put down the struggle of peoples for liberty and democracy, and discredit policies of peaceful coexistence.[8]

Not only do the "forces of aggression and reaction" in the imperialist camp strive to sabotage detente and disarmament, so also does the present Peking regime. "The Chinese leadership acts as one with world reaction" in efforst to create an anti-Soviet front and create "hatred and hostility between peoples."[9] Maoism is defined as answering the "selfish interests of the Maoist leadership alone, who are ever more closely tied with the darkest forces of imperialist reaction in the battle against peace, democracy, and the national and social liberation of peoples."[10] Again and again, "China's new leadership . . .

ranges itself . . . with the most reactionary forces";[11] "China has joined the alliance."[12]

Soviet armed strength is described as having been and remaining the only bulwark against imperialist encroachments. In its infancy it was vital to the survival of the "Socialist Fatherland,"[13] while as yet an impotent bystander to the demise of even neighboring fellow travellers (such as Bela Kun in Hungary). Aid to foreign revolutionary aspirations was cramped by lack of means.[14] After World War II, however, growing Soviet might did suffice to defend the "conquests of socialism," first in Eastern Europe and then, gradually, further afield: "The defence of the conquests of socialism, this is not only a national, but also the most important international task of the land of socialism."[15] Or, as another author put it,

> The greatest merit of the Soviet state and its armed forces stands . . .
> in the fact that after the Second World War they did not permit im-
> perialist counterrevolution to burst into a number of countries in
> Europe, into Asian countries or into Cuba . . . they helped those coun-
> tries retain their revolutionary conquests and found and strengthen
> the position of socialism. This historical mission the army of the
> Soviet state is carrying out with honour at the present time.[16]

Great emphasis is placed on the growth of Soviet strength. The increased ability to provide aid is deliberately advertised: "In modern conditions the extent (of aid) has grown and the concrete forms of military aid on the part of the Soviet Union to many young developing states, which have taken the road of a deeper social-political transformation, have expanded."[17] It is pointed out that "this aid seriously restrains the reactionary forces of imperialism from crude interference in the affairs of developing countries and has acted to prevent direct acts of aggression against them."[18]

Furthermore, Soviet aid is painted as the "decisive" difference between success and failure.[19] Due to the

> deep change in the relationship of forces in the international arena.
> . . . The imperialists were not able to obtain victories in wars against
> the peoples of Algeria, the Yemen and Bangladesh. They were forced
> to seek to terminate the war in Viet Nam and at present are not able
> to suppress the liberation battle of the peoples of Africa and the
> Near East.[20]

Conversely, "the possibilities of victory for the progressive forces in national-liberation wars is growing. In this the all-sided aid of the U.S.S.R. and all lands of the socialist commonwealth to the struggling peoples is of decisive significance."[21] In fact, "it is impossible to conquer a people . . . on whose side stands the Soviet Union, all countries of the socialist commonwealth, and the progressive forces of the whole world."[22] The victory in Vietnam proved the "triumph of the effective and militant solidarity of the socialist countries."[23] It was "with massive assistance from the Soviet Union and other socialist countries . . . (that) the liberation struggle of the peoples of the Portuguese colonies was crowned with success."[24] Thus, in Angola, a "most important factor that guaranteed the victory of the . . . people was the all-sided help and support given Angola by the U.S.S.R. and other socialist countries."[25] With regard to Ethiopia, Moscow declared herself to be providing the "appropriate material and technical assistance to repulse the aggressor."[26]

Purported lies about self-serving Soviet motives[27] and frenetic Western attempts to subvert new-found independence[28] are cited as testimony and desperate reaction to Soviet steadfastness. In turn, of course, they render that steadfastness all the more vital:

> When the so-called "ideological component" of foreign policy . . . is stuffed with primitive anti-communism, the inevitable deviation from truth this causes leads to inability to assess realistically the complicated situations in a changing world, . . . the absurd accusations hurled at the Soviet Union, Cuba and other socialist countries of allegedly "destabilizing the situation" by siding . . . with the young states in the consolidation of their independence and in their sovereign right to follow the path of progress.[29]

Moscow describes Western claims that "Soviet armed forces are a weapon of communist expansion" as an "evil lie. The Soviet Armed Forces have never been used for aggressive purposes . . . only against those who infringe on the Soviet homeland, on its liberty and on the socialist conquest of the people."[30] Soviet military cooperation and support is said to be extended only upon request, "whenever Afro-Asian countries need them to achieve political independence or protect it from imperialist encroachments."[31] What the West labels "interference" is described as "nothing short of legitimate aid (to the victim of aggression), entirely in accord with elementary notions of right and justice."[32]

At the same time, the very fact that the ideological struggle has intensified, while of course due entirely to imperialist reaction and based on perverted premises, does serve to put yet a greater premium on Soviet steadfastness.[33] Imperialism's very reaction inevitably bared its baser instincts; it inevitably took the form of closer ties with reactionary and racist regimes.[34] Herein lies the crux. Not only is Soviet support vital to success, but increased Western support to *ancien régimes* and established privilege combined with Western encouragement of the divisive potential of minority nationalism and chauvinism ("divide and conquer"), in fact, make Soviet support vital to survival.[35]

Soviet stress on the import and steadfastness of their support for "just" causes was a necessary antidote to the legacy of the past, the accumulating historical record of occasions when their means and/or will had not sufficed.[36] Soviet protection lacked credibility and therefore held little pragmatic appeal.

The depth of the frustration and of the lesson shines through in the scorn poured on the "Maoists." Where Soviet aid persevered in its cause-orientation and finally became "decisive," Chinese frustration led rather to a scurrying for imperialist crumbs, revealing both the emasculated potential of Chinese means and the shallowness of "Maoist" commitment.[37]

The stress on Soviet effectiveness and on the uniqueness of this effectiveness has not only served to elbow the Chinese out from perceptions of ideological credibility and relevance. It has also served another purpose. One of Khrushchev's many depatures from Stalinist orthodoxy was his willingness to accept non-marxist nationalist movements as confreres. Their inherent anti-colonialism made for common ground against imperialism; the raising of their "social consciousness" could wait.[38] To an extent, the Khrushchevian formula was a recognition of weakness, as well as shrewdness, in that it implied both awareness of the advantages of the alliance and of the fact that the alliance could not be consummated without ideological compromise. Today, on the other hand, there is evidence that confidence and successfully demonstrated strength is leading at least to a limited reversal of the Khrushchevian compromise. Now Soviet strength is projected as self-sufficient and no longer in need of dubious alliances, while recent history is said to demonstrate imperialism's unwillingness to reconcile itself to the loss of dependencies, imperialism's continued intrigues and subversion, and the fact that only Soviet protection can succeed in thwarting such designs.[39]

The shoe is now seen to be on the other foot. Moscow no longer needs to swallow the same indignities as in the past[40] but can afford to be more selective. The recipients' greater need allows Moscow to be more insistent on congenial social goals. The only national-liberation movement that Moscow now cares for is one that can be defined as "a current of the world revolutionary process and an ally of the socialist community, it is increasingly siding itself with the forces of social progress."[41] It is pointed out that "our successes in the military sphere are successes aimed at defending and securing ourselves and our socialist friends."[42] The Soviet Union is willing to provide extensive aid, civilian, economic, and educational as well as military,[43] but only to people "upholding their independence and fighting against imperialist aggression."[44] This means not only in the domestic arena:

> Especially now echoes the Leninist definition, according to which
> to be an internationalist signifies to do "the maximum in one country for the development, support of and victory of the revolution in
> all countries." . . . This help may be expressed in a moral-political
> and in a material way, and in necessary cases also in military support
> for the toilers who are battling with imperialist aggression.[45]

Moscow has never seen any contradiction between support of such revolutionary movements and designs and the simultaneous pursuit of detente and peaceful coexistence. Before delving into the appropriate quotations, however, one must note a definitional and perceptual peculiarity. The Russian language does not have an exact equivalent of "detente," nor do the Soviets use that word. They tend rather to employ the term "razriadka," and the context in which they use the term makes it quite clear that they see razriadka/detente as an extension of peaceful coexistence. It portrays the defusion of the threat of general war in accordance with the recognition that such is likely to be rendered mutually suicidal by contemporary military realities but no amelioration of the basic conflict with the opposing social system. On the contrary, with the de-emphasis of war as a practical instrument of policy (at least as concerns the interaction of the main protagonists), the struggle will be intensified correspond-ingly on other planes, ideological, economic, and the like.[46] The only real dif-ference between razriadka and peaceful coexistence is that the former does not appear to be encumbered with the same definitional time constraints, although it does connote or allow for the possibility of sudden termination.

Moscow is adamant that detente does not and cannot entail "any obliga-tion to guarantee the social status quo in the world or to stop the processes of class and national liberation struggle."[47] Or, to use another formulation, "De-tente does not mean—and will never mean—a freezing of the social and political status quo in the world, or a halt to the anti-imperialist struggle . . . and against foreign intervention and repression."[48]

Soviet authors disclaim any intention to use detente as an instrument to "prod" these processes.[49] On the other hand, "the principle of coexistence . . . has nothing in common with class peace between exploiters and exploited, the colonialists and the victims of colonial oppression, or between the oppressors and the oppressed."[50] Thus, Western contentions that such acts as moral and material assistance to Angolan (or other) freedom fighters do not accord with the spirit of detente "only testifies to a false understanding of the meaning of detente, which never implied and cannot imply a free hand to aggressors."[51]

Moscow frankly admits that detente inherently provides favorable condi-tions for "the national-liberation process,"[52] allowing participants "to step up their efforts."[53] Detente is, after all, nothing but symbolic recognition of the reality and consequences of the "changing correlation of forces."[54] "What is detente, after all, in its global dimensions, if it is not a worldwide restructuring of international relations on the principles of a just and democratic peace?"[55]

Soviet writers pursue the point:

> It is precisely the U.S. that has demonstrated that most vulnerable area of its politics . . . in a number of regions, where the vestiges of colonialism are on the way out, they have found themselves not on the side of social change but on the side of the forces paddlling against the stream. . . . The important thing is never to lose sight of the fact that detente cannot serve as an excuse for reversing one's attitude to racialism, to the exploitation of Africa and other areas by

monopolies, to the acts of violence by mercenaries, and to encroachments on the sovereignty and integrity of the emergent states anywhere.[56]

The emphasized alignment with "natural justice" is central to the Soviet
posture. While asserting and stressing the decisiveness, resoluteness, and hence
reliability and attractiveness of its aid, Moscow is careful to ascribe to it the
motives of the angels, anti-racism and anti-colonialism in particular. If one looks
at the areas of explicit Soviet commitment, these two motherhood issues have
been at the forefront of Soviet involvement in the dissolving Portuguese colonial
empire, Guinea-Bissau, Mozambique, and Angola, as well as in its aid to "liberation" endeavors in Namibia, Rhodesia, and (still only putatively) South Africa.
In the other areas of assertive commitment, the justifying moral has been that of
"defending territorial integrity" against aggression, another issue that carries
motherhood connotations in contemporary Africa.[57] Where the issue has appeared purely ideological, as in opposition to "fascist" or "puppet" but nevertheless ensconced and established regimes, Moscow has been cautious to restrict
explicit support to the philosophical realm, couching support in terms of sympathy rather than commitment.[58]

Soviet interventions are said in no way to threaten detente, since they are
aimed only at the elimination of crude colonial relics which all but the most
obdurate of imperialists realize are beyond the pale of morality; the interventions do not strike at the true national interests of capitalist nations. The Soviet
Union is fighting only against the discredited aims of imperialism, "to eliminate
the remnants of the colonial system, against neo-colonialism, racism, apartheid
and Zionism."[59] "A durable peace cannot (after all) be ensured while there is
still colonialism, racism, discrimination and foreign domination."[60] While imperialist force inherently entails deprivations of liberty and democracy, due to
capitalism's intrinsic systemic need for ever wider, ever more exploitative spider-
webs of control, socialist initiatives are impelled by the contrary systemic imperative of equal justice.[61]

This propaganda posture and the careful tailoring of actions so as to conform of the posture has served a number of interrelated purposes. Its political
impact has cramped, minimized, and nearly emasculated the possibility of resollute U.S. opposition (a not immaterial consequence in view of persisting U.S.
physical potential). It has secured for Moscow the benevolent neutrality and
sometimes outright support of regimes which under any other circumstance
would have gravitated elsewhere.[62] It has procured a rare no-risk or minimum-
risk environment for the establishing of resoluteness and credibility. Moscow's
insistent stress on subscribing to formalistic legality, except when such is superseded by universally sanctioned moral imperatives, mirror its recognition both of
the uniqueness of the opportunity and of the fragility of the oiling environment.[63]

It should be noted at this point that the core of the oiling, or perhaps one should say peculiarly facilitating environment, namely, South African apartheid and continued Western tainting-by-association (through abiding historical and economic ties), is likely to persist well into the 1980s, and perhaps the 1990s. It might be relevant to point also to the apparently accelerating trend of less than dynamic and often all too obviously corrupt regimes turning to erstwhile colonial masters for protection.[64] It is not just that French military personnel today operate in more African countries than do those of Cuba; rather, the "colonialist" propaganda beacon lit by their presence could confer legitimacy on future interventionary, or subversive designs.[65] Whereas the "anti-communist" moral does not override formalistic legality and the related imperative of upholding national integrity, the motives of anti-colonialism and anti-racism do. This unquestioned fact of contemporary African perception and priority presents Soviet policy councils with a manipulable advantage of considerable consequence.

There is dynamic license potential in the perceptional flexibility of definitions of "colonialism" and "neocolonialism." Conversely, there is also interesting and possibly portentious blurring of the definitional parameters of "socialist," the regime category with automatic call on guaranteed Soviet armed forces protection. This category used to be narrowly circumscribed to Eastern European states, Mongolia, and (in those days of yore) China; later it was extended to include Cuba, Vietnam, and North Korea. The presumably deliberate vagueness of current usage suggests that some African and other nations may for de facto security purposes have become, or be in the process of becoming, part of the "socialist commonwealth" core.[66]

In conclusion, it should be mentioned that definitional ambiguities can be manipulated in various ways. There have been sceptical mutterings about darker Soviet motives, "new colonialism," and so on.[67] Nevertheless, it is equally clear that majority (U.N. and O.A.U.) opinion deems this charge unproven and therefore chooses to disregard it in favor of action against the "proven" wrongs and consequences of past colonialism and against the "proven" and ultimate cancer of apartheid.[68] The increased sensibility that past blunders have forced on Soviet policy making, the acquired sophistication and caution that smooth the edges of current Soviet assertiveness do give one reason to expect that Moscow's advantage may be perpetuated. (Although a sceptical historian might well insert that that very expectation would be bound to lead to its demise!)

Finally, the dynamism and "purity" that flow from Moscow's elastic ideological stance must of course be seen in conjunction with the dynamism associated with its recent assertion of distant "state interests" (a term of equally elastic definition, covering land as well as ocean contingencies), and its inherent right to protect them.[69] There is room for overlap between the stressed "socialist" character of national liberation and the consequent "international duty" of the Soviet Armed Forces to come to its "aid," and the sphere of "state interests." The measure of future Soviet success, and its permanence, is likely to mirror the degree to which Moscow proves able to paint the latter in the hues of the former—and to circumvent others' attempts to reverse the painting process.[70]

NOTES

1. See Chapter Two.

2. D. E. Davis and W. S. G. Kohn, "Lenin's Notebook on Clausewitz," in *1977 Soviet Armed Forces Review Annual*, ed. D. R. Jones (Academic International, 1977).

3. S. Tiushkevich, in *Voenno-Istoricheskii Zhurnal* no. 1 (1978): 8. Hereafter this journal will be referred to as *V-IZ*.

4. E. Nikitin and V. Khalipov, *Vestnik Protivovozdushnoi Oborony*, no. 2 (1976): 9. Hereafter this journal will be referred to as *VPD*.

5. A. Kramar, *Morskoi Sbornik*, no. 1 (1974): 11-15. Hereafter this journal will be referred to an *MS*.

6. Ibid.

7. Editorial, *Voennyi Vestnik*, no. 3 (1977): 4-5. Hereafter this journal will be referred to as *VV*.

8. V. Kulikov, *VPO*, no. 1 (1976): 13.

9. Transcript of speech by D. F. Ustinov, *Kommunist Vooruzhennykh Sil*, no. 5 (1978): 18. Hereafter this journal will be referred to as *KVS*.

10. N. Konstantinov, *KVS*, no. 5 (1978): 93.

11. See litany in Y. Tarabrun, "The National Liberation Movement: Problems and Prospects," *Mezhdunarodnaya Zhizn'* no. 1 (1978). Hereafter this journal will be referred to as *MZ*.

12. *New Times*, February 2, 1978.

13. A. A. Epishev, *KPSS—Organizator i Rukovoditel' Vooruzhennykh Sil* (Moscow: Znanie, December 1977), p. 63.

14. Pre-World War II "internationalist aid" is surveyed in M. Trush, *VPO*, no. 4 (1976): 21-22; and M. Filimoshin, *V-IZ*, no. 10 (1977): 82-87. See also N. G. Kuznetsov, *Nakanune* (Moscow: Voenizdat, 1966), especially his discussion of the Spanish Civil War and Soviet supply problems of the time. Note also testimony in M. Djilas, *Conversations with Stalin* (London: Pelican, 1969), p. 141.

15. M. Trush, *VPO*, p. 21.

16. B. Orekhov, *VV*, no. 12 (1976): 28-29.

17. Ibid.

18. Ibid.

19. Ibid.

20. G. Malinovsky, *V-IZ*, no. 5 (1974): 97-98; see also V. A. Golikov, *Soviet Union: Political and Economic Reference Book* (Moscow: Progress, 1977), p. 526.

21. G. Malinovsky, *V-IZ*. The Soviet terms are "vsestoronnaia pomoshch'" (all-sided aid), and "reshaiushchee znachenie" (decisive significance).

22. Ibid.

23. Words of L. Brezhenv, quoted by G. Shirokov and A. Khazanov in "The Soviet Union and the National Liberation Movement," *Narody Azii i Afriki*, no. 1 (1978).

24. V. A. Golikov, *Soviet Union*, p. 526.

25. V. Kirsanov, *V-IZ*, no. 3 (1977): 78-79.

26. *New Times*, February 2, 1978; and see, for example, V. Razmerov, *VPO*, no. 12 (1975), especially pp. 7–8: "The strength of the proletarian party is in the ability . . . for an unstinting battle for the general international cause of the revolution and socialism"; as in the case of Vietnam the U.S.S.R. will (always) render help "in the interests of world socialism."

27. Editorial, *VPO*, no. 2 (1974): 4.

28. See, for example, *Pravda*, February 5, 1978 (Soviet-Yemeni communique); *Izvestia*, February 7, 1978; and *New Times*, February 2, 1978.

29. "Commentary," *APN*, February 3, 1978.

30. Ustinov speech, *KVS*; and N. Churkanov, *VPO*, no. 8 (1974): 10–14. Churkanov notes that the "defense of socialism" has of course now acquired an "international character"!

31. *APN* summary of, "The Soviet Union and the National Liberation Movement," p. 4.

32. *Izvestia*, March 1, 1978.

33. N. Maltsev, *VV*, no. 5 (1974): 27.

34. *Izvestia*, March 18, 1978; and see, for example, *New Times*, February 2, 1978.

35. *New Times*, February 2, 1978; *Pravda*, February 5, 1978; *Tass*, February 14, and March 20, 1978.

36. N. G. Kuznetsov, *Nakanune*; and Djilas, "Conversations with Stalin."

37. G. Mos'ko, *V-IZ*, no. 12 (1977): 85; *MZ*, no. 1 (1978); *New Times*, February 2, 1978; and *KVS*, no. 5 (1978).

38. Adam Ulam, *Expansion and Co-existence* (London: Secker and Warburg, 1968). See also R. Löwerthal *Model or Ally: The Communist Powers and the Developing Countries*, (Oxford: Oxford University Press, 1976), pp. 359–64.

39. Ibid; (compare with following quotes and footnotes).

40. Such as her expulsion from Egypt.

41. "The Soviet Union and the National Liberation Movement," p. 9.

42. *Pravda*, April 1, 1978, (quoting Brezhenv); see also V. Kortunov, *International Affairs* (Moscow), August 1974, p. 3.

43. "The Soviet Union and the National Liberation Movement," p. 5.

44. Ibid.

45. V. Ustimenko, *VPO*, no. 1 (1975): 12–13. See also V. Razmerov, *VPO*, no. 12 (1975); in *Kratkii Slovar'–Spravochnik Agitatora i Politinformatora* (Moscow: Politizdat, 1977), p. 282, the "national liberation movement" is described as "one of the basic contemporary revolutionary strengths. It unites the battle for national independence of peoples of colonial and semicolonial countries with the battle of young independent states for peace and social progress. The upsurge of the national liberation movement and its transformation into a powerful international revolutionary force is tied directly to the growth of the strength of world socialism, and with the strengthened union of all three of the basic contemporary revolutionary streams."

46. See definition in *1961 CPSU Program*. (Moscow: Novosti, 1961).

47. B. Pyadyshev, *USSR-USA: Confrontation or Normalization of Relations?* (Moscow: Novosti, 1977), p. 99.

48. V. Matveev in *Izvestia*, quoted in W. Inglee, *Soviet Policy towards Angola*: Library of Congress Research Service, Washington, D.C. 1977.

49. B. Pyadyshev, *USSR-USA*, p. 99.

50. M. Suslov, *Kommunist*, July 21, 1975.

51. Editorial, *New Times*, no. 2 (1976): 1.

52. V. Sidenko, *Soviet Military Affairs*, November 1975.

53. Golikov, *Soviet Union*, p. 526.

54. A. Sorokin, "Year of Great Achievement" *MS*, no. 2 (1977): 7.

55. "Commentary," *APN*, February 27, 1978.

56. Ibid.; see also N. Shumikin, *VPO*, no. 1, 1977, p. 20: "Revolutionary and national liberation wars, and wars in defence of the conquests of socialism, are deeply just."

57. Refer, for example, to Nigerian coverage of President Carter's spring 1978 visit to Lagos.

58. *Pravda*, May 31, 1978.

59. Y. Tarabrin, *MZ*.

60. Ibid.

61. D. F. Ustinov *KVS*.

62. Kaunda's Zambia is a prime example. Juxtapose Kaunda's mid-May 1978 Washington speeches accepting the legality and beneficence of Soviet-Cuban African policy with his visceral epithets of "tiger" and "cubs" in the early days of the Angolan crisis.

63. The conditional nature of Nigerian support is symptomatic. See, for example, report in the Toronto *Globe and Mail*, July 20, 1978.

64. *Time*, June 5, 1978. See also *The Economist*, May 27, 1978, p. 60: "The regimes in both Zaire and Chad . . . have obvious political weaknesses which arouse valid opposition. Mr. Giscard d'Estaing has to be careful not to fall into the trap of perpetuating discredited governments on their request."

65. *Pravda*, May 31, 1978.

66. Note, for example, the ambiguity of the treatment of "socialist commonwealth" in the leading editorial article in *VV*, no. 2 (1974), compare pp. 3–4 and pp. 116–17; or see treatment in Ya. Yanborisov, *MS*, no. 5 (1977).

67. Epitomized by Somalia, as in their presentations to the late July 1978 Belgrade conference of nonaligned natiions. Note, however, that the majority opinion at the conference was one of cautious support for Soviet-Cuban engagements. *CBS News*, July 25, 1978.

68. Nigeria's stand, as presented in the above-mentioned *Globe and Mail* report, July 20, 1978, is illustrative. See also I. Ivanov and L. Mogila, *V-IZ*, no. 12, (1976): 87, 93.

69. J. M. McConnell, Admiral Gorshkov, quoted in "Soviet Coercive Naval Diplomacy, the Rules of the Game" (Talk given at Carleton University, Ottawa, April 5, 1976). The quotation is taken from this author's notes from the oral presentation. Note also the statements of Brezhnev and other Soviet authors cited in Chapter Two.

70. Confidence on this score lies at the essence of U.N. Ambassador Young's advice to the Carter administration. His sometime ostracized status within that administration reflects scepticism as to its potential and, hence, leeriness and disinclination as to the policy course that would be required.

4

SOVIET INTERVENTION: HOW?

This investigation will look at recent Soviet writings on the kind of physical capabilities that are intrinsically suited or adaptable to interventionary designs and on the preferred tactics for their utilization. The context of the writings is not always clear. Sometimes references are to Europe, sometimes to distant arenas, sometimes, and perhaps deliberately and judiciously, to no particular geographical locale. The selection criterion used, therefore, has been that of potential rather than explicit relevance. European-oriented data are hence included to the extent that they are considered also to have wider ramifications, to the extent that they appear applicable to possible interventionary scenarios. Statements and information on nuclear and chemical-bacteriological (C-B) environments are also included when they appear explicitly or implicitly related to local scenarios and not solely or exclusively to wider conflagrations. The particular topics focused upon by Soviet writers are the need to guarantee viable lines of communications; the combined operations requirement of unified command, insuring optimal coordination of the force potential of different service elements; and the unique operational tasks of each functionally specific service contingent. The common denominator is provided by constant attention to the tactical as well as strategic import of the evolving "scientific-technological revolution in military affairs." The topics will be treated in the order indicated, although it should be emphasized that Soviet authors consider them inherently interrelated and interdependent.

THE NEED TO GUARANTEE LINES OF COMMUNICATION

There have been a number of recent articles in Soviet journals on the vital role played by "lines of communication." Some of these articles are clearly oriented

37

to strategic contingencies, the navy's strategic ability to destroy the opposing alliance's ports, their logistics and supply bases, and their supporting eco-omic-technological complexes; these revolve exclusively around missile and nuclear means.[1] Other articles are clearly "local" in their concern, although they nearly all take cognizance of the possibility of (partial) escalation, of the chance that nonconventional weaponry might come to play a part.

A favored approach is to view World War II and later experiences, with running commentary as to contemporary relevance. One such review concludes the survey of wartime events with the following lessons for the future:

> 1. The experience of the Second World War . . . supports the objec-
> tive historical tendency towards an expansion of the scope of
> the battle for (lines of) communications and a rise in its signifi-
> cance in the general system of armed battle.
> 2. In the strategic plan the breaking of the enemy's supply lines must
> be considered . . . as a composite part of the armed struggle. . . .
> The experience of the War upholds the close ties and interdepen-
> dence between the battle actions on ocean communications and
> the operations of land troops in continental theatres. . . .
> 3. The War demonstrated that the absence of a strictly scientific
> approach to planning and waging the battle for communications
> on the part of the fleet commands of the capitalist states led to a
> number of major miscalculations and errors. The most characteristic
> of these were:
>
> an incorrect direction in the building and preparing of fleets for con-
> ducting a battle of communications;
> the limited nature and adventurism of accepted operational-strategic
> conceptions; efforts to resolve all missions with only a single
> type of force, and the absence of co-operation between various
> types of strike forces and their requirements;
> the incompatibility of the goals set and the real abilities of the forces
> drawn into action along sea (lines of) communications;
> the incorrect choice of objectives for influence and areas of concen-
> trated effort, the dispersal of force, attempts to achieve opti-
> mum results on sea lines of secondary importance, with the
> weakening of influence/pressure on the supply lines that were
> most important to the enemy.
>
> 4. The basic type of weapon in the battle . . . was the submarine.
> The War's experience also demonstrated the great, real possibilities
> of aviation and the perspectives open to mine weapons.
> 5. In modern conditions the greatest effect in the battle on (the lines
> of) communications will be achieved by the combined use of various
> types of forces, branches of arms and combat material, with all the
> basic elements of communications and organization between them.[2]

The author ends by asserting,

> Today the growth of the combat abilities of our Naval Fleet, the appearance in its inventory of new classes of ships and types of aircraft and the equipping of them with modern nuclear missile weapons allows one to set still more decisive objectives in the battle of (lines of) communications and to conduct them on a qualitatively new basis. . . . (One must consider the) changes in the composition and armament of fleets in the post-war period.[3]

Another article, which reviewed North Baltic, and Black Sea "communications" engagements during 1941–45, disparaged the Germans for having paid insufficient attention to the problem. The "highly maneuverable character" of war made—and makes—the battle for communications vital, both on land and sea:

> The whole course of the war with Fascist Germany demonstrated the tremendous significance of naval communications for guaranteeing the operations of both armies and fronts. And therefore the battle for the sea lanes rapidly passed beyond the limits of operational significance and acquired a strategic character.[4]

Yet another war-review article stresses the fluidity of circumstance and the differing peculiarities affecting different theaters of conflict. The author emphasizes the war lesson that in theaters of "overwhelming" enemy superiority, "the defense of naval communications demands the conduct of special operations." He stresses the need to study "the tendencies of the development" that shape naval communications defense problems and prospects.[5]

There are, of course, two quite distinct types of "communications" problems that come into play when considering interventionary potentials. There is the need to establish and be able to defend the umbilical cord "lines of communications" with the homeland, and there are the very different yet complementary problems of insuring the security and efficiency of tactical "communications" during the operation itself.

With regard to the first requirement, Soviet authors have long recognized it as being dual-natured, necessarily resting on interdependent long-range air and sea power projection capabilities; aviation and "sea control ships" are both essential to the struggle for "mastery at sea" and to protection of lines of communications.[6] The impressive evolution of Soviet air and naval projection potential lies outside the scope of the present effort and is treated elsewhere.[7] However, one quote from the naval side of the equation might be warranted as an indication of Soviet perception and confidence:

> Now the Soviet fleet is capable of having an essential influence on the course and outcome of armed battles in the (most) extensive

theatres of military operations. Included in its make-up are atomic submarines with rockets and torpedoes, rocket-carrying aircraft, surface vessels . . . auxiliary vessels . . . coastal rocket units and the naval infantry, which is based on contemporary armament. . . . (In fact, in many important aspects Soviet ships) surpass analogous vessels of capitalist states.[8]

With regard to local combat contingencies of air-sea landings, proper communications are seen to be vitally important. The question of effective communications demands "Special attention, all the more so as in contemporary conditions their (landing operations) role has grown considerably."[9] Examples are provided of the conflict situations for which this dictate has "particular" relevance:

> With an offensive along a coast a landing of the strength of a motor rifle battalion may be charged with such tasks as seizing the enemy's means of nuclear attack, or of preventing/interdicting the arrival of his reserves. In joint operations with a tactical air landing (TVD) a battalion may be used also to take possession of a port, an airfield or a small island.[10]

In cases of this type, communications are organized on the commanding officer's directive by the "chief of communications," who is supposed during the preparatory period to set up a radio net that includes all units and vehicles (tanks, BMDs) in the battalion, as well as the supporting vessels whose fire will aid the landing (KOP), and also air cover units.[11] "Secrecy of preparation and surprise" are noted to "have immediate decisive significance" for a landing operation; "secure coordination with fire support vessels (KOP) and aviation" will also "greatly further . . . accomplishment of the mission of the naval landing operation."[12]

COMBINED OPERATIONS REQUIREMENTS

Combined operations are a Soviet predilection with long antecedents and general applicability. The World War II phenomenon of "fronts," in which air and naval units were integrated as component parts together with land formations proper was typical.[13] With regard to landing operations and tactical actions of possible Third World import, the dictum continues to reverberate. Both for offensive and defensive purposes, Soviet authors harp on the necessity to integrate land, naval, air, and indeed National Air Defense Forces (PVO) means. History is called upon again and again to demonstrate the need for combined operations[14] and combined command[15] (though with contingency emphasis on individual unit initiative and creativity).[16]

The "communications" literature's emphasis on operations involving combined arms has already been noted. The combining of rifle battalion landings from the sea with air drops to block enemy reserve and retreat routes is a favored modus operandi for actions against coastal regions.[17] Land and air-borne troops and capabilities are also constantly linked; in complicated conditions where movement is problematic and supplies limited "aircraft and helicopters have proved the only way of landing infantry, moving heavy armament, general and direct fire support and other forms of guaranteeing battle."[18]

Larger shore-landing and leapfrogging air mobile formations are essentially ground troops, ground units, naval rifle brigades, and motorized rifle battalions.[19] (These last are said to need no more than eight to ten hours of instruction to prepare them for helicopter-borne operations and assaults.[20]) The modern naval infantry is elite, intended as a landing's "advanced detachment," the "storming detachment."[21] So also with the paratroop divisions; they are seen as advance commando units, tasked with temporary seizure, disrupture, and, when possible, destruction—but with staying power limited by presumptions of extraction or else relief from advancing units of greater substance.[22]

But combined operations require not only command integration of different service units, air, sea, and land, they also require incorporation of different service elements within each. You have air scouting,[23] strafing, and even drops into the enemy rear as component parts of naval landing operations;[24] and artillery, air strikes, air mobility, and air defense as part and parcel of ground advances further inland.[25] Furthermore, tank divisions now have incorporated engineer battalions and motorized rifle regiments.[26] Artillery is combined with tactical air strikes, helicopter, and BMD and tank potentials.[27] Naval and air landing forces have incorporated specialized nuclear and chemical-bacteriological protection and defense units,[28] a consequence partly of their own training to utilize and follow up on offensive strikes,[29] partly of their anticipation that an inferior enemy is himself likely to initiate the use of nuclear/C-B means (if such means are available to him).[30] Finally, these landing forces also have integral PVO air defense detachments, for offensive as well as defensive purposes.[31] The general presumption is, "In present conditions it is impossible to count on success without making use of rapid manoeuvres and surprise attacks on the flank and rear of the objective's defence, without having recourse to military guile and without making every possible use of new weapons and technical equipment."[32]

There is great stress on the amending "corrections" which the "scientific technological revolution" has wrought with respect to World War II experiences and lessons.[33] There is acute awareness of the fact that "new means of combat are creating a revolution in all areas of military . . . art."[34] One consequence recognized and emphasized in Soviet writings is that war today acknowledges no real "rear." "Everywhere is the front."[35] The literature evinces recognition of the double-edged nature of this phenomenon, of the complexities attending the effectualizing of their theoretical predilection, and of the need for constant rethinking of the impact of ever newer technologies, yet it also exudes confidence that the basic prescription is right.[36]

Finally, with particular reference to interventionary-type scenarios, it may be useful to review the lessons that Moscow draws from recent localized wars. Vietnam was, of course, seen to demonstrate the efficacy and potency of partisan warfare (though "not separable from the valuable aid and support given by the Soviet Union"[37]). But it is also said to have demonstrated the following tendencies:

> the growth of troops' fire power;
> an increase in mobility on the field of battle, the violent develop-
>   ment of aeromobile forces, (and) strengthening of the role of
>   helicopters, which were drawn into a wide circle (variety) of
>   missions;
> the intensive introduction of radioelectric means into the systems of
>   direction and various forms of providing for the troops;
> the wide conduct of battle operations at night;
> the growth in the role of small subunits in carrying out not only
>   tactical, but also operational missions;
> a broadening of the scope of operations of diversionary-reconnais-
>   sance units and subunits; (as well as extended use of metero-
>   logical and geophysical warfare).[38]

Another lesson drawn from a review of local wars in general is the

> recognition of the fleet as the most universal and mobile form of
> armed force, and one that is especially suitable for actions against
> any weakly developed country. . . . (Fleets are also used because)
> they provide a hidden concentration of military power (anywhere
> on the globe, although their use is obviously conditioned by geo-
> graphic circumstances). . . . (Still) the despatch of troops, their sup-
> ply and evacuation would be impossible without a fleet. . . . (Fleet
> missions in local wars are) (1) aerial support of land troops; (2) the
> conduct of seaborne landings; (3) artillery support for troops along
> the coast; (4) the naval blockade of coasts and ports; and (5) the sea-
> borne transport and the guarantee of the deployment and evacuation
> of troops. . . . (This is) evidence of the growth in its (the fleet's)
> role in the armed battle of opposing sides.[39]

The use of missiles is also thought noteworthy:

> One more tendency in naval tactics: this consists of an extension of
> "small scale operations" which bring significant advantages. The
> actions of a large number of small groups of rocket launchers, in-
> dependently or in cooperation with similarly small groups of air-
> craft, have a great effect and lower their losses. . . . Rocket vessels

and aircraft, just like atomic submarines, now provide the possibility of carrying out large missions in a short time with a limited force.[40]

Yet, there is apparently some unease about total conversion to missiles. Drawing on U.S. experience in Vietnam, some authors insist that artillery, "guns of calibre up to 203 mm," can in certain circumstances be more effective than "non-nuclear rockets" (a vital caveat).[41]

With regard to air power, both naval and air force, Moscow is clearly appreciative of its impact. Yet it emphasizes that Western interventionary success in this field has been due largely to the absence of opposing air defense systems; it is an emphasis that draws attention to the dual-purpose impact of Moscow's own integrated PVO detachments.[42]

OPERATIONAL TASKS OF THE PARTICULAR SERVICES

The services focused upon will be those with peculiar relevance to intervention scenarios, the navy, the air force, and the PVO in particular. As concerns the navy, there are two distinguishable spheres to note, namely, its ability to establish and secure supply "lines of communications" and its ability to engage and land in the chosen locale. The former has been treated elsewhere,[43] it will suffice here to point up Soviet confidence with one quote: The fleet is asserted to be capable of "reliably defending . . . state interests in the ocean spaces."[44]

With regard to naval ability to engage and land, there is a considerable body of literature. The fleet's landing capacity is said today to have benefited from "new forms and capabilities of action."[45] The requirements of sea landing schemes are described as follows:

> For the preparatory period . . . maintaining secrecy about the plan of operations, and especially the region and time of the landing; hidden preparations; the concentration of forces and means; the use of darkness and bad weather; passing disinformation to the enemy in every possible way; the battle with enemy reconnaissance and the conducting of one's own on a wide front. . . . During the period of deploying forces and the landing force's crossing of the sea, apart from those (measures) listed above, effective (ones) are to vary the route of the crossing; actions in other directions to draw off the enemy's strength; careful attention to hiding lights and radio silence; the use of technical camouflage means and radio countermeasures; and the concealed deployment of hydrographic means. . . . With the opening of the battle for the landing (it is necessary) to continue demonstration actions and the battle with aerial reconnaissance. In the future, in conditions of the possible use of nuclear weapons, special attention must be paid to making the landing on a broad front. . . . The development of reconnaissance aviation, radar and

other technical means of observation necessitates an increase in the
volume and an improvement in the ability and means of camouflage.
Night must be abandoned as a natural (sufficient) cover for the force
of the fleet in both the open seas and oceans. Yet the skillful use and
combination of other means of camouflage in combination with the
dark hours of the day and bad weather conditions can remain effective in modern circumstances.[46]

Another source, one which also proceeds from a review of World War II
landings, stresses the need for surprise and the various methods (camouflage,
secret sailings, radio silence, and so on) of achieving surprise. It emphasizes the
necessity for coordination of command and proper reconnaissance and naviga-
tional-hydrographic measures. Experience is seen to demonstrate "the importance
of achieving high tempos of the landing of all echelons of the landing force so as
to guarantee in the shortest time the seizure of the necessary beach-head in conditions of the enemy developing resistance." Dawn or night are viewed as the
most propitious times to attack. The author concludes that the history of World
War II and of "the local wars of the subsequent period, convincingly demon-
strates that naval landings are an important and inalienable part not only of
armed battle at sea but in the overwhelming majority of armed actions in general." He predicts that "in the future landing actions will remain an essential
component of armed battle at sea."[47]

A third source discussing naval landing requirements, problems, and prospects deserves quoting in some detail:

> Modern means of inflicting defeats and making landings expand the
> possibilities of making seaborne landings and allow all subunits to
> master this complicated form of battle activities and in a brief time
> to carry out the mission of defeating the enemy defending the
> coastal region. The most important conditions for the success of a
> seaborne landing are its careful and concealed preparation, the sur-
> prise of the landing and an all-sided guarantee of swift and active
> operations of the subunits. . . . The combat operations of a tactical
> seaborne landing comprise three stages: the loading of personnel and
> the ferrying of combat technical equipment onto the landing craft,
> the crossing of the sea and the battle for the landing, the develop-
> ment of an offensive and the carrying out of the missions set.
>
>   The enemy will naturally take measures in order to observe
> the landing and to bottle it up with successful operations. During
> any of these stages he may launch a nuclear strike or use chemical
> weapons. As a result the coastal section of the region and the basins
> may be contaminated, and the landing will have to re-establish com-
> bat potentiality.
>
>   To render help to the troops in carrying out measures of de-
> fence and to liquidate the consequences of the enemy's use of wea-

pons of mass destruction, chemical defence subunits are included in a tactical landing force. In the battle's first stages they are most frequently used in a decentralized manner, chiefly in the interest of those motor rifle, tank, artillery and other subunits with whom they act jointly. With the development of success in the enemy's rear, the efforts of chemical reconnaissance patrols and the means of special treatment are concentrated to handle tasks of a chemical nature that suddenly spring up.[48]

There is general stress on the need for small units to be trained for independent work.[49] The so-called advance detachments, the naval infantry, is said to have been reorganized "on a new basis" so as to be able to "land in the rear of an enemy together with units of the ground forces."[50] They are said to be equipped with "the latest combat technology and armament . . . capable effectively and quickly of fulfilling difficult missions in battle."[51] Their "ability to act independently and attack decisively" is proclaimed as fact.[52] "Today's naval infantry . . . are a qualitatively new branch of the force of the naval fleet."[53]

Finally, before turning to air force potentials and landings, there are two summary comments of potential relevance that ought to be made. One concerns the earlier quotations' stress on preparation, hydrographic and other surveying, and transport. It should be said that Admiral Gorshkov and other military spokesmen have testified that the formidable Soviet oceanographic research, fishing, and merchant fleets are considered for contingency purposes as "components" of the Soviet Navy.[54] The second comment concerns "peacetime" naval visits. Between 1969 and 1975, for example, Soviet ships apparently visited 65 countries and called on 150 foreign ports.[55] Soviet ships and sailors are described as conscious ambassadors, charged with demonstrating Soviet social and technological prowess and with repudiating Western "influence . . . propaganda and racist ideas."[56] The visits "play an exceptionally great role in the resolution of the foreign political tasks of our country in peace-time."[57]

On the subject of air force landings and air-borne interventions, there are again a number of sub-themes that can be distinguished within the body of Soviet writings on the topic. As with the navy, one should probably start with the security of the "lines of communications." Soviet authors acknowledge that airborne troops are today "under (potential) threat of attack from the very moment of concentration at the airfield in the departure area."[58] Having recognized the threat, however, they proceed to emphasize the great improvement in capabilities; the force is now "capable of preparing airborne landings, ferrying troops and of conducting modern battle and operations in the enemy rear; . . . Soviet airborne troops can appear in the enemy's rear with everything needed for the successful conduct of a battle, and they are capable of carrying out great strategic missions." Furthermore they can now sustain "prolonged action" in the enemy rear.[59]

As is the case with the navy, the air force is also asserted to have benefited from impressive improvement in equipment, both qualitatively and quantitatively.[60] They ferry troops in An-22, An-12, and Il-75 transports (capable of carrying 40 tons at 900 kilometers an hour, 5000 kilometers non-stop, and landing on unpaved airfields).[61] Much improved air transport, "air-borne technology," and general "full mechanization" is said to have accompanied "stronger organization" and led to a much more "mobile" and "formidable" force potential.[62] The introduction of the BMD, to supplement the longer standing air-borne battalion complement of tanks, anti-tank guided missiles, (PTURS), an air-defense battery, armoured personnel carriers (APC), ASU-57s, self-propelled artillery, 122-mm howitzers, mortars, guns, other small arms, and special searchlights for night operations,[63] is touted as being particularly significant.[64]

There is also a good bit of attention paid to the leapfrog ferrying of motor rifle battalions.[65] This is conducted with helicopters, at low altitude to avoid radar, with both helicopter gunships and fighters providing cover.[66] It is recognized that enemy air and ground (tank) attacks may occur during the landing operation,[67] but there appears to be confidence that defense equipment and inculcated ability to engage immediately will prove sufficient.[68]

As concerns the PVO air defense component of landing groups, Soviet commentators return to the theme that the uninterrupted air defense of (landed) ground units is an essential part of attempts to gain supremacy in the air.[69] The importance of air defense is described as having growing significance, due to its "sharp growth in possibilities."[70]

The primary non-nuclear threat against sea and air landings is clearly seen to lie in helicopter and tank assaults; it is on these eventualities that PVO (and PTURS and BMD) landing elements focus first. There are a number of Soviet articles that describe the pivotal role of PVO in warding off helicopter and tank assaults.[71] But PVO is not only seen as needed for defense; it is also seen as a fine complement to the offensive use of helicopters.[72] (Helicopters, which are now "confirmed in the system of armament of contemporary armies,"[73] "have become a new means of battle with tanks. At the same time they are also the reliable ally of tanks.")[74] In general the effectiveness of PVO, seen to have been proved in Vietnam and the Middle East,[75] is said to be testified to by "American and other military specialists of NATO" who now view it "as the main danger to their aviation."[76]

There is one final theme in the literature, the theme of blockades, that also deserves attention as of possible import for distant designs. Two basic varieties are treated, aerial blockades and naval blockades. With regard to the former, one Soviet author asserts, "Battle against enemy transport aviation during the destruction of encircled groups . . . has not lost its significance."[77] On the topic of naval blockade, it is suggested its wide use in postwar local conflicts points to the lesson that it "has not lost its significance and in a future war . . . will unconditionally find a wide application."[78] Naval blockades are "part of armed battle as a whole." Their basic aims are "to cut communications by sea; to destroy groupings of surface and undersea vessels at sea and in their bases; and to create in a blockaded zone conditions which will hinder or prevent the enemy's vessels from crossing it."[79] They employ both maneuverable and positional means and, depending on the objective, may have either "strategic or operational significance."[80] The following are the lessons of history, with an appended contemporary caveat; one must consider:

1. The presence of a scientifically worked-out theory for using the fleet's forces in blockade operations;
2. The availability of force and means sufficient and capable of realizing the blockade;
3. The geographical-military position of the warring sides;
4. The rear provision of the forces of the fleet committed to a marine blockade;
5. A reliable and stable system of illuminating the surface, undersea and aerial circumstances in the blockaded zone and in the approaches to it;
6. The organization of the co-ordination of the blockading forces, and the reliability and continuity of their direction; . . . However, the scientific-technological revolution in military affairs has obviously introduced definite corrections.[81]

In concluding, it appears evident that a substantial body of Soviet military writings is today concerned with emerging capabilities and tactics of obvious relevance to future interventionary-type contingencies. The types of equipment and the types of exercises prominent in Soviet literature testify to growing confidence that successful distant intervention falls within the scope of the present-day Soviet armed forces' capabilities. The necessary well-rounded tactics and wherewithal for complex landings against capable defenders are being developed and perfected.

NOTES

1. See Gorshkov quotes in Chapter Two.

2. G. Morozov, *Morskoi Sbornik*, no. 5 (1976): 28. Hereafter this journal will be referred to as *MS*.

3. Ibid.

4. I. I. Markov, "Bor'ba na Morskikh Kommunikatsiiakh i ee Vliyanie na Khod Voennykh Deistvii na Sushche," *Vtoraya Mirovaya Voina*, 3 vols. Moscow: Voenizdat, 1966) III: 106–07.

5. A. Basov, *MS*, no. 2 (1976): 36.

6. See, for example, Yu. Nefedev, *MS*, no. 8 (1974): 96–100.

7. See Chapter Five. But note awareness of the vulnerability and exposure of air transport, for example, in V. Margelov, *Voennyi Vestnik*, no. 7 (1977): 62–63. Hereafter this journal will be referred to as *VV*.

8. G. Bondarenko, *MS*, no. 7 (1974): 3.

9. D. Moskalenko, *VV*, no. 5 (1974): 107–11.

10. Ibid., p. 107.

11. Ibid. The details of a network of this type, intended for tactical training, are provided, with illustrative charts; the equipment used included BTR, R-107, and R-126.

12. Ibid., p. 110. See also V. Shlomin, *Voenno-Istoricheskii Zhurnal*, no. 4 (1977): 27–33, for "operations" requirements relating to, respectively, the preparatory, the development, and the battle phases. Hereafter this journal will be referred to as *V-IZ*.

13. Harriet Fast and W. F. Scott's book, *The Soviet Armed Forces* (Boulder, Colo.: Westview Press, 1978) provides an admirable exposition of the historical evolution of the concept.

14. L. Ol'shtynskii, *MS*, no. 11 (1974): 20–26.

15. This is required not only to optimize the coordination of functionally different service elements but also to optimize the coordination of same service elements provided by coalition allies. See A. Rodinov, *MS*, no. 7 (1976): 21–26.

16. A. Golubkov, *VV*, no. 1 (1975): 80–83.

17. D. Moskalenko, *VV*.

18. V. Katin, *MS*, no. 6 (1974): 86.

19. Regarding naval rifle brigades, see, for example, N. Belous, *V-IZ*, no. 11 (1976): 29–38; on motorized rifle battalions see, for example, D. Moskalenko, *VV*.

20. K. Urtayev, *VV*, no. 3 (1971): 33.

21. N. Belous, *V-IZ*, no. 11 (1976): p. 38.

22. See, for example, A. Golubkov, *VV*, no. 1 (1975): 80–83; I. Zuev, *VV*, no. 2 (1976): 85–89; G. Kuvitanov and V. Dediukhin, *VV*, no. 1 (1976): 46–49; A. Bykov, *VV*, no. 8 (1974): 67–70; and later quotes.

23. Yu. Khramov, *MS*, no. 10 (1974): 20–23.

24. P. Beregov, *VV*, no. 6 (1974): 19–25.

25. V. Grechnev, *VV*, no. 12 (1977): 74–77.

26. J. Erickson, 11 Trends in the Soviet Combined-Arms Concept *Strategic Review* (Winter 1977): 43–44.

27. Ibid., p. 49. Note review article in *VV*, no. 2 (1974): 124–26; and see articles by A. Gorbachev and V. Subbotin in *VV*, no. 10 (1975): 62–66, 89–92, respectively.

28. As concerns naval landings, see G. Zhavoronkov and V. Tkachev, *VV*, no. 9 (1976): 107–10; for air landings see M. Naumov and D. Dregal, *VV*, no. 1 (1978): 53–56.

29. V. Margelov, *VV*, no. 7 (1977): 61–65.

30. Zhavoronkov and Tkachev, *VV*.

31. M. Govorov, *Vestnik Protivovezdushnoi Oborony*, (hereafter referred to as *VPO*); no. 10 (1975): 83–88; A. Gorbachev, *VV*, no. 10 (1975): 62–66. The defensive emphasis and its implied respect for U.S. helicopter potentials in particular (see Chapter Two) is quite prominent. See P. Levchenko, *VV*, no. 9 (1977): 2–6; M. Kiriukhin, *VV*, no. 3 (1975): 86–91; and P. Chaplygin and Yu. Rodnikovskii, *VV*, no. 10 (1974): 51–54.

32. I. Tikhomirov and A. Panasenko, *VV*, no. 2 (1975): 51.

33. M. Stepanov and L. Zamulin, *MS*, no. 6 (1974): 23.

34. B. Makeev, *MS*, no. 2, 1977; p. 19. The specific reference is to naval affairs, but there is no doubting the general applicability of the awareness (see above quotes).

35. V. Pepelin, *VV*, no. 3 (1975): 62–63, discusses the tactical implications of this for air landings; as concerns the wider strategic recognition, *Nedelia*, no. 6 (1965), provides early testimony.

36. V. Kulikov, *Kommunist*, no. 5 (1976): 38–47.

37. G. Berdnikov, *V-IZ*, no. 1 (1975): 64–72.

38. Ibid., p. 72, and (regarding the final bracket) p. 65.

39. S. Stalbo, *MS*, no. 9 (1976): 23–29.

40. N. V'iunenko, *MS*, no. 10 (1975): 21–26.

41. Yu. Galich, *MS*, no. 12 (1974): 72–75; and N. Petrov, *MS*, no. 9 (1975): 99–100.

42. V. Katin, *MS*, no. 6 (1974): 87–92, 95.

43. See Chapters Three and Five.

44. Editorial, *MS*, no. 1 (1978): 3–6.

45. G. Ammon, *MS*, no. 11 (1975): 32.

46. V. Shlomin, *V-IZ*, no. 4 (1977): 27–33.

47. K. Stalbo, *V-IZ*, no. 8 (1977): 37–43.

48. G. Zhavoronkov and V. Tkachev, *VV*, no. 9 (1976): 107.

49. Ibid.

50. N. Belous, *V-IZ*, no. 11 (1976): 38; and N. Smirnov, *V-IZ*, no. 7 (1976): 33.

51. P. Yakimov and V. Petukhov, *V-IZ*, no. 11 (1974): 33.

52. G. Sinitsa and M. Egorov, *MS*, no. 8 (1976): 27; see also N. Setrov, *MS*, no. 2 (1977): 83: "The skillful use of geographic and hydro- and meterological conditions, initiative and careful planning are the guarantee of successful combat activities" (commenting on naval infantry requirements); and see *MS*, no. 1 (1975): 15–16 (on naval infantry standards).

53. I. Spirkin, *MS*, no. 4 (1974): 38–41.

54. S. Gorshkov, *Pravda*, July 25, 1976; see also L. Panomareva and D. Naumov, *MS*, no. 1 (1978): 87–90, and N. Kozhevnikov, *MS*, no. 4 (1977): 11–15.

55. N. Smirnov, *V-IZ*, no. 7 (1976): 36.

56. Editorial, *MS*, no. 7 (1977): 6–11; S. Gorshkov, *MS*, no. 11 (1977): 10–11; A. Perepelitsa, *MS*, no. 2 (1976): 58, and G. Zhuravel, *MS*, no. 5 (1976): 42–45.

57. I. Tarkhanov and M. Ovanesov, *MS*, no. 7 (1974): 91–94; and see interview with S. Gorshkov, *VV*, no. 2 (1978): 25.

58. V. Margelov, *VV*, no. 7 (1977): 62–63.

59. V. Margelov, *V-IZ*, no. 1 (1977): 52–59.

60. As concerns the navy, see earlier quotes, and, for example, V. Maslov, *V-IZ*, no. 4 (1977): 88.

61. *Tass*, December 28, 1977; see also V. Margelov, *V-IZ*, no. 1 (1977): 58–59.

62. V. Margelov, *VV*, no. 7 (1977): 62–63.

63. V. Margelov, ibid., and idem., *V-IZ*, no. 1 (1977); also G. Bondarenko, *VV*, no. 2 (1977): 59–61; N. Kononov, *VV*, no. 3 (1977): 57–60 (Kononov described BMD protective shield); and A. Bykov, *VV*, no. 8 (1974): 67–70. On the searchlights, see V. Molianov, *VV*, no. 5 (1977): 58–60; for further information on night landings, see R. Salikhov, *VV*, no. 6 (1977): 64–67.

64. I. Zuev, *VV*, no. 2 (1976): 85–89; N. Kononov, *VV*, no. 3 (1977): 57–60; G. Bondarenko, *VV*, no. 2 (1977): 59–61.

65. V. Subbotin, *VV*, no. 10 (1975): 89–92; D. Moskalenko, *VV*, no. 5 (1974).

66. V. Subbotin, *VV*.

67. On the former, see I. Bliznik, *VV*, no. 2 (1975): 47–50; and V. Margelov, *VV*; on the latter, see N. Naumov and D. Dregal, *VV*, no. 1 (1978): 53–56.

68. Ibid.; and V. Margelov, *VV*, no. 7 (1977).

69. N. Nikitin and S. Petrov, *V-IZ*, no. 11 (1974): 87. Most of the citations below relate to air landings; for a description of the vital necessity of naval-PVO cooperation, see M. Govorov, *VPO*, no. 10 (1975): 83–88.

70. F. Shesterin, *V-IZ*, no. 10 (1977): 77.

71. See, for example, P. Levchenko, *VV*, no. 9 (1977): 2–6; G. Bondarenko, *VV*, no. 2 (1977): 59–61; M. Kiriukhin, *VV*, no. 3 (1975): 86–91; A. Gorbachev, *VV*, no. 10 (1975): 62–66; and P. Chaplygin and Yu. Rodnikovskii, *VV*, no. 10 (1974): 51–54 (dis-

cussing armanents and capabilities of U.S. helicopters and countering tactics open to troops and air-borne force).

72. V. Zaitsev and A. Naumov, *VV*, no. 2 (1977): 76–79, and Yu. Zakharov, *VV*, no. 8 (1977): 63–65.

73. M. Belov, *VV*, no. 4 (1975): 117.

74. Review article, *VV*, no. 2 (1974): 124–26.

75. Khoang Ngok Z'en, *VPO*, no. 2 (1975): 21 (claims 4181 U.S. aircraft were downed over North Vietnam); and F. Shesterin, *V-IZ*, no. 10 (1977): 75–81.

76. M. Shelekov, *VPO*, no. 6 (1974): 52.

77. M. Kozhevnikov, *V-IZ*, no. 11 (1974): 26.

78. V. Sysoev, *MS*, no. 12 (1976): 32–36.

79. M. Stepanov and L. Zamulin, *MS*, no. 6 (1974): 20–23.

80. Ibid., p. 20.

81. Ibid.

5

SOVIET PROJECTION CAPABILITIES

The 1960s and 1970s have seen the emergence of significant Soviet distant power projection capabilities, both air and naval. While the original impetus for their development at least in the case of the new naval means, was strategic and defensive, it is clear that distant state and client interests, Third World presence requirements, have today become a major developmental determinant. The appearance of a high seas Soviet Navy will be treated first, as behooves the most commented upon, visible, and intrinsically flexible component of Soviet projection capacity. This will be followed by a look at the complementary Soviet development of long-range air potentials and of aeromobile forces whose impact on distant scenarios may prove as portentous as their contiguous abilities.

The emergence of the Soviet Navy from a coastal defense formation to a force of global strategic impact unfolded through the 1960s and early 1970s. There were two original rationales. The most important was strategic and defensive. There was a need to counter the threat to the homeland posed first by U.S. carrier-based nuclear-armed aviation (since the mid 1950s) and later and more dramatically by the Polaris-Poseidon fleet of strategic submarines. Subsequently, with the development of a Soviet sea-based strategic capability, the defensive requirement for forward deployment came to be supplemented by an offensive dictate. (This offensive dictate could, of course, also be seen as defensive if one adheres, as most do, to the tenets of deterrence theory.) Early submarine launched ballistic missiles, SLBMs, had a limited range. It was a technological restraint that was seen by Washington to require forward deployment, both in the Mediterranean and especially the Norwegian Sea. Moscow was faced with the alternative of analagous deployments in the western Atlantic or of securing the surge potential to suitable firing positions of forces deployed beyond their natural firing range. The latter alternative was preferred. The support vessels required for surge protection were procured.

51

The situation changed in the early 1970s. The Soviets began to deploy their long-range Delta class SS-N-8 (and later SS-NX-18), submarine-launched ballistic missiles capable of hitting "San Diego, California, Quito, Recife, Mozambique, Indonesia and Hawaii from the haven of the Kola inlet."[1] The still modern Yankee class was also scheduled to receive improved range missiles.[2] Older SLBM platforms began to be phased out. Developments were obviating the need for surge capabilities and their protection. A similar trend toward homewater basing could be discerned in the U.S. procurement of the long-range Trident system, scheduled for consequential deployment in the 1980s.[3] Mid-ocean ASW (anti-submarine warfare) and counter-ASW capabilities, the never perfected but hauntingly plausible threat against the viability of the sea-based deterrent (a viability crucial to prevailing strategic perceptions), were becoming redundant.

This is reflected in the changing composition of the Soviet strategic fleet charted below. As will be seen, its dramatic growth tapered off after 1968, when numbers of hunter-killer submarines began to contract markedly. Through the mid-1970s, the continuing growth of the SLBM "offensive" strategic submarine force barely sufficed to offset the dimunition in numbers of attack submarines. So also with surface vessels, the numbers of which stagnated after 1968. One should note that all major Soviet surface combatants have ASW designations. On the other hand, the fact that numbers have steadied does not reflect on quality. It could be argued that quantitative stagnation or, in some cases, contraction, has been more than offset by qualitative improvements. But it should be noted that qualitative improvements have been catholic, focusing on the amalgam of needs associated with distant sea control ambitions; at least until very recently they did not noticeably favor ASW requirements (see sections and tables below).

With the apparent easing of the defensive requirement for a high seas fleet, of the need to defend against the ocean-based threat per se and defend the sea-going deterrent, there appears to be emerging a greater Soviet capacity for sustained distant operations of a more general nature. Moscow is procuring capabilities which invite the entertainment of limited command of the sea notions. Emerging capabilities may be related to the previously described trends in Soviet strategic literature toward increased interest in interventionary-type concepts and increasing stress on the navy's role as defender of state interests abroad.[4] In the former case there may be room for debate as to whether expressed interests were causal or whether they are post facto rationalizations, whether such have in fact been an abiding consideration in the shaping of the fleet's growth or whether they reflect the search for a new raison d'être for emerging and future capabilities at a time when the old justification may be being undermined.

As concerns the protection of state economic interests, however, there can be little doubt that this is a function with deeper roots. Although perhaps secondary to the strategic imperative, it was clearly a consideration of substance at the genesis of the buildup. Since the late 1950s, and especially through the 1960s, there has been a dramatic growth in distant Soviet merchant shipping, fishing, and other ocean wealth exploration and exploitation activities.[5] By the late 1960s, Soviet "ocean development" endeavors reached to every major expanse of the world's seas; of particular interest to this analysis, "blanket coverage" might be said to have been established in northern waters. The Soviet Union had developed the one condition, distant ocean financial interests, that has traditionally been seen to justify and even demand protective naval potential.[6]

Furthermore, while the Soviet Union's existence might not yet depend on the inviolability of trade routes to the same extent as did traditional maritime powers, in view of the reality of greater residual self-sufficiency in most basic resources, it had come to depend on the inviolability of ocean wealth extraction prospects. The harvesting of fish, crustaceans, krill, and algae had come to constitute an important part of the nation's protein intake. It had become an increasingly indispensible supplement to the output of the still problem-plagued agriculture, and its excess capacity was becoming an increasingly important source of foreign exchange, a source of disproportionate value to a nonconvertible currency nation. The harvesting of ocean and ocean-floor mineral and energy potentials, while perhaps less urgent, was similarly associated with superficially disproportionate promise, due to the severity of the geophysical and climatological restraints hampering the full exploitation of land prospects. The value of excess production exports of these products were, of course, also at a premium due to the very fact of its being convertible.[7]

Soviet "civilian" fleets clearly serve an auxiliary military function. Their character is determined by the Soviet proclivity towards a degree of military-civilian integration, where possible. This proclivity is a function of the all-embracing, part-Clausewitzian, Soviet concept of strategic power, a concept which sees economic, military, political, and other levers of power as explicitly intertwined and interdependent; no component has absolute worth but gains relative weight through a calibration of domestic and external circumstances and requirements.[8] Admiral Gorshkov's testimony that Soviet "civilian" fleets are regarded as part and parcel of "Soviet naval might"[9] should, therefore, occasion no surprise.

Moscow's civilian fleets provide reserve naval transport and intelligence monitoring capacity. They "survey and mark future battle fields"; they play an important role in the distribution and control of underwater devices of strategic import; and they perform a significant role in the perfecting of command and control means and practice.[10] To the extent that their inherent capabilities and normal deployment patterns allow them to satisfy routine naval requirements at minimum cost to their other tasks, to that extent are they so assigned.

But under normal peace conditions, free of such tension requirements as exemplified by the Cuban crisis of 1962, the capabilities and tasks of the civilian fleets are correlated with military requirements only to the extent that is possible without seriously jeopardizing their nonmilitary endeavors. Not only are the civilian functions cost-effective (to the extent that even marginal efforts, like the Capelin fisheries off Labrador, unprofitable to Canadian fishermen, become economical under the different contextual parameters of a Soviet-type economic system), but they have become vital to the satisfaction of the standard-of-living commitments upon which the nation's establishment has chosen to stake its legitimacy.[11]

The fact that distant Soviet ocean financial interests have not only been established but may be said to have acquired crucial import for domestic prospects is rarely appreciated fully by Western analysts. The flow of responsibilities between the civilian and military fleets is no longer (and perhaps never was entirely) a one-way street. Calculations of Soviet naval designs must take cognizance of the reality that the Soviet Navy of today has a significant new responsibility qualitatively distinct from those hitherto presumed to underly its modus operandi.

With this in mind, it is possible to conceive of at least two scenarios in North America (Canadian)-claimed waters that might see Soviet naval involvement. One relates to Canadian fisheries' jurisdiction in the event of a recurrence of the Soviet crop failures of the early 1970s, especially should such a repetition coincide either with climate-caused harvesting short-falls in the West or with politically motivated restrictions on Western agricultural exports. Under such circumstances, Moscow might well consider the protein potential of a dramatic increase in Grand Banks fishing, bursting the seams of internationally-sanctioned quotas, to be vital—in the literal sense of the word. Is it likely that existing international agreements would deter Moscow under the hypothesized circumstances? Would it be plausible to expect challenge from the rather meager enforcement means at Canada's disposal if Soviet naval elements were to provide protection to the fishing fleet? Would it be plausible to expect Washington or other third powers to intercede? The continuing lack of an international law concensus on either the principle or the particulars of unilaterally declared extensions of coastal states' rights beyond the confines of traditional territorial seas (namely, the 200-mile economic zones) adds an additional element of uncertainty.[12]

The other scenario that might be postulated concerns Canadian Arctic ocean waters and beds. A few facts stand out. Neither the USSR nor the United States have fully sanctioned Canadian sovereignty claims. Canadian surveillance is of questionable efficacy (as indicated a couple of years ago, in the case of the Polish "yacht" Gdynia, when search efforts failed to determine its location and indeed failed to determine if it was, in fact, in Canadian waters at all).[13] There are analysts who doubt whether recent procurement decisions promise consequential improvements for the late 1970s and the 1980s.[14] Canadian scientific and exploratory endeavors in these areas have also been scant, whether one talks of geological or biological surveys to locate and determine the extent of resource concentrations; of surveys of factors that affect operational efficacy, such as salinity, currents, water temperature (and seasonal and other variations thereof); or of resource wealth extraction technology, be it related to alimentary, mineral, nodule, or energy spheres.[15] Canadian law enforcement means as pertains to these regions are equally questionable, with few suitably trained forces and limited equipment of relevance. Meanwhile, it is clear that the scientific endeavors of the Soviet Union (and the United States) in Canadian-claimed Arctic waters and ocean floors have been far more extensive than those of Canada.[16] They are also uniquely advanced as concerns Arctic wealth extraction technologies. Finally, they both have more relevantly trained and equipped military personnel.

It may not be too remote to suggest that the superpowers have or soon will have the capacity to establish northern ocean floor wealth extraction operations without Canadian knowledge, a prospect with obvious common-law ramifications. Their ability to defend such installations upon discovery would, of course, have similar juridical consequences. The point must be made that a Soviet initiative along these lines might not have to be pioneering and thus possibly disruptive to the Washington-Moscow equilibrium but might conceivably be able to rest on U.S. precedent(s)—in light of current U.S. Law of the Sea positions in general, U.S. attitudes to Canadian Northern claims in particular.

Visions of the Soviet Army marching across Canadian Arctic islands do indeed appear rather far-fetched. But the same cannot be said of certain ocean or ocean floor scenarios, especially when under ice and beyond the certifiable inspectoral concern or capacity of the claimant power. Both superpowers carefully distinguish between respect for Canadian Arctic island suzerainty and considerably less accommodating views on Canadian claims over Arctic seas and seabeds.[17] The latter are treated as more dubious than, say, Norway's Svalbard associated claims. Since Canada has not established the same presence in the more northerly reaches of its claimed sovereignty, as has Norway, a point of some international law significance, Canada could be said to be at a double disadvantage.

In the southern hemisphere, too, one can now conceive of Soviet economic requirements dictating Soviet military engagement. The mentioned krill harvesting off southeast Africa, for example, entails an investment of such intrinsic scale, potential, and importance as could not be dispensed without domestic dislocations.[18] In the unlikely event of Soviet inability to insure continued access to Mauritius or other conveniently located repair, supply, and replenishment facilities, there would be a major incentive for assertive action.

Still, while such scenarios of economically dictated military embroilments cannot be ruled out, the extremity of premises is perhaps unlikely to eventuate.

What may be more important is the early-1970s trend in Soviet doctrinal promulgations toward a more catholic, broader definition of state interests. This trend has been treated elsewhere; so also has the corresponding but nevertheless startling fact that the naval duty to "protect state interests," the task of "peace-

time naval diplomacy," now ranks immediately behind the priority task of protecting its own ranks immediately behind the priority task of protecting its own
strategic potential—and ahead of the earlier priority requirement of grappling
directly with NATO's strategic fleets.[19] The point is that the increasing trend to
identify Soviet interests with Third World contingencies and the assertive willingness to pursue and protect these interests inevitably entail a requirement for improved interventionary potentials.

The corollary Soviet stress on the operational ability to establish and defend distant lines of communications has also been dealt with elsewhere.[20] But
there is one element that deserves mention here, that is, the consequent need to
offset the countering capacity of U.S. carriers on the supply routes and in the
locale in question:

> The removal of attack carriers from the first echelon of the reserves
> of strategic forces in a general nuclear war in no way excludes their
> wide utilization for resolving important tasks. The command of the
> U.S. Navy recognizes at least three of them. Firstly, seaborne aircraft
> remain in the forefront of tactical aviation in local wars; secondly
> aircraft carriers are an integral part of the forces that guarantee
> "mastery of the sea"; and thirdly, aircraft carrier formations are an
> irreplaceable instrument in "gunboat diplomacy," providing a mili-
> tary presence where this is needed in peacetime.[21]

By the early 1970s, Moscow had standardized "anti-carrier task groups":

> The core of Moscow's Third World diplomacy of force lies in its
> capabilities for countering U.S. carrier task groups. These capa-
> bilities seem to be organized in what we refer to as anti-carrier task
> groups, each typically consisting of a cruise-missile submarine, a
> couple of torpedo attack submarines, a surface-to-surface missile
> ship and a surface-to-air missile ship.[22]

And Moscow appeared until recently to be content with the potency of its
counter: "Although capabilities continued to improve, Soviet investment since
1970 in countering the carrier has not been as intensive as in previous periods."[23]

In 1977, however, the number of Soviet attack submarines jumped noticeably, past the peak that had been established in 1968 (see below). The time lag
since the early-1970s enunciation of doctrinal interest in greater interventionary-
type commitments, needs, and requirements suggested that the increase might
be attributed to attendant prospects of greater "lines of communication" demands. Moscow clearly was not intending to revert to the near futile aspiration
of the 1960s, general "combat against the enemy fleet," and there was no
evidence of increased Soviet dissatisfaction regarding its ability to guarantee the
survival of its strategic fleet and hence allow for the option of withholding.

There were other possible reasons for the 1977 spurt in numbers of attack submarines. One was contemporary U.S. advocacies for additional carriers, although it must be said that U.S. budgetary and political realities always appeared likely to squeeze such aspirations to the minimum. Another plausible Soviet motive lay in sales of attack submarines to Third World clients and possible expectations that these would increase.[24] Finally, there was the modernization drive, the appearance and deployment of new improved vessel types. To the extent that the latter considerations operated, one would expect the numbers bulge to deflate or at least stagnate under the impact of sales and the phasing out of older submarines. In other words, the bulge might prove to be an aberration.

However, if the late-1970s bulge proves not a hiccough of planning but the signalling of a trend, then the "leadtime" (research and development time lag) consideration outlined above would indeed appear to convey the most logically compelling explanation.

It would seem appropriate, here, to return to the original thrust of our inquiry, the question of the changing character of the navy. The focus will be on the Soviet Northern Fleet, preeminent among the Soviet fleets. The reason for this focus is partly geopolitical, in that it is the only one of the three "western fleets" that can be secured access to open seas. As will be shown in the following chapter, this uniqueness was appreciated from the first days of the Soviet regime and remained a constant policy consideration through the first four decades of its existence. Since the late 1950s, strategic considerations have provided additional rationales for and hence further cemented Soviet perceptions of the crucial nature of the Northern Fleet (see Chapter Six).

These considerations led to a Soviet decision to assign all its western-based strategic submarines, and in fact a very large portion of its overall number of strategic submarines, to the Northern Fleet (with the residual being assigned to her Pacific Fleet). The figures in Table 1 are based on a composite of sources.

The privileged position of the Northern Fleet in the procurement of strategic submarines and in the allocation of the more modern elements of the hunter-killer fleet finds an echo in surface fleet trends—although to a less marked extent.[25] The surface fleet is on the whole far more evenly distributed among the four base areas. Still, if one focuses on larger modern units capable of sustained distant operations, then the North does appear advantaged. The trend in numbers of modern cruisers, for example, is indicated by the fact that the Northern Fleet was allocated four of the nine units completed between 1968 and 1975. Overall, its complement of such units grew from five in 1968, to ten in 1975 (the increase included also one of older vintage), as compared, for example, to a growth from seven to ten for the Pacific Fleet. It has not yet been assigned permanent carrier capability, but while the two helicopter carriers have remained based in the Black Sea, they have frequently visited the Northern complex; the new Kiev V/STOL carrier prolonged the visit initiated when it sailed north from its southern launching area in the fall of 1976. From 1976 to

TABLE 1

Soviet Fleet Distribution of Attack and Strategic Submarines, 1950–77

Type of Submarine	Number																					
	Northern						Baltic				Black Sea				Pacific			
	1950	1968	1973	1975	1976	1977	1950	1968	1975	1977	1950	1968	1975	1977	1950	1968	1975	1977
Strategic SLBM-armed																		
Nuclear	0	14	34	38	44	56	0	0	0	0	0	0	0	0	0	6	11	16
Diesel	0	21	16	15	15	15	0	0	0	0	0	0	0	0	0	14	8	8
Attack with torpedoes and cruise missiles																		
Nuclear	0	18	27	28	30	31	0	0	0	0	0	0	0	0	0	10	12	12
Diesel	0	13	16	16	16	16	0	6	2	2	0	0	1	1	0	3	9	9
Attack with torpedoes																		
Nuclear	0	10	22	26	32	34	0	0	0	0	0	0	0	0	0	5	6	7
Diesel	30	105	72	55	40	55	135	63	74	83	40	40	44	48	110	62	46	46

	1950	1968	1975	1977
Total attack	315	335	319	344
Total attack and strategic	315	390	391	439

Notes: Exact 1975–77 distribution is not known; the breakdown above reflects the presumption that 1968–75 distribution trends have continued. There is one exception to this pattern. For shorthand purposes, the 1975–76 net retirement of 15 diesel attack-torpedo submarines is ascribed solely to the Northern Fleet, where previous attrition had been the most marked; the 1977 increase in newer model units of the category is described as reestablishing 1975 numbers in the Northern and Pacific Fleets, focuses for earlier contractions, with the residual added to the other fleets in accordance with past growth rates.

SALT I permitted the USSR up to 62 "modern" ballistic missile submarines. Since Moscow has already deployed some 34 Yankee and 26 Delta I and II vessels, totalling 60, it is clear that Moscow views the older shorter missile-range classes, such as Hotel and Golf, as excluded from the calculation.

The period 1968–77 saw the nuclear percentage rise from 21 percent to over 58 percent in the Northern Fleet, and from 19 percent to 36 percent in the Pacific Fleet. The newest category, the formidable Deltas, were at least initially allotted only to the Northern Fleet. The qualitative favoring of the Northern Fleet (and, to a lesser extent, the Pacific Fleet) is further evidenced by apparent priority call also on newer diesel categories; Baltic and Black Sea increments obscure transfers of older types.

Numbers of attack submarines began to decline in 1968, and continued to contract until 1976 (a reflection of the de-emphasis of the task of "combat against the enemy fleet"). Until the mid-1970s, the rapid growth in numbers of strategic submarines only barely balanced the withdrawal of attack numbers. The consequential 1977 increase in attack submarines is hence quite arresting. The increase would seem to transcend the sea-control requirements of northern "withholding." It clearly reflects the stress on distant "state interests" and the concomitant requirement to be able to protect "lines of communication" and to assert localized sea control.

Sources: J. F. Skogan, *Sovjetisk Flaateoppbygging i Nord*, N.U.P.I. Notat, Oslo, November 1976; *Jane's Fighting Ships 1950/51, 1973/74, 1975/76, 1976/77 and 1977/78*; and J. L. Moulton, *British Maritime Strategy in the 1970's*, (London, England: Royal United Services Institution, 1969). (1968 figures are culled from this source.) Somewhat different (current) figures are provided in *The Military Balance 1977–78*, IISS, 1977. The composite figures presented should thus not be viewed as absolute; they are approximations, portraying the concensus of the best available data.

December 1977, the Kiev participated in Northern maneuvers as an apparently integral component of that fleet.[26] One does not know of permanent basing dispositions for either this carrier or for its two sister ships now being completed, but the Northern Fleet would likely be involved.

There was a clear break around 1968 as concerns surface fleet distribution patterns. Between 1950 and 1968, the number of Soviet destroyers had increased by 34; nearly half of these (15) had been assigned to the Northern Fleet. Since 1968, however, Northern numbers have stagnated, decreasing, in fact, from 24 to 22 in 1973, at a time when overall navy totals rose slightly, from 104 to 106 (the beneficiary being the Baltic). But the disfavoring of the Northern Fleet on the destroyer issue was more than made up for by the increasing privilege it was accorded after 1968 in the assignment of larger ships. That privilege is emphasized by a consideration of qualitative trends, specifically, the ratio between missile-armed and conventional cruisers. By 1975, the Northern Fleet had acquired a far higher proportion of missile cruisers than other fleets (seven of its ten crusiers were in fact missile ships). It is indicative to note that it had six of the ten Kresta-class cruisers in the Soviet Navy, or 60 percent. (Its seventh missile cruiser was of the even newer Kara class; yet another unit of this type appears to have been added by the end of 1976, and one may presume current and prospective numbers to reflect similarly disproportionate allotments from the ongoing production rate of one a year.)[27]

This dichotomy between trends concerning larger and smaller-type vessel categories in the Northern Fleet is further testified to by a consideration of smaller escort ships and coastal defense vessels. In these categories, the Northern Fleet was second only to the Black Sea Fleet as late as 1973. By 1975, its complement of these types had shrunk from 36 to 31, putting it behind the Baltic Fleet and not far ahead of the Pacific Fleet (whose numbers had also contracted, from 32 to 27).[28]

It is thus clear that the favoring of the Northern Fleet, while definitive, has also been discriminating and not universal. Among surface vesséls it is in the category of larger modern ships capable of sustained distant operations that Northern preeminence is clear. And it is, of course, this surface category that we are concerned with when speculating on future Soviet potentials in areas such as the northwestern Atlantic (or the South Atlantic).

The qualitative if not quantitative trend has clearly been to assign to the Northern Fleet the greater part of what appears to be an increasingly traditional-type offensive capability. While it may have peaked in overall numbers, the Soviet Navy appears to be in the process of transforming itself into a very different and potent animal.[29] The focus for that transformation is the Northern Fleet.

It is now some years since NATO commanders first queried their ability to penetrate the Norwegian Sea in the event of a conflict.[30] Today Moscow may have succeeded in acquiring or be procuring an ability to establish local sea control in areas far further afield. In the process it appeared that the Soviet Union might be further obviating the fetters of the Svalbard/Spitzbergen constellation (see Chapter Six):

> The Soviets have been sending their highly sophisticated Delta-class 14000-ton nuclear submarines, armed with SSN-8 missiles (range: nearly 5000 miles), ever deeper into the Arctic Sea. Says Willy Øs- treng, research associate at the Norwegian Arctic Research Institute: 'For the first time the Soviets have direct access to the high seas, even if under ice, without having to go through international straits. From that area they can shower any part of the U.S. with nuclear missiles.' NATO naval forces, moreover, find it difficult to detect Soviet subs under the constantly shifting ice.[31]

It also appeared that the USSR at the same time might be minimizing whatever residual efficacy Western barrier aspirations (across the so-called G-I-UK gap), might retain against those of its submarines that still suffer from range restrictions and therefore need closer-to-target firing locales. Soviet capabilities now flank traditional bottlenecks to encroach on the nominal responsibility of scantily prepared Canadian and NATO Arctic defense forces: "The Danish Ministry of Defence now believes that Soviet subs can passage between Ellesmere Island and Greenland and, furthermore, that Soviet submarines . . . station themselves under Arctic ice."[32]

One might interject that one presumes the Ellesmere Island-Greenland passage and other potential passages through Canada's Arctic Islands can be closed to hostile traffic. But such closure presupposes a warning time that might not be warranted by the suggested predispositioning. Also, the submarine element in question might in fact not find it necessary to transit through the potential "chokepoints"; the "Canadian basin" would itself serve as a fine stand-off local for "Yankees" SLBMs.

Whether for strategic purposes in the northernmost reaches, or for other "state interests" and designs in the southern hemisphere, Moscow must be acknowledged to have acquired the capacity to establish control over limited areas of its own choosing. In a sense, the very recognition of the futility of more embrasive aspirations has entailed significantly improved prospects for more circumscribed actions. On the other hand, since some of these more restricted, more manageable steps can be hazarded in times of relative peace, their accumulation may prove of far greater potency than could have been ascribed to earlier policies.

SOVIET AIRMOBILITY FORCES

The extraordinary 1970s growth of Soviet airmobile force and potential was not effected by dramatic expansion of the elite paratroop formations, nor was it effected by emulation of the U.S. procurement of functional airmobile units. Moscow chose instead to focus on the larger potential of regular units, in particular the Motor Rifle Brigades, trained and prepared for airmobile employment. The paratroopers as well as the naval infantry were retained as elite commando or shock-troop elements, as the "advance detachments" of air drops and landing assaults. But it was believed, apparently, that the follow-up would be constricted unnecessarily by a designation of particular units. Soviet strategists appear persuaded that regular units can be air or sea-lifted after a minimum of training and that this fact promises greater flexibility and greater potency.[33]

Soviet experiments with helicopter transport of men and material began in the early 1950s, spurred by U.S. airmobile operations in Korea. But it was not until the mid and late 1960s that the concept became a prominent theme in Soviet strategic literature. Again, U.S. airmobile practices in Vietnam provided the acknowledged base for much of the attention and debate.[34]

By 1965, Major General Bochkarev, writing about the high tempo and fluidity requirements of modern conflict, noted the need to integrate tank, armored transport, and helicopter potentials.[35] The vital nature of the helicopter component was increasingly recognized by the late 1960s and through the early 1970s. The mobility increment inherent in the helicopter came to be seen as a crucial partial answer to the lethality potential of a modern battlefield. As the 1970s progressed, it became clear from both Soviet literature and Soviet deployment patterns that the helicopter was becoming central to Soviet tactical concepts.[36]

However, the helicopter was not the sole focus of Soviet airmobility efforts. Distant air projection capability was dramatically upgraded.[37] The 1965 development of the Antonov An-22 (maximum payload 176,350 pounds; speed 460 miles per hour, range 6,800 miles with 99.200-pound payload) was followed by the 1971 appearance of the Ilyushin Il-76 (records include payload of over 70 tons, 154,590 pounds, lifted to a height of 38,390 feet, and a speed of 532.9 miles per hour around a 1000-kilometer circuit with the same load; its maximum range is 4,163 miles). The years 1976–77 saw reports of a follow-up Antonov An-40 (a new, very large, turbofan-powered transport in the class of the USAF's Lockheed C-5 Galaxy) and the wide-bodied Ilyushin Il-86 (the prototype for which flew for the first time on December 22, 1976; cruising speed 560–590 miles per hour at 30,000–36,000 feet; maximum range 2,858 miles). Paratroopers were trained to jump from these craft, a development which significantly extended possible reach and scope.[38] The new means permitted "personnel and armament to be moved over tremendous distances, and allows landings to be made in a short time at any locality at any time of the day or night and in difficult weather conditions."[39] The "great load-carrying capacity, considerable range of flight and high cruising speed" of contemporary transports, together with the fact that they can nonetheless use unpaved airfields,[40] means that one can "put into the place of the landing all that is necessary for conducting prolonged battles."[41]

But the change of greatest consequence lay in the procurement of a family of helicopters, medium and heavy helicopters for general troop mobility, helicopter gunships, helicopters designed to provide attack cover as well as defense against enemy tank and helicopter formations.[42] The 1960-developed Mi-6 (capable of lifting tanks) provided the technological base for the 1970s emergence of the Mi-10 flying crane and the giant Mi-12 (with four engines, it can lift 50 tons or 200 combat troops and has no Western equivalent). The 1970s also saw the appearance of the turbine-powered Mi-2, comparable to U.S. utility helicopters, and the Mi-8, a now standard medium troop carrier (up to 24 troops, or 5 tons of cargo). Finally, there was the introduction of the impressive Mi-24s, one an assault transport, the other an advanced gunship with secondary transport capacity (eight combat troops; machine gun in nose; mountings for four anti-tank missiles; plus rocket pods, each designed for 32 57-millimeter rockets, under the stub wings).

It is believed that regular Motor Rifle troops will need only eight to ten hours of instruction to prepare them for airmobile operations.[43] Two or three hours are allotted to studying the technical characteristics of helicopters, particularly as they affect tactics. The remaining six to seven hours are devoted to boarding and landing procedures, the rapid loading and unloading of combat equipment, the requirements of organization and execution. It is stressed that the whole operation, the dispatch, the in-flight and the landing and deployment phases, may have to be conducted under attack. Cover will be provided by escorting fighting craft (planes and helicopters) and, where applicable, by land and/or naval artillery.[44] But the airlifted soldiers themselves must be prepared to engage in flight as well as immediately upon landing.[45] They are taught "to be ready to repel enemy attacks that will grow in strength and, above all else, (those) of tanks and the strikes of aircraft and battle helicopters."[46]

Airmobile troop formations are slotted to perform a variety of tasks and missions. One of the foremost of these concerns the offensive and defensive imperatives of an actual or feared nuclear environment. Offensively, "Their high mobility allows surprise and the rapid carrying of battle into the enemy's rear so as to utilize the results of nuclear-missile strikes."[47] "The airborne troops are viewed in the capacity of forces who are capable of most effectively and rapidly utilizing the results of the nuclear attacks of the rocket troops for accomplishing the rout of the enemy."[48] The defensive or defensive-offensive dictate is to follow up high priority reconnaissance and intelligence efforts with drops into the "enemy" rear to destroy opposing nuclear systems, the missile sites, the nuclear storage depots, and the command and control facilities.[49] "Initiative," "creativity," and "military guile" are stressed as troop qualities essential to success.[50] The second half of the nuclear mission will be conducted generally by smaller company or platoon-size units and terminated by subsequent helicopter extraction.

Airmobile troops are said to be able "to seize great military-industrial regions and centers" and to hold these until link-up is effected by over-land forces.[51] Airmobile units are also expected to accomplish a number of more specific tactical tasks. "One of the most important and complicated missions assigned to the airborne troops is the seizure and crossing of water barriers."[52] Operations to secure river crossings are conducted with a functional division of the attacking force into a small, heavily armed, seizure group of motor rifle troops, combat engineers, and skindivers, a larger support group to take, hold, and reconnoiter the surrounding terrain, and a platoon-size battalion reserve that can be inserted if and as needed.[53]

Other tasks include the seizure of mountain passes, coastal and inland beachheads, airfields, road junctions (an interesting subtheme in the literature focuses on the Arctic variant, where climatological conditions can impose critical restraints on off-road maneuverability), desert oases, and other potential mobility-affecting focuses and chokepoints.[54] Deep operations to cut off enemy retreats or to intercept enemy reinforcement aspirations are also favored topics of literature and exercises, as is the ability to engage under adverse weather conditions, night or day.[55] Finally, there is, of course, appreciation of the helicopter's more orthodox supply, logistical, and evacuation utility.

Standard air-borne troop equipment includes the BDM tracked infantry combat vehicle, a vehicle sturdy enough to be air-dropped without a platform and with a land speed of 65 kilometers per hour, an in-water speed of 8–10 kilometers per hour; the AUS-57 and AUS-85 air-borne assault guns (helicopter-lifted, with their own speed of 45 kilometers per hour); the 140-millimeter M-1965 heavy mobile rocket launcher (towed, and used by naval infantry as well as air-borne troops); and the 85-millimeter SD-44 auxiliary self-propelled anti-tank gun (helicopter-lifted). To this is mated the impressive array of helicopter platforms noted above, including the Mi-24 gunships.[56]

The Motor Rifle Brigade, the described focus of the Soviet stress on using non-air-borne troops in heliborne assault operations, is normally composed of three companies, each divided into three platoons of three squads each. Normal organic capacity includes anti-aircraft, mortar, and signal platoons, maintenance and medical subunits, and armored personnel carriers. For air-borne missions the MRB can be reinforced with additional mortar and howitzer batteries, combat engineer and anti-tank guided missile platoons, a chemical reconnaisance squad, demolition experts, and skindivers; usually organic elements can also be discarded if superfluous to the mission. There is considerable scope for juggling components for tailoring to specific mission requirements.[57] Helicopter potentials are, furthermore, not integral but organized into regimental units of a separate Tactical Air Army, to be allocated as deemed necessary by the front commander.[58] This is thought to be optimal to considerations of maximum flexibility.

The versatile BDM is given particular stress in the literature as "a basic factor of success."[59] Yet its vulnerability to enemy armor is recognized. It is therefore noted that it needs to be accompanied by PTURS anti-tank missile batteries.[60] The threat to both from enemy helicopter attack may be countered by the addition of ZSU-24-4 air defense (PVO) units and helicopters.[61] Aside from being flexible, mobile, heavy-load carriers, the helicopter's armament potential (including PTURS, non-guided missiles [NURS], aerial machine guns [mgs] and cannon, napalm, and other bombs) is appreciated and emphasized; as a corollary, it is noted that these characteristics of the assault helicopter entails unique ambush potentials, the ability to rise and engage from close cover, and the ability to strike with little warning at armored columns in the flank and rear.[62] But a combined-arms approach is vital. PVO, helicopter, BDM, and other units must be coordinated, for attack and for defense, with particular advantages of one covering the vulnerabilities of the others. The dual or multi-purpose possibilities of each must be accommodated and utilized. Typically, "helicopters have become a new anti-tank weapon; at the same time they are a reliable ally of tanks(!)"[63]

Great emphasis is placed on organization, communication, and execution. "The airborne forces have grown stronger in an organizational respect," as required by the fact that "the sphere of their application in battle has expanded."[64] MRB troops are now expected to be ready to move into organized, full-complement attack within 10 to 15 minutes of landing.[65] (It is presumed that fire from escorting fighters and attack helicopters can hold off an enemy during this short organization phase.)[66]

In-flight communication is facilitated by a common frequency linking the heliborne forces with the escorts.[67] Upon landing, communications are organized, on the commanding officer's direction, by a designated chief of communications.[68] He utilizes the preparatory period to set up a radio net to include all vehicles (tanks, BDMs, and other) in the battalion as well as supporting vessels whose fire will aid the landing (if it is from the sea) and all air cover units. A 1974 description of such an exercise referred to communications equipment (BTRs), R-107s, and R-126s as among the equipment used.[69] This and subsequent articles stress that the question of effective communications is vital to the success of any landing operation. The priority focus on internal communications is complemented by a follow-up emphasis on the disruption of enemy communications.[70] Up to platoon-size sabotage and reconnaissance units are dispatched for this purpose. Effective communications are acknowledged to have been of tremendous importance in the past, too. But it is asserted that they have been made even more crucial by the peculiarities of today's battlefield. Contemporary weapons, nuclear and chemical-biological (C-B) means in particular, impose a previously unknown imperative on the need for flexibility, initiative, and control. Battlefield conditions have become more fluid. There is no longer any easily discernible front or rear. Hence, it is more difficult, although also more essential, for the commander to control the course of battle.[71]

It is of course this factor of communications control that makes the problem of execution a matter of foremost concern. "Combat coordination," "pre-

FIGURE 1

Organization of a Soviet Parachute Battalion

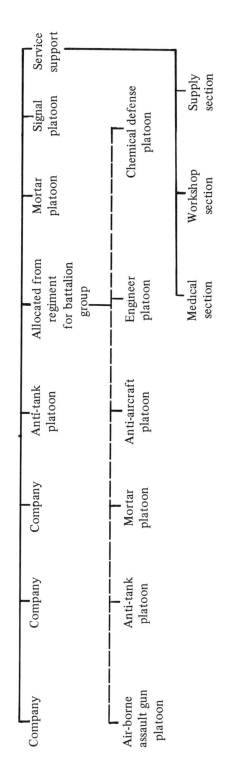

Source: D. R. Jones, ed., *Soviet Armed Forces Review Annual* (Gulf Breeze, Fla.: Academic International, 1978).

FIGURE 2

Organization of a Soviet Air-borne Division, 1976–77

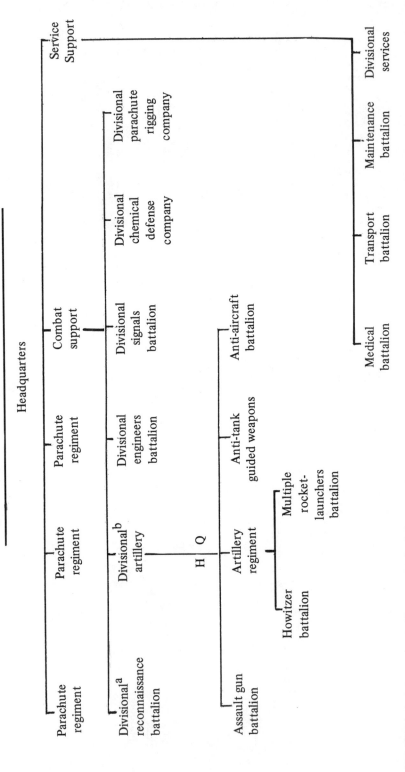

Vehicles:

533 GAZ-69s
703 GAZ-66s
1082 trailers

Artillery:

45 Mortars (in Parachute Regts)
18 122mm howitzers
18 Multiple rocket launchers

127 BMD combat vehicles
18 battle rescue vehicles
18 ASU-85 self-propelled assault
   guns
18 12-millimeter howitzers and field guns

30 Anti-tank guided weapons (ATGW)
36 Anti-aircraft guns
18 ASU-85 mobile airborne assault guns
27 ASU-57 mobile assault guns

138 85-millimeter heavy anti-tank guns and
   missiles
+ the 122-millimeter mortars and 16-tube 140-millimeter
   rocket launchers.

Notes: By 1976–77, U.S. sources had expanded the division's complement to include a reconnaissance battalion. It now contains some 7,500 officers and men, whose mobility and combat capability have been increased by re-equipment with UAZ quarter-ton truck/jeeps, BRDM armored cars, and BMD-1 air-borne combat vehicles. Its table of equipment now includes:

Official British sources in the early 1970s estimated an air-borne division comprised 737 officers and 6,560 non-commissioned ranks, for a total of 7,297 men, and equipment as indicated.

[a]By 1975–1976 American sources included the ATGW and assault gun battalions, but not the anti-aircraft battalion, within the division's artillery regiment.

[b]These units were officially identified in the US Army's *Handbook on the Soviet Armed Forces of 1975.*

Source: D. R. Jones, ed., *Soviet Armed Forces Review Annual* (Gulf Breeze, Fla.: Academic International, 1978).

FIGURE 3

Organization of a Soviet Parachute Regiment

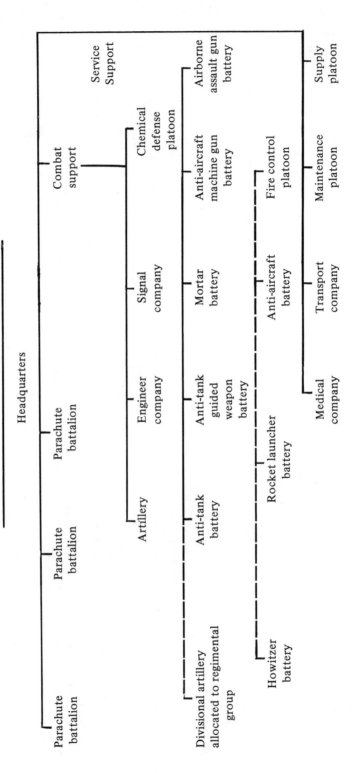

Source: D. R. Jones, ed., *Soviet Armed Forces Review Annual* (Gulf Breezes, Fla.: Academic International, 1978).

paredness to enter battle immediately after landing and ability to use the surprise of their drop and to carry it on at a rapid tempo, boldly, resolutely and actively" is sought from every airmobile exercise.[72]

By 1977, a prominent Soviet strategist felt able to assert:

> At present airborne-landing troops are equipped with the most modern means of battle. There is not another type of troops in which one finds so concentrated such varied forms of weapons and technical equipment. Soviet airborne troops can appear in the enemy's rear with everything that is needed for the successful conduct of a battle (operation), and they are capable of carrying out great strategic missions in contemporary war.[73]

With the approach of the 1980s, U.S. airmobile forces remained quantitatively and perhaps qualitatively superior to those of the USSR.[74] But the innovative expansion of Soviet capabilities appeared favored by greater dynamism. The gap was closing. The totality of the Soviet preference for airmobile (and/or seamobile) employment of regular troop formations also appeared to promise greater potency, though there remained sceptics who queried the consequences of real-life battle conditions. (For organization of air-borne troops, see Figures 1, 2, and 3.)

Yet, to the extent that elements of the USSR's airmobile potential had been tested by real battle, in the Ogaden conflict of 1978, they had shown up well. The decisive stage of the conflict was said to have begun with the Soviet employment of 225 long-range transports. As a Western source described it, "For three weeks the big Antonov planes were launched continuously from different bases." The operation was seen to demonstrate that "the Soviets could move at least three divisions into the Middle East or Africa within ten hours, catching countries in the region by complete surprise."[75]

NOTES

1. *Jane's Fighting Ships 1977/78*, (London, 1977), p. 119.

2. Ibid., p. 117.

3. There is of course a dichotomy here. The Trident missile was designed to have the requisite range to be fired from protected home waters, thus obviating the potential threat of hostile ASW. Yet, while some analysts had pursued the logic of the missile with suggestions ranging down to cheap anchored concrete platforms, decision-making bodies chose instead to fund the mammoth Trident submarine, whose sophistication and consequent expense was a direct corollary of a design intended to challenge that same potential ASW. Hence, "the Trident controversy."

4. See Chapter Two, especially quotations from Kulish and Gorshkov. See also "The Evolution of Soviet Theory re Intervention in Distant Areas," *1978 Soviet Armed Forces Review Annual*, (Gulf Breeze, Fla.: Academic International, 1978).

5. U.S., Senate, *Soviet Oceans Development*, prepared for the Committee on Commerce (Washington, D.C.; Government Printing Office, October 1976).

6. Ibid.

7. Ibid.; see especially "The Civilian Fleets."

8. C. G. Jacobsen, *Soviet Strategy—Soviet Foreign Policy*, 2nd ed. (Glasgow: The University Press, 1974). See also Jacobsen, "Soviet Military-Party Relations . . .", (Ottawa: Carleton University, Current Comment Series no. 10, 1976).

9. *Pravda*, July 25, 1976.

10. See "The Civilian Fleets," in *Soviet Oceans Development*, pp. 257–86; and *Jane's Fighting Ships 1977/78*, p. 117.

11. *Soviet Oceans Development*, pp. 257–86; See also pp. 331–46 and pp. 377–463.

12. For Soviet attitudes, see, for example, S. Pavlov in *Pravda*, February 12, 1976; or I. Gorev in *Novoye Vremya*, no. 11 (March 12, 1976); and *Council of Ministers' resolution* of February 24, 1977.

13. See, for example, J. Best, *The Ottawa Journal*, September 10, 1975.

14. Note, e.g., Canada, Department of National Defence, *ORAE E-M.P.* Ottawa, February 1978.

15. Information based in part on telephone interview with G. D. Hobson, Director, Polar Continental Shelf Project, Ottawa, February 17, 1977; and on Hobson to Jacobsen, April 26, 1977.

16. The wall map in the office of the Director of the Arctic and Antarctic Institute in Leningrad, which charts the impressive array and scope of Soviet scientific endeavors in the area, makes Canada's corresponding programs seem rather weak.

17. See, for example, Canadian Press story, "Soviets on Islands Claimed by Canada," *Ottawa Citizen*, June 12, 1976.

18. *Soviet Oceans Development*, pp. 257–86; and Chapter Seven.

19. See Chapter Two.

20. See Chapter Four.

21. R. Tumkovskii, *Morskoi Sbornik*, no. 7 (1974): 95–99 (hereafter referred to as *MS*); also, for example, V. Evseev, *MS*, no. 9 (1974): 96–100.

22. J. M. McConnell, "Doctrine and Capabilities," in forthcoming book sponsored by U.S. Center for Naval Analyses, Arlington, Va., pp. 1–21.

23. Ibid., pp. 1–22.

24. *Jane's Fighting Ships 1977/78*, p. 117, notes, for example, "Foxtrot" class sales to Libya.

25. See source note for Table 1.

26. See coverage in *Time*, June 27, 1977; or "Soviet Aerospace Almanac 1978," *Air Force* (March 1978): 67.

27. Skogan, *Sovjetisk*; Table 5, p. 20, and *Jane's Fighting Ships 1977/78*, p. 690. (Continuing Kresta II production rate is similar, while that of Krivak destroyers is four per year. See *Jane's Fighting Ships 1977/78*, pp. 691, 696.)

28. Skogan, *Sovjetisk*, Table 8, p. 27.

29. *Jane's Fighting Ships 1976/77*, p. 121, and see Kara cruiser description, p. 702.

30. See, for example, *New York Times*, November 1, 1971.

31. *Time*, June 27, 1977.

32. CBC Report from London NATO Conference, 6:30 PM Atlantic Time, May 10, 1977.

33. A. Golubkov, *Voennyi Vestnik*, no. 1 (1975): 80–83 (hereafter referred to as *VV*); V. Saprunov, *VV*, no. 9 (1977): 61–64; N. Belous, *Voenno-Istoricheskii Zhurnal* (hereafter referred to as *V-IZ*); Noll, (1976): 38; and V. Margelov, *VV*, no. 7 (1977): 61–65,

refers to the specialized elements. On the airmobility potential of regular forces, see, for example, V. Margelov et al., *Bridgehead from the Clouds*, Moscow, 1972 (JPRS57507, p. 27); K. Urtayev, *VV*, no. 3 (1971): 33.

34. I. S. Lyutov and P. T. Sagaydak, *Motostrelkovyi Batalon' v Takticheskom Vozdushnom Desante*, (Moscow: Voenizdat, 1969), pp. 89–90; D. A. Bramlett, *Military Review* (January 1977): 14–25; and see *VV* issues cited elsewhere.

35. M. Bochkarev, et al., "The Modern Revolution in Military Affairs and Its Meaning," in *The Nuclear Revolution in Soviet Military Affairs*, ed. Kintner and Scott, Norman, Oklahoma, 1968, p. 131

36. Yu. Zakharov, *VV*, no. 8 (1977): 63–65; V. Zaitsev and A. Naumov, *VV*, no. 2 (1977): 76–79.

37. "Soviet Aerospace Almanac," *Air Force* (March 1978): 102–03; *Tass*, December 28, 1977; V. Margelov, *V-IZ*, no. 1 (1977): 52–59.

38. A. Dynin, *VV*, no. 8 (1976): 58–62.

39. V. Margelov, *VV*, no. 7 (1977).

40. E. Otlivanchik, *VV*, no. 10 (1976): 53–54.

41. K. Kurochkin, *VV*, no. 2 (1975): 42–46.

42. Yu. Zakharov, *VV*, no. 8 (1977); P. Levchenko, *VV*, no. 9 (1977): 2–6; *Air Force* (March 1978): and *Military Review* (October 1975): 3–15, (November 1975): 3–13, and (January 1977): 14–25.

43. Margelov et al., *Bridgehead*; and K. Urtayev, *VV*, no. 3 (1971): 33.

44. V. Subbotin, *VV*, no. 10 (1975): 89–92; D. Moskalenko, *VV*, no. 5 (1974): 107–11.

45. K. Urtayev, *VV*, no. 3 (1971): 33.

46. V. Margelov, *VV*, no. 7 (1977).

47. I. Bliznik, *VV*, no. 2 (1975): 47–50.

48. V. Margelov, *VV*, no. 7 (1977).

49. V. Margelov, *VV*, no. 1 (1977): 52–59; and see sources referred to in *Military Review* articles cited above.

50. V. Saprunov, *VV*, no. 9 (1977): 61–64; I. Tikhomirov and A. Panasenka, *VV*, no. 2 (1975): 51–54.

51. V. Margelov, *VV*, no. 7 (1977).

52. V. Grechnev, *VV*, no. 12 (1977): 74–77.

53. Lyutov and Sagaydak, *Motostrelkovyi*, pp. 21–22.

54. B. Dregal, *VV*, no. 4 (1977): 74–77; P. Beregov, *VV*, no. 6 (1974): 19–25; I. Dynin, *VV*, no. 7 (1974): 62–65; and see Bramlett, *Military Review* (January 1977): 14–25.

55. Ibid.; also R. Salikhov, *VV*, no. 6 (1977): 64–67; and A. Bykov, *VV*, no. 8 (1974): 67–70.

56. From charts prepared by C. N. Donnelly for the 1978 *Soviet Armed Forces Review Annual* (Gulf Breeze, Fla.: Academic International, 1978); and "Soviet Aerospace Almanac," p. 106.

57. V. Chernyak, *VV*, no. 6 (1968): 29–34; Margelov et al., *Bridgehead*, pp. 30–31.

58. G. H. Turbiville, *Military Review* (October 1975): 5.

59. N. Kononov, *VV*, no. 3 (1977): 57–60.

60. Ibid.

61. Yu. Zakharov, *VV*, no. 8 (1977).

62. Ibid.

63. Review in *VV*, no. 2 (1974): 124–26.

64. V. Margelov, *VV*, no. 7 (1977).

65. V. Urtayev, *VV*, no. 3 (1971): 41.

66. V. Subbotin, *VV*, no. 10 (1975).

67. S. Goryachkin, in Bramlett, *Military Review* (January 1977): 14–25.

68. D. Moskalenko, *VV*, no. 5 (1974): 107–11.

69. Ibid.

70. G. H. Turbiville, *Military Review* (October 1975): 12.

71. P. Pavlenko, *VV*, no. 11 (1974): 52–55.

72. V. Saprunov, *VV*, no. 9 (1977): 61–64.

73. V. Margelov, *V-IZ*, no. 1 (1977).

74. G. H. Turbiville, *Military Review* (October 1975) provides comparative figures. See also *The Military Balance, 1978-79*, IISS, London, 1978, p. 8.

75. "Soviet Aerospace Almanac."

6

MOSCOW AND THE NORTHERN RIM: GEOPOLITICAL DETERMINANTS

Soviet northern rim policy is shaped by geopolitical restraints and imperatives. Moscow has always focused on the larger amalgam of northern concerns; its policy toward particular national-territorial or ethnic groupings in the north has been a reflection of the abiding Soviet perception that they are interdependent components of a more important totality. An analysis of Soviet policy towards Finland, Norway, or, indeed, Scandinavia as a whole would be crippled if divorced from the larger context of Soviet military-political, strategic policy in the north. The perceptual totality is precisely strategic. Its core is military-political rather than political-ideological or economic. Considerations affecting the latter spheres have always taken a back seat to considerations flowing from the former. Furthermore, it is quite clear that the military-political priority concern has been and will continue to be dictated by geopolitical determinants.[1] The following analysis will proceed from an introductory survey of the concept of "Finlandization" that is, of the political arena. It will then focus on the crux of Soviet concern, the Svalbard-Kola problem complex, the strategic parameters that define and circumscribe Soviet exit to the high seas. A final section will then look at the circumstances affecting Soviet strategic prospects at the North American, western reach of its Arctic thrust.

MOSCOW'S NORTHERN RIM POLICY: A BACKGROUND SURVEY

During the interwar period, the war years, and, to a lesser extent, through the first postwar decade and a half, the primary determinant of Soviet policy lay in the perceived geographic threat to the Leningrad heartland. Even in these early years, however, there was—as evidenced in the wording of the Brest-Litovsk

Treaty—an astonishingly prescient awareness of Svalbard's potential import. The relative weight assigned these two linchpins of Soviet policy began to shift during World War II. During the last two decades, with the emergence of the Murmansk base complex as the indisputably most vital single strategic nerve center in the USSR, priority has been focused squarely on the strategic imperatives of Svalbard and the Kola exit.

Before proceeding to this analysis, however, it would appear appropriate to present some comment on the concept of "Finlandization," which will also provide a useful point of departure. Ironically, its utility derives perhaps less from its validity than from the extent to which its emotive projection is at variance with reality. Finnish governments of the postwar era have consistently termed Western concepts of "Finlandization" as very far off the mark as concerns the reality of the Soviet-Finnish relationship.[2]

The "Paasikivi line," the embodiment of Finnish neutrality and foreign policy ever since Juhu Kusti Paasikivi was appointed Prime Minister in October 1944, has seen the Lilliputian-Goliath relationship as determined by different premises and therefore as having different consequences than believed or feared by outside commentators.[3] Paasikivi and current President Kekkonen were convinced that the historical experience disproved the thesis of inherently aggressive Soviet intent, be it military, political, or ideological. They emphasized the consistent restraint and limitation of Soviet policy posture and initiatives at times of Finnish weakness. They stressed the continuity between the prewar demands of a Moscow too feeble to expect compliance and the postwar moderation of a Moscow capable of enforcing much further ranging designs. Paasikivi and later Finnish leaders became persuaded that the Soviet stance embodied and mirrored the natural and, hence, in the historical context legitimate security concerns and prerogatives of a major power. Accepting the defensive nature and legitimacy of Moscow's posture they determined to satisfy its implied requirements, expecting *quid pro quo* freedom to pursue Finnish preferences in the domestic political, economic, and cultural domains. They interpret history to have proved that Moscow will forego opportunities to affect these as long as it remains satisfied that its security needs are met. The Finnish interpretation sees Soviet policy as a Monroe doctrine in miniature, a denial to outside power involvement. The harsher realities of Finnish-Soviet history encourages one to presume a supporting motivational instinct of self-preservation: it is essential that the Bear continue to feel that minimal control satisfies its interests; it is essential that one does not provide ammunition to those Soviet quarters which might seek pretexts to justify further ranging demands. Still, this does not alter the fact that the above *prima facie* Finnish arguments do find considerable historic justification. While they may provide only a partial explanation, too orthodox a denigration of their sincerity may be akin to throwing the baby out with the bathwater.

Finnish official sentiments might be seen to echo those of Canadian Prime Minister Trudeau addressed to the National Press Club in Washington, in March 1969:

> Americans should never underestimate the constant pressure on Canada which the mere presence of the United States has produced. We're a different people from you and we're a different people partly because of you. . . . Living next to you is in some ways like sleeping with an elephant. No matter how friendly and even-tempered is the beast, if I can call it that, one is affected by every twitch and grunt. . . . But it should not therefore be expected that this kind of nation, this Canada, should project itself . . . as a mirror image of the United States.[4]

Finnish government spokesmen would note that their elephant has, in fact, twitched and grunted less, or at least in a less all-encompassing fashion. Finnish foreign security policy is as neighbor-determined as Canada's, but its economic, cultural, and, perhaps, political freedom to maneuver is not as encumbered by neighborly involvement as is Canada's. Certainly formal or demonstrable Soviet control or influence over Finnish economy and culture seems much less extensive than that of the United States in relation to Canada.[5]

An analogy with Austria[6] might well be more apt, although Vienna's distance from the elephant's belly cushions the impact. The Austria analogy is useful because Vienna's more prominent exposure in the Western consciousness has generated both a more widespread appreciation of its domestic freedoms and a more benevolent understanding of its foreign policy restraint. The positing of the analogy is, therefore, an antidote to what is integral to most Westerners' concept of Finlandization, namely, the element of specter. While the concept has contained an element of bewildered admiration (some Finns would say a mistakenly premised admiration) at Helsinki's continued integrity, it has also always had a distinctly negative connotation, an odor of helplessness. Perceptual reality might be better served if Finland were called Austrianized, and if the phenomenon usually associated with the term Finlandization was renamed Canadianization or Romanianization. The reality of Canada and Romania, both on occasion flamboyantly independent in words, yet both accommodating extensive outside influence not only on security concerns but also in the domestic arenas of economy and culture, is probably closer to the emotive context of Finlandization than is the reality of Finland.[7] Ultimately, it is perhaps impossible to balance truly the undoubted psychological scars of Finland's unique invasion memories against, say, the far greater degree of *pro forma* dependence of Canada's current fiscal and social health. All that can be said with confidence is that measurable indices favor Helsinki.

This does not mean that the Western specter of Finlandization can be dismissed as a distortion occasioned solely by distance and ignorance. It is certainly due in part to the Western penchant for generalization and categorization (in this case into Cold War stereotypes) and the consequent inability or unwillingness to accommodate uniqueness. Nevertheless, the traditional concept of Finlandization cannot be said to have been totally alien to Scandinavia.

The concept clearly commanded some support even in Finland itself, although vocal support appeared restricted to certain non-establishment circles and usually took the form of a fear of a trend rather than a conviction of actuality.[8] The concept found a similarly limited resonance in Sweden. There is scant evidence that Swedish government quarters ever considered the specter a threat to Swedish society as such. Its occasional positing by Swedish officials to Western colleagues appears always to have been couched with reference to Finland and in terms of Stockholm policy having to guard against initiatives which Moscow might perceive to warrant or demand increased Soviet pressure on Helsinki. The skeptic might toy with the idea of tactical bargaining value. Swedish policy retains its prewar roots and cannot be shown to have been significantly affected by the origin or evolution of the Finlandization concept. The moralizing aspect of Swedish neutrality has remained evenhanded, former Prime Minister Palme was an contemptuous of Husak as he was scathing of Thieu.

In Norway, the Western concept of Finlandization has enjoyed somewhat greater prominence in the outward posture of the pro-NATO establishment elite. But here also it has been given a peculiar twist. The negligible electoral support of pro-Moscow parties (see below) always undermined the credibility of a domestic threat. Instead, the concept came to serve as a cornerstone of the Norwegian theory of Nordic balance. This is the theory that postulates that Norway's NATO ties counter Soviet pressure on Finland, that Norway's freedom to lift the self-imposed qualifications of its NATO association (no nuclear weapons, no foreign troop contingents, no NATO exercises near Soviet territory, and so on) serves as a deterrent to Soviet designs vis à vis Helsinki.

Finnish government spokesmen have disputed the premise, and voiced concern that the supposed deterrent could become the midwife, spurring rather than discouraging the eventuality against which it is purportedly designed.[9] Notwithstanding the possible fallaciousness of Norway's pro forma argument, however, the theory has served Norwegian interests well. One might even venture to say that it is its very fallaciousness that has guaranteed its utility—or is that postulation too colored by a cynic's taste for irony?

Norway's theory of Nordic balance might be accepted at face value. But there are at least two other very different yet compelling ways of looking at it, both suggested by a retrospective approach. On the one hand, the theory proved to be the vehicle for Norway to obtain the security guarantees of NATO membership at a uniquely low price of NATO obligations. The desire for security guarantees was a consequence of the establishment's perception of the lessons of April 1940, and of its profound sense of itself as a Western-oriented entity; the minimizing of obligations could be seen as necessary obeisance to residual neutralist aspirations and to an equally traditional isolationist and ethnocentric distaste for continental embroilments. The second line of reasoning, one which would be perfectly compatible with that outlined above, would focus on considerations of *real-politik*. Norway after all, is itself close to the beast, particularly in the north. As will be seen below, Norwegian policy makers would have had reason to shy away from the sharper edges of confrontation. Established Soviet sensitivity in the north encouraged alarmist projections of the consequences of too close a NATO presence. There was reason to fear the limits of Soviet tolerance, the limits of deterrence, and the dividing line between deterrence and counterproductive provocation.

Some further comment on the subversion element of the Finlandization concept appears warranted at this juncture.[10] Finland is the only Scandinavian country with an indigenous communist movement in the same league as, say, those of France or Italy. It is a movement with early twentieth-century roots. But, compared to its French and Italian brethren, it seems stagnant and with scant prospect of further growth. As a vehicle for Soviet influence it might even be said to have had a retarding effect; its electoral appeal has been inversely affected by sometime perceptions of Soviet or ideological assertiveness.

In Norway, Sweden, and Denmark, pro-Moscow parties have suffered from a miniscule but equally stagnant base (a base swelled only slightly and temporarily in the immediate postwar glow of alliance memories and of exemplary Soviet conduct in and withdrawal from northern Norway). Soviet-oriented communist parties languish at one to three percent in opinion polls. The Marxist-attracted Socialist People's Parties also appear to be wallowing, at less than ten percent. One ought in any case be leery indeed of the view that these might serve as conduits for Moscow. They denounce Soviet policy as being all too often the antithesis of Marxism. They have no regard for Soviet directives, strive for national models of socialism, and cooperate with the left wing of the (pro-NATO) Social Democratic parties. They are "national socialists" seeking wider left-wing coalitions, but in competition rather than alliance with the Communist Parties.

Iceland's case is peculiar in that here the Communist Party did merge both with other Marxist groupings and with those traditional archenemies of Moscow and the Third International, the Social Democrats, thereby winning 18 percent of the vote and occasional government representation. But the Icelandic Communist Party is a breed apart from the norm. It has muted doctrinal preferences and focused instead on more secular issues, such as wages, unemployment, housing, inflation, and economic policy. Anti-imperialism has taken second place to pro-independence and national pride. To a degree this has, of course, made them more effective. There is no real evidence, however, to substantiate a fear that Moscow could manipulate this effectiveness. Nor, on the other hand, should this fact necessarily cause solace in NATO capitals. Radicalized nationalism, because of its greater appeal potential, might well come to pose a more formidable, if less extreme, threat to NATO potentials than could ever have been engineered by an orthodox Communist Party. One could argue that a Sovietized Iceland had never been credible, that the denial of Soviet presence had never been challenged, but that the real threat of denial "tous azimuths" (as de Gaulle would have said) loomed as a distinct possibility.

One is forced to conclude that subversion, or at least the type of subversion postulated by the Finlandization concept, is not in the cards as far as today's Scandinavia is concerned. This would appear to be acknowledged both in Moscow and in Scandinavian capitals. Policy revolves instead around strategic and geopolitical dictates, perceptions and misperceptions.

THE SOVIET EXIT: THE SPITZBERGEN CONTROVERSY, GEOPOLITICAL SENSITIVITIES, AND CONSEQUENT SECURITY PREROGATIVES[11]

Sovereignty over the Svalbard/Spitzbergen archipelago has long been a subject of extreme concern and sensitivity to Soviet security organs. Towards the end of World War II, in a discussion with then Norwegian Foreign Minister Trygve Lie, Molotov presented a succinct synopsis of Soviet anxieties. His words indicate the enduring character of Moscow's concern. They followed Norway's refusal to a Soviet demand that Norway give up its suzerainty over Svalbard and Bear Island (the former was to be put under a joint Norwegian-Soviet administration which was to act "as a condominium"; the latter to be transferred outright) and were frank and to the point:

> The Dardanelles . . . here we are locked in . . . Oresund . . . here we are locked in. Only in the North is there an opening, but this war has shown that the supply line to Northern Russia can be cut or interfered with. This shall not be repeated in the future. We have invested much in this part of the Soviet Union, and it is so important for the entire Union's existence that We shall in future ensure that Northern Russia is permitted to live in security and peace.[12]

Molotov acknowledged that the Norwegians were friendly neighbors but persisted: "Shall we settle this in a friendly manner, or shall there be a dispute?"[13] Admiral Golovko summed up, "Without the Kola inlet the Northern fleet cannot exist . . . the Kola inlet is necessary to the state."[14]

The dynamic postwar expansion of Kola base facilities and the introduction and buildup of strategic naval forces underlined the area's significance. The basis for the abiding Soviet concern is clearly to be found in the field of security. Its acute sensitivity reflects strategic realities. Defense activation procedures entail certain time requirements vis à vis incoming strikes,[15] while offensive prospects must be secured against such countermeasures as might jeopardize their employment (for example, the now legally defunct but nevertheless technologically plausible potential of Polaris/Poseidon-based BMDs proximate enough to intercept during ICBMs' vulnerable ascent phase).[16] Moscow could not accept active hostile utilization of adjacent lands and water.[17]

Norway has consistently acknowledged the legitimacy of this position by refusing to permit the stationing of offensive missiles on Norwegian soil, by vetoing NATO exercises within about 300 kilometers of the border, and by insisting that it has not and will not permit the peacetime integration of Norwegian radar facilities into U.S. strategic submarine targeting designs.[18] The Norwegians clearly conduct some tactical electronic and other surveillance of Soviet developments in the area. The fact that the Western coast of the Ribachi Peninsula is within visual, naked-eye surveillance distance from the border makes such activity inevitable.[19] But this limited intelligence seeking can be tolerated by the Soviet Union. It is surveillance integrated into hostile strategic systems that could not be tolerated. Any act or tendency that promised such integration would clearly tread on very sensitive Soviet corns.[20]

This is evidenced by articles like that printed by *Krasnaya Zvezda* in spring of 1969,[21] forcefully condemning alleged radio and radar communications between northern Norwegian installations and U.S. nuclear submarines on patrol in northern waters. There appeared little reason to doubt the Norwegian assurances that the charge was mistaken. The Soviet Union must furthermore have known it to be inaccurate since it presumably had means of verification. One must infer that the Soviet allegation mirrored not belief but rather fear regarding potential activities. The allegation belonged to the realm of declaratory policy, a warning of the unacceptability of any such communication. This sensitivity and posture was if anything reinforced through the 1970s.[22]

If Soviet statements have been correctly interpreted then it would be logical to conclude that the type of intelligence integration referred to would be not only theoretically unacceptable but could provoke countering actions. A Norwegian departure from its tacit concessions to Kola security requirements might well be seen to constitute an invitation to "a Cuba in reverse"; Kola security demands are so essential that Moscow would likely accept the risks associated with intervention.[23]

The astounding Soviet buildup of strategic and maritime facilities in the north at one time stirred Western fears for northern Norway's fiords.[24] This concern now appears less acute. Nuclear and other developments shrank the expected burgeoning of Soviet naval base requirements; the long-range character of emerging fishing and merchant fleets similarly defused the expansionary base requirements of its civilian fleets. It is clear that Kola base prospects have not been exhausted. A cursory glance at relevant maps, furthermore, suggests that they are unlikely to be exhausted.[25] The notion of physical Soviet need for Norwegian space is untenable, and the associated specter of Soviet strategic need is no more viable. The offensive benefice of a westward movement of its base complexes was always logically offset by the defensive advantages of status quo—so long as the practical neutrality of the intervening territory remained unquestioned. The Soviet strategic need, or imperative, as regards northern Norway lies in its exclusion from active participation in hostile strategic designs.[26]

By the late 1960s, basic Soviet security requirements appeared to have been met. The failure to acquire Svalbard and Bear Island facilities was compensated for by the establishment of military bases (and radar installations) on ice floes in the Barents and White Seas and on Franz Josef's Island.[27] Electronically equipped surface vessels and the presumed employment and integration of ocean floor monitoring devices[28] further supplemented early warning capabilities. Finally, the establishment of such a North Sea naval presence as promised effectively to isolate Norway behind (that is, east of) potential front lines[29] secured against a possible future Norwegian abnegation of self-restraint.

The early 1970s, however, brought new anxieties. On the one hand, technology had outstripped reigning international law. The Geneva Convention of 1958 had stipulated coastal states' authority to extend to depths of 200 meters, or such depths to which exploitation was feasible. But, whereas 200 meters had originally been thought the limit of technological feasibility, by 1970, one could already envisage oil drilling at depths of 400 meters and ocean-bed mineral extraction at depths to 1,500 meters,[30] and all bets were off regarding future potentials. The early 1970s thus saw the entire ocean floor between northern Norway and Svalbard placed in the "exploitable" category. And while the logic of the Geneva text and of Norway's 1963 assertion of sovereignty over its continential shelf was unequivocal,[31] the continued absence of a more realistic international law consensus on the outer limits of coastal states' rights did inject an element of uncertainty. The element was all the more disturbing in view of the discovery that the geological structure of the shelf between Norway and Svalbard was extremely favorable to oil and gas prospects.[32] The specter of a multinational scramble to install rigs in the area, a specter of some urgency following the oil crisis subsequent to the 1973 Middle East War, spurred emphatic Norwegian reassertions of sovereignty,[33] and Norwegian-Soviet negotiations.[34] The security implications of a forest of rigs in the area was a nightmare to Moscow; knowledge thereof was a nightmare to Oslo.[35]

But before delving further into the legal status of the Svalbard archipelago and the Norwegian shelf and into ongoing negotiations, some further note must be paid to the geopolitical peculiarities of the situation, the more so since these exacerbate the area's sensitivity.

Svalbard is sensitive not only because of its proximity to Kola. What makes its status of vital concern to Moscow is its command of the northern shore of the mouth of that natural ice-bound fiord through which Kola-based vessels must pass on their way to and from western seas. The ice limit goes south from Spitzbergen to about Bear Island and then arches eastward until finding its continental anchor at Mys Svjatoi Nos.[36] Northern Norway and northwestern Kola form the southern shore of the "artificial" fiord, the distance from the Norwegian border to the ice limit being 240 nautical miles—not counting the smaller fiord leading into Murmansk and the numerous bays.[37] The integration of Svalbard and/or northern Norway into active anti-Soviet military activities would obviously be intolerable. They control not just one but the only approach to Kola.

The minimum demand of Soviet and, in earlier years, Russian policy has therefore always revolved around effective Svalbard neutrality. It is symptomatic that even the chaos and civil war embroiling the early revolutionary regime did not suffice to drown the concern; the 1918 Brest-Litovsk Treaty between the still young government of Lenin and that other outcast, defeated Germany, contained a clause demanding equal rights on the archipelago. Although Moscow finally acceded to the Svalbard Treaty of 1920,[38] which allowed for Norwegian suzerainty in return for demilitarization and equal exploitation rights for all signatories' subjects, in February 1924,[39] it remained a jealous guardian of the conditional clauses. Concern as to German wartime activities sparked the above-mentioned Molotov initiative as well as a followup initiative aimed at giving the Soviet Union shared responsibility for Svalbard's defense (this demand was only refused by the Norwegian Storting in January 1947, as a by-product of the emerging Cold War).[40] Similar concern arising from Oslo's 1949 adherence to NATO was only defused by Norway's late-1951 assurances that the action did not affect the provisions of the 1920 Treaty.[41] Continued sensitivity was manifest when Norway began constructing an airfield in the early 1970s (Norwegian reassurance of nonmilitary intent was here to be supported by the agreed stationing at the field of a Soviet contingent to service Soviet planes and helicopters) and when Moscow demurred as regards the July 1971 Norwegian-imposed petroleum exploration regulations.[42]

The current status of international law concerning Svalbard and the surrounding waters and ocean beds is best approached from the vantage point of Norwegian interpretation, partly because its basic suzerainty is not questioned and partly because Norway commands a consensus on most points at issue:[43]

> The point of departure must be paragraph 1 of the Svalbard Treaty. According to this all signatories recognize Norway's "full and absolute sovereignty over the Spitzbergen archipelago." Article 2 of the treaty stipulates certain concrete restrictions to this sovereignty. But it is clear from the treaty that these special restrictions are specifically enumerated. Outside of these restrictions article one's main principle operates without limitations.
>
> As will be shown, the Svalbard Treaty does not affect the Continental Shelf. The same comment applies to the sovereignty restrictions that are specifically enumerated in the Svalbard Treaty.

According to the Svalbard Treaty's article 2 all contracting parties' subjects have equal rights to hunting and fishing "within those areas mentioned in article 1 and their territorial waters." That is, article 2 clearly and unequivocally asserts that it concerns not only the land areas mentioned in article 1 but also the territorial waters surrounding the islands.

It is likewise stipulated in article 3 that all Treaty members' subjects shall have equal opportunity to conduct any maritime, industrial, mining and trade activity "both on land and in the territorial waters." Again, this means on islands, large and small skerries, and the territorial sea.

The equal rights principle the Treaty prescribes in articles 2–3 applies according to its wording only to Svalbard's land territory and Svalbard's territorial waters. As concerns these specific areas there are certain concrete restrictions to the Norwegian exercise of sovereignty. Beyond these specially enumerated instances and certain other exceptions expressly mentioned in the Treaty, article one's main principle operates without restrictions. . . . When articles 2–3 of the Svalbard Treaty also refer to territorial waters, and not just "land area," then this is due to the fact that both articles cover "fishing and maritime activities." Territorial waters is not mentioned in the Svalbard treaty's articles 7, 8, which deal specifically with "Ownership" and "Mining."

It follows that the Norwegian Continental Shelf is clearly not affected by the Svalbard Treaty's decisions. This interpretation is reinforced by other Treaty clauses.

This article 7 decrees that as regards the acquisition and exploitation of ownership rights, herein included mining rights, Norway commits herself to accord equal treatment to Treaty partners' subjects, but only for those areas mentioned in the Treaty's article 1. The Treaty's article 1 is explicitly limited to the Svalbard archipelago's land areas, that is to islands and large and small skerries. The equal rights clause of article 7 ought therefore in principle not even apply to territorial waters.

Article 8 provides further support for this interpretation in that this article commits Norway to establish mining regulations for areas mentioned in article 1, which again in principle means the land areas of Svalbard. . . . Paragraph 1 of the mining regulations (enacted in August of 1925) refers only to islands and large and small skerries. Paragraph 9 contains clauses regarding claim demarcations which demonstrate that they focus on land areas. Claims must be demarcated with markers in hard rock or through other lasting means . . . in the field.[44]

(Anyway) . . . the continental shelf in the area off Troms/Finmark and Svalbard—constitutes a natural extension of the land masses of the Norwegian mainland. Under Norwegian and international law, based on the exploitation criteria, Norway therefore has sovereign rights over these areas, regardless of the Svalbard Treaty.[45]

Norway thus tried to preempt speculation by foreclosing debate on the continental shelf and by presenting such a strict definition of Svalbard Treaty clauses as would also reserve unto itself petroleum and mineral extraction rights in Svalbard territorial waters. However, what appeared to be a backup bargaining position as regards the territorial waters issue was noted at the same time. It reflects the more conciliatory range of Oslo's perception of possible negotiating parameters: "Article 2 of the Treaty mentions measures for protecting the natural environment of the island group. . . . Under the exercise of their legislative and administrative authority, the Norwegian authorities are obligated to undertake the balancing involved here."[46]

The late 1976 unilateral Norwegian imposition of a 200-mile fisheries zone around Svalbard, a zone to be regulated and policed (albeit "impartially") by Norwegian agencies, testified to the immutable core of Norway's posture.

Initial Soviet reaction to the Norwegian stance was cool.[47] As a growing maritime power the Soviet Union was loathe to countenance the freedom of the seas implications of vague extensions of ocean states' jurisdiction; as an established actor on the Svalbard scene it was loathe to accept regulations of possible restricting import. Finally, it was clearly loathe to make concessions regarding Svalbard proper at a time of ongoing negotiations to delineate the boundary between Norwegian and Soviet continental shelves.

Soviet opposition to Norway's assertion of continental shelf sovereignty jarred with its own traditional espousal of the sector principle and its corollary of Soviet suzerainty over that part of the Arctic Ocean bounded by the longitudinal extremities of the Union's northern territories (with an eastward identation between the Svalbard archipelago's southern and northern latitudinal limits, drawn along the longitudinal median between Svalbard and Franz Josef's land).[48] The Soviet position reflected general antipathy towards the early 1970s' somewhat anarchic proliferation of unilaterally promulgated coastal states' assertions of ocean sovereignty claims, and it reflected the natural concerns of free passage of what had become one of the world's major maritime powers.

But the Soviet position softened appreciably during the first half of the 1970s. In part, this was no doubt due to its realization that the mushrooming trend to extend coastal states' ocean and ocean-floor exploitation rights could be seen to complement and indirectly sanctify its view of the sector principle. One might point to the fact that the southern reaches of the Arctic Ocean, the Barents, Kara, Laptev, and East Siberian Seas, are extraordinarily shallow; the ocean floors here involved are all within rather easily exploitable depths.[49]

Another motive for Soviet flexibility might be inferred from a presumed reluctance to jeopardize its self-espoused role as protector of Third World interests; most of the more assertive coastal right's nations were counted among those otherwise less privileged. It should also be said that Moscow has in fact succeeded in circumventing some of the restrictions inherent in coastal states' rights extensions (see Chapter Seven).

There emerged a careful differentiation of the rights of free passage and the rights of exploitation. As regards the former, Moscow's firmly stated complementarity of interests with Washington, London, and other maritime powers appeared likely to insure the perpetuation of traditional concepts. As regards the rights of exploitation, evolving Soviet attitudes tended more and more to complement the aspirations of Third World nations. While continuing to insist on a 12-mile territorial waters limit through the mid-1970s, the trend of the Soviet policy stance was indicated by its suggestion that continental shelf rights extend to whichever was greater, the 500-meter isobath or 100 nautical miles beyond the baselines from which territorial seas were measured.[50] Moscow's position moved towards acceptance of the 1972 tenet:

> In view of the practice chosen by a number of Latin American states and other developing nations, it is . . . politically unrealistic to believe that a distance of less than 200 nautical miles off shore would be acceptable as a criterium of international law. The alternative depth criterion might be suggested to be 500 or 1,000 meters.[51]

By 1975, four years, two relatively unsuccessful Law of the Sea Conferences (Caracas and Geneva), and a further proliferation of unilateral claims later, it appeared clear that nothing less than the outer limits suggested in the above quotation would prove acceptable. Law of the Sea consensus was moving towards 200 nautical miles and/or 1,000-meter isobath coastal states' reserve exploitation zones,[52] with at least some kind of "common heritage of mankind" stipulation to cover exploitation of unaffected ocean areas.

The year 1976 saw the codification of these trends, as most developed nations chose to anticipate or force Law of the Sea progress through unilateral declarations of 200-mile economic exploitation zones off their shores. The Soviet Union joined the procession in December, with the justification that the closing of other venues put a premium on the protection of adjacent resources.[53]

The developments promised considerable benefit to Moscow. Soviet fleet movements, naval and civilian, would remain basically unfettered. On the other hand, as regards ocean floor exploitation, it secured for itself a disproportionately vast expanse of geologically highly promising real estate.[54] In addition, it was surely not lost on Moscow that the trend would, conversely, serve to restrict the less fortunately endowed U.S. access to noncontiguous shelf riches. By restricting the "common heritage of mankind" acreage to more dramatic depths, the Soviet Union might furthermore effectively retard the United States' ability to draw maximum benefit from residual U.S. deep sea mining technological superiority, while the Soviet Union pursued its now very impressive priority research efforts.[55] As regards non-mining exploitation of deep sea resources, the Soviet Union was of course already in a highly favorable position as a result of the dramatic quantitative and qualitative expansion of its fishing fleets it had effected through the previous decade.[56]

But while international law on ocean floor exploitation rights was tending both to buttress Soviet northern policy and to reserve for Norway the sensitive depths between its northern counties and Svalbard, there remained the uncertainties of continuing delimitation differences. There remained substantial discrepancies between the delimitation suggested by the Soviet-championed sector principle and that suggested by the 1958 Geneva Convention clause, to which Norway had adhered, on the median line principle.[57]

Preliminary negotiations were initiated in 1970, a fact which in itself could be taken to reflect a degree of flexibility on the part of Moscow. But negotiations proceeded slowly. By 1975, Norwegian sources were acknowledging a new Soviet willingness at least to concede Norway's basic position on the northern shelf issue (as a practical corollary of the evolution of Moscow's position on the larger Law of the Sea issue) as well as Norway's interpretation of the import of the Svalbard Treaty.[58] But the demarcation issue remained vexing. The fourth negotiating session, in the fall of 1976, again failed to resolve the impasse. June 1977 finally saw movement of possible import, with the initialling of a temporary fishing agreement covering disputed waters (an area comprising about 34.2 percent west of the sector, 61.5 percent of the "gray area" and 4.3 percent east of the median line was opened to joint fishing, with each authority responsible for its own vessels).[59] The issue was diffused somewhat with the ratification of this agreement, but continued tension potential was evident in Oslo's subsequent refusal to extend the compromise with an analagous resolution of the territorial dispute as such.

Still, while Oslo continued to hold out for a more beneficial territorial apportionment, the very fact that Moscow proved willing to acquiesce in even an implied departure from earlier sovereignty claims was dramatic. The degree of Soviet flexibility thus evinced stems, as indicated, from a number of considerations. First and foremost among these is that of security. With the specter of a multinational oil and gas scramble in the area being well nigh intolerable from a security viewpoint, Moscow was clearly finding it preferable to make some concessions to Norwegian claims. The promised perpetuation and extension of the now traditional de facto military quasi-neutrality of Finmark was far preferable to any conceived alternative, and it was surely the paramount, crucial nature of this concern that also induced Soviet flexibility on the formal delimitation issue—just as the converse Norwegian willingness to compromise, as evinced through its presence at the negotiating table, surely demonstrated Norwegian recognition of the fact that too great an exacerbation of tensions in the area could prove dangerously counterproductive. Moscow could find relative comfort in the low-risk promise of present-type Norwegian control over the "fiord-mouth."[60] If such a solution proved unfeasible, however, then geopolitical realities would appear to dictate consideration of higher risk alternatives.

One other consideration may have been present in Soviet calculations. As demonstrated by the 1975 Norwegian development of the revolutionary concrete drilling platform "Condeep," Norway has emerged in the forefront of world ocean drilling technology and has become an alternative source of the most advanced deep sea oil and gas extraction technology. This may have been a factor in inducing Moscow's willingness to countenance the limited fishing compromise, a compromise which by its very nature held precedent connotations for the question of territorial delimitation.[61]

Yet finally, one must remember that the linchpin for all Soviet policy initiatives in the area lies in the Kola base complexes and that the character of these initiatives is determined by the geopolitical realities and constraints of the Kola Peninsula. Geopolitical facts dictated the development of Kola as the most vital core area of expanding Soviet naval and civilian fleets. Geopolitical facts dictated these fleets' dependence on unimpeded passage through the Norway-Bear Island gap. Soviet missile tests into disputed waters since 1975, and the stepped-up pace of Soviet naval maneuvers in the northern Norwegian Sea testify to the limits of its flexibility.[62]

Moscow could no more tolerate hostile control over that gap than it could tolerate hostile control over the mountain ranges of western Czechoslovakia (east of which the plains stretch flat, if marshy, to Moscow). If Moscow considered Svalbard sensitive enough to warrant thoughts of intervention in November 1944, then there can be little doubt that its much increased strategic value today would be seen to justify and, indeed, demand intervention in the event of its future hostile utilization.[63]

Still, it must be noted with regard to another variant of "Finlandization" that the fact that Norway now finds itself behind probable front lines does not appear to have affected its will, nor does the conceded de facto neutralization of Finmark (the northernmost county) appear to have sapped its determination. Defense budgets have increased. Sentiment today is more pro-NATO than it was ten years ago. Norway might not be able to defend the easily traversed plateau of Finmark, but it appears quite confident that it could defend the wild crags of Troms. The Cuban analogy is indeed apt. Castro's need to desist from offensive missiles, from providing a base for strategic submarines, did not deflect him from Angola, from the general pursuit of his revolutionary ambitions. Similarly, Norway's tough bargaining stance in the north on territorial delimitation, fisheries, and so forth does not appear weak (even in the face of Soviet missile tests into the disputed region). Comparative power realities have changed dramatically over the last decades, but they have also become more complex.

SOVIET POTENTIAL IN "NORTH AMERICA'S"
ARCTIC: OPPORTUNITY KNOCKS?

The parameters defining Moscow's strategic exit, the Svalbard-Kola constellation, have evolved through decades of hard bargaining, carefully calibrated
adjustments, and constant scrutiny and monitoring by the affected parties. But
the late 1960s and 1970s saw an extension of Soviet military, scientific, and
economic deployment through pan-Arctica which was not to encounter similarly
touchy restraints. The panoply of Soviet Arctic endeavors is treated elsewhere.
The focus here will be on the relative paucity of assertion capacity on the part
of the *pro forma* claimant power in most of "North America's" Arctic, namely
Canada. Soviet and, to a lesser extent, U.S. capacities will be referred to only for
purposes of comparison, to place Canadian capabilities, such as they are, in
sharper relief.

The Canadian government today advertises increased Arctic interest and
capability.[64] Yet the facts show a continued paucity of both information and
means. The cartographic situation is typical. For complete topographical map
coverage of Canadian land areas, the interested party has to make do with a
1:250,000 scale (on which one inch represents close to four miles of terrain).[65]
While southern Canada is well covered by 1:50,000 scale maps, more northerly
regions are not.[66] Furthermore, while maps of southern Canada are based on
land surveys, those of the north (and, in fact, most areas down to 56 degrees
northern latitude), rely on aerial photography alone.[67]

The Canadian Hydrographic Service is unable to provide comprehensive
nautical charts even of the waters between the Arctic Islands.[68] There remain
many "holes." For example, there have been no real surveys between Victoria
Island and Prince of Wales Island, in Committee Bay by the Melville Peninsula,
or between Prince Charles Island and Foxe Peninsula. Resources expended have
been and are being concentrated on narrow route surveys for ships and pipeline
developments.[69] Even Baffin Bay has not been surveyed systematically. There
have been many track soundings, a number of which are rather dated today, but
no systematic survey. What has been done has been focused on uncertain passage
areas.

There has been relatively systematic surveying (that is, with measurements every kilometer or so) off northwest Banks Island, off Prince Patrick Island, off Borden Island, and around to north of Ellef Ringnes Island. But there
has been no systematic surveying at all from northwest Axel Heiberg Island and
right around north of Ellesmere Island. A limited amount of surveying has been
done in the fiords of Ellesmere Island. But there have been no ocean proper
measurements in these northern waters. It is only at their eastern extremity that
one again finds measurements, at the northern exit of the Nares Strait (which,

incidentally, while too difficult for surface passage, has good water all the way through for submarine transit).[70]

The surveys that have been done have measured depths and vertical and horizontal movements of water but not, as a rule, chemical composition. In fact, "almost no chemical oceanographic studies have been done in the eastern Arctic in spite of the obvious relevance of such work to the overall understanding of a very large part of the country."[71] The first physical-chemical expedition to the eastern Arctic took place in the fall of 1977, under the sponsorship of the Bedford Institute of Oceanography, of Dartmouth. Concentrating on the Baffin Bay and adjacent regions it investigated the chemical and biological constituents of water samples (in the process hoping to collate a modicum of nutrient and trace metal data), collected some sediments from the ocean floor, and did oil tows (collecting floating tar balls, chunks of oil). Although scattered oil tows had been conducted for some time, this was said to be the first scheme for "extensive" analysis for hydrocarbons in the waters traversed.[72]

A reasonable number of salinity and temperature measurements were conducted in the early 1960s, and some were done in conjunction with the project described above. But little had been done in the meantime, certainly "not enough for people to think they understand watermasses in general in the region."[73] Rudimentary measurements of salinity, temperature, and oxygen have been done between Ellesmere Island and Greenland. The Soviet Union and the United States apparently have done considerable physical oceanographic (salinity and temperatures) studies in Baffin Bay and the Davis Strait, but little is known of chemical oceanographic and possible sound propagation studies or of nutrient measurements.[74]

Canada has received but the scantiest of information from the known extensive Soviet program for aerial aeromagnetic data collection. While a limited amount of generalized data is passed on, the crucial data base has never been provided.[75] Canadian bathymetry charts of Arctic waters reflect the lack of knowledge in this sphere. Their scales range between 1:2 million and 1:6.75 million (as opposed, for example, 1:300,000 for the Halifax to Sable Island region).[76] Canada's Polar Continental Shelf Project has prepared some gravity charts and also some hydrographic charts of Arctic waters (the latter for the Earth Physics Branch). But coverage is still spotty, nowhere extending more than between 100 and 150 miles offshore.[77]

"Canada has not charted the biological and geological characteristics of the Arctic Ocean waters and floors."[78] As a result of its involvement as a sometime participant in certain U.S. efforts, it has gained some information, for example, from mud samples and shallow cores taken from the U.S. ice station T-3 (finally abandoned in October 1974, when it stranded on the north shore of Ellesmere Island). Bottom photographs were taken in conjunction with participation in the U.S.-organized Arctic Ice Joint Experiment (AIJEX) project in the Beaufort Sea. But the limited extent of the resultant information is indicated by the fact that the bottom photography in question was conducted only from one of thirteen major AIJEX locations, and only for a period of a few weeks out of a year and a half.[79]

There is no doubt that overall U.S. research, air, surface, and subsurface, has been more extensive.[80] It is clear that Soviet Arctic research is more extensive still. By 1967, Soviet researchers were able and authorized to release public tectonic (structural) maps of the Arctic floor, going right up to the Canadian Arctic Islands(!).[81] The exact location of sample and exploratory work involved is not known, but the details of the maps testified to a considerable scale of effort.[82]

Canada's knowledge of the existence, location, or extent of Arctic Ocean floor geological phenomena is negligible, as is that of all analysts without access to classified Soviet or U.S. material. Placer deposits (concentrations) of gold, tin, titanium, and platinum-bearing minerals are found on Arctic shelves, and exploitation of some of them has begun (of tin in the Laptev Sea, of gold off Alaska).[83] Placer deposits are apparently relatively easy to exploit, either with mining techniques or, at shallower depths, with suction methods. The point in this context is that while concentrations are rich they are also very much concentrated in small areas, and therefore their location demands detailed knowledge of the ocean floor. Canada does not have such knowledge; Soviet tectonic/metalogic maps, considered in conjunction with Soviet preeminence in the field of geochemistry[84] and the extraordinary level of ongoing Soviet Arctic research in general, indicate that Moscow may have or be acquiring such knowledge.

The same comment applies to possible ferro-manganese nodule presence. Most nodules have been found at deeper and more southern depths, but there are exceptions. They have also been found, for example, on Blake Plateau off Florida and on some sea mountains; furthermore, some have actually been found off the Soviet Arctic coast.[85] Possible scepticism as to their presence in Canadian-claimed sectors can, in view of the limitations of Canadian effort, only be described as speculative; available knowledge is too limited. On the question of strategic mineral deposits in the Arctic, Canada does not have the same awareness as the Soviet Union or probably the United States, nor does it appear that it would have the same capabilities to exploit them if given the opportunity.[86]

Canada has been involved in some ice dynamics measurements, but again only in restricted locales. The AIJEX project collated data for parts of the Beaufort Sea. A second project involved Department of National Defence and civilian researchers in ice dynamics measurements in Robeson Channel, between Ellesmere and Greenland (ice behavior in this location was found to be only 40 percent wind affected, 60 percent current affected, due to the narrowness of the channel and the tidal variations of the end oceans).[87] There have also been some Canadian measurements of turbulence of water under ice in the Beaufort Sea.[88] But while there are general water level reports for parts of the Arctic and Hudson Bay, there are no daily current predictions even for the more southerly reaches of these areas.[89]

But if Canada's knowledge of the biological, geological, and other characteristics of Arctic waters and beds appears scanty, this can hardly surprise observers knowledgeable about Arctic land regions; surveys of Canada's Arctic land areas are often equally weak.[90] Thus, the geology and surface material maps in the *National Atlas of Canada* have a discrimination ten times worse than the now decade-old Soviet tectonic/metalogic charts of Canadian ocean floor regions.[91] The Canadian map is accompanied by this stricture: "Note: The map is based on a large number of surveys with varying degrees of reliability. . . . The map should be regarded as a prediction . . . not as a precise portrayal of surface material distribution."[92] The doubts expressed refer primarily to northern regions where the data required for better discrimination maps remains largely unavailable.

The scarcity of Canadian knowledge on Arctic expanses within Canadian-claimed borders is partly due to low government priority. Ottawa has never chosen to subsidize or otherwise encourage either the habitation or the economic exploitation of its Arctic to the same extent as other nations with Arctic territories.[93] This low government priority presumably has been due partly to limited perceptions of needs. As concerns security, for example, no physical threat was perceived as credible, and while military-technological and resource scarcity and developmental trends and techniques are today revolutionizing Arctic accessibility and potential,[94] this has not yet resulted in any significant revision of traditional attitudes.[95]

Another reason for the low government perception of need has been economic. Until recently it was presumed that southern natural wealth would suffice to guarantee continued prosperity. The shock of scarcity realization over the past few years appears to have put a new premium on the higher-cost energy and other prospects of the north. Still, before presumed riches can be extracted, they must be located and surveyed. The government-appointed Berger Commission and NEB (National Energy Board) hearings of 1977 make it clear that Canada still has a long way to go before it will be able to exploit fully the economic potential of the north.

The final reason for the low priority traditionally accorded the north in government corridors is surely to be found in its low political profile. Canada's northlands are the world's most sparsely populated; with 57,000 inhabitants (1971) distributed over an area of four million square kilometers, northern Canada's population is spread far more thinly than Greenland's.[96] What might be called "the northern constituency" is miniscule in political terms.

The limited clout of the "northern constituency" is, in fact, due not only to low numbers; it is clearly also due to past government policies. The colonial status of the northern regions was perpetuated through a policy of benign neglect.[97] The Royal Canadian Mounted Police (RCMP) and other government agents provided sufficient protection and sometime benign cuddling to undermine autonomy sentiments and divert attention from developmental neglect, thus seeking at minimum cost to perpetuate Ottawa's prospects of maximizing the economic corollary of unfettered suzerainty in the event of improved future exploitation potentials.[98] The recent breakdown of this calibration, as witnessed by the increase in native assertiveness attendant upon Ottawa's now more urgent attitude to Arctic wealth extraction, may have profound impact on future northern developments. But the fact that popular southern attitudes are perceived to be perhaps even more distant from that of the natives than Ottawa's is not comforting.[99]

The final and main reason for the "northern constituency's" lack of clout, and for past government policies, may be said to be prevailing southern attitudes. There have been times when Ottawa has indicated willingness to review its attitudes towards the north, in the early Trudeau and early Diefenbaker administrations for example. But apparent movement towards change always foundered on eventual apathy. The Diefenbaker case of two decades ago is classic. The image,—"this is the vision—a Canada of the north"—of northern development that Diefenbaker conjured up and people supported in the 1958 election turned out to be a mirage.[100] The fact that the north referred to was on the whole a misnomer for "middle Canada" was perhaps irrelevant, if illustrative. The point is that the "immediate response . . . touched off . . . among that overwhelming majority of the nation's citizens who never venture further north than their summer cottages" proved ephemeral.[101]

Southern attitudes have a crucial electoral impact on both northern development prospects themselves and on the general question of northern stability. It is not at all clear that past indifference is changing. Most current evidence points to a continued lack of interest. The romanticism and adventure of the north is extolled in children's books, but as a subject of serious concern the north still seems to be very far from the forefront of most adult minds. The most prominent Canadian bibliographical "guide to Canadian history, government and politics" since 1867 contains eight chapters divided into 97 sections; in the latest mid-1970s edition not a single section deals with Arctic topics, Arctic problems, or Arctic prospects.[102] A recent perusal of some of the issues of one of the most prominent Canadian journals revealed but one article with a suggestive name, "The True North Strong and Fettered"; but it turned out to be a review rather than an article, and "North" turned out to refer to Canada rather than northern Canada or the Arctic.[103]

Attitudes, are, in fact, crucial—to development prospects, to security, and to concepts of legality. Thus, the extraordinary Norwegian encouragement of the development of their north has always found perhaps its prime justification in the explicit premise that sovereignty demands presence. Sovereignty claims must have some relationship to control, surveillance, and sovereignty-enforcing capabilities. This traditional supposition of international law may have little relevance for claims that are not contested. The history of general (if recent) world acceptance of Canada's claim to the Arctic islands to its north may be seen to dispense with the demand for "presence" as far as these are concerned. But the case of surrounding bodies of water and ocean beds is considerably more contentious. Both Washington and Moscow hold that the Northwest Passage is an international waterway; neither sanction Ottawa's claim that it is to be regarded as among Canada's internal waters. Furthermore, both continue to demur on Ottawa's Arctic sector claims and refuse to acknowledge or recognize Canadian sovereignty over, say, the "Canadian Basin" (or the parts thereof that fall within the "sector").[104]

The all too limited state of Canadian presence in the claimed areas still might not be too detrimental to Canadian interests had sovereignty demurrals remained merely verbal. Unfortunately, they have been backed up by a significant level of presence on the part of dissenting nations. Most Canadians know of the odyssey of the U.S. tanker Manhattan. Few know of the level of established U.S. presence in the "sector" (through the AIJEX project, ice stations, such as T-3, and other air, surface, and subsurface activities). Few know of the size of Soviet efforts, as exemplified by the fact that the last Soviet ice station in Canadian waters, the NP-22, had a runway of 5000 feet, 1000 feet longer than the longest recently completed runway in "mid-Canada" (on the south coast of Baffin Island)[105] and, in fact, long enough possibly to accommodate the Soviet supersonic bomber Backfire.[106] Over most of these areas Canada's presence is restricted to a maximum of two, or perhaps three, overflights per month.

The discrepancy in the level of actual presence and in the ability to perpetuate and protect this presence in the north oceanic regions of Canada's self-proclaimed realm is unfavorable to Canada and undermines its jurisdictional position. This position is also undermined by Ottawa's hesitancy to enunciate and define that position. It is over half a century since Canada first proclaimed sovereignty over the northern acreage bounded by its longitudinal extremities, the "sector."[107] In the intervening years Canada has never departed from that position; in fact, government cartographers have consistently been instructed to depict the area in question as Canadian. But Ottawa did not emulate the Soviet pattern of physical exploitation and follow-up to sovereignty assertion. Canadian government spokesmen (as opposed to their cartographers) shy away from even verbal emphasis of the claim; they tend rather to engage in apparent and ironic efforts to avoid espousing the claim too strongly while yet not voiding it.[108]

Government spokesmen defend traditional claims only in terms of extraordinary vagueness on the specifics of extent and consequences.[109] They shy away from confrontation. When a CBC investigative team visited the Soviet NP-22 in late spring 1977, they reported that no Canadian government, Defence or External representative had attempted to visit the ice station at any time since it first drifted into the Canadian "sector" over a year previous; a follow-up report noted that while some government members had reacted to the initial program with an inclination to protest, the collective had decided against it—purportedly because such a protest would have to be followed also by protests against analagous cases, U.S. as well as Soviet. Then there was the recent homicide case on a U.S. ice island in the Canadian Arctic; Ottawa "in effect waived jurisdiction" and thus avoided challenging the legitimacy of the subsequent New York trial.[110]

The evolution at the Law of the Sea conferences of recent years, with apparently steadily increasing acceptance of the principle of extensions of coastal states' rights in adjacent waters, might be seen as having favorable implications for Canada's northern posture. Yet, the extraordinary tradition of disproportionate outside power presence, not just inside the larger sector but even at times within line of sight from Arctic island shores,[111] is not only perturbing to Canadian nationalists. The fact of territorial differences between the NATO power most active in the area and the NATO power claiming suzerainity chips away at concepts of optimal coordination of defense planning and activation. It has given at least a measure of license to Soviet penetration designs, a tempting geopolitical context for the circumvention of areas of more concentrated NATO effort (the "G-I-UK gap" in particular). While the trends of current Soviet strategic SLBM designs and deployments tend to lessen the requirement for forward deployment, they do not obviate the advantages of superior familiarity, either with Arctic vistas in general or with the waters of the Canadian-claimed sector and archipelago in particular.

NOTES

1. C. G. Jacobsen, *Soviet Strategy–Soviet Foreign Policy* (Glasgow: The University Press, 1972). See also A. Rubinstein, ed., *Soviet Foreign Policy Towards Western Europe*, (New York: Praeger, 1978); Sections below are based on this author's chapter on "Moscow and the Northern Rim" in the Rubinstein volume, pp. 151–182.

2. Max Jacobson, *Egna Vägar* (The Best of Both Worlds) (Stockholm: Norstedts, 1968).

3. Ibid., p. 56.

4. W. H. Pope, *The Elephant and the Mouse* (Toronto: McClelland and Stewart, 1971), p. vii.

5. The extraordinary extent of U.S. economic penetration and control in Canada has been documented in a number of Canadian government-sponsored analyses over the last decade. The most prominent of these are the "Watkins Report," *Foreign Ownership and the Structure of Canadian Industry* (Ottawa: Queens Printer, 1968); the "Gray Report," *Foreign Direct Investment in Canada* (Ottawa: Queens Printer, 1972); and the *Foreign Direct Investment Act* of 1974, and its subsequent annual follow-up studies. See also debates and analyses engendered by these, in journals such as the *Canadian Journal of Economics* and, in particular, *Canadian Forum*. Pope, *The Elephant and The Mouse*, provides additional data of relevance.

The U.S. cultural penetration of Canada is symptomized by Canadian newspapers' astonishing dependence on U.S. wire services for political, economic, cultural, and sports stories, for verbatim headlines, synopses, and contents in general. Only in Quebec do non-U.S. wire services have much impact (notably Agence France Press). Direct Soviet control over elements of Finnish economy or culture is miniscule by comparison. The indirect control potential inherent in established trade and economic cooperation ventures is also not of an equatable order of magnitude; nor is the cultural control/restraint potential of indirect Soviet influence.

6. G. Ginsburgs and A. Rubinstein, "Finlandization: Soviet Strategy or Geopolitical Footnote," (Paper presented to American Association for the Advancement of Slavic Studies Conference, Washington, D.C., October 1977); see Rubinstein, *Finlandization.*

7. See Canadian government reports cited in footnote 5, above.

8. Jacobson, *Egna Vägar.*

9. Ibid.

10. N. Ørvik, "Security and Politics in 'The Northern Rim,'" *National Security Series: Canada and the Northern Rim,* (Kingston, Ontario: Queens University, Fall 1977).

11. Based on chapter in author's *Soviet Strategy–Soviet Foreign Policy*, a version which was also published in U.S., Senate, *Soviet Oceans Development,* prepared for the Committee on Commerce (Washington, D.C.: Government Printing Office, October 1976).

12. V. Molotov, as quoted by Trygve Lie in *Hjemover* (Oslo: Tiden Norsk Forlag, 1958).

.13. Ibid.

14. A. Golovko, *With the Red Fleet. The War Memoirs of Admiral Golovko*, (London: Pitman, 1965) p. 40.

15. See, for example, *International Affairs* (Moscow), no. 12 (1969).

16. For elaboration, see C. G. Jacobsen, *Soviet Strategy–Soviet Foreign Policy,* chap. 6.

17. Ibid.; and see footnote 59, below.

18. See, for example, Norwegian Minister of Defense G. Harlem in *Parliamentary Debates (Stortings forhandlinger),* 1964–65, vol. 7, p. 2475. Note also footnote 22, below.

19. See map "The Kola Coastline, from Nordkapp to Mys Kanin Nos including the White Sea," (London: Admiralty, 1958).

20. *International Affairs,* no. 12 (1969).

21. *Krasnaya Zvezda,* March 30, 1969.

22. The Lorang controversy of mid-summer 1977, with its Norwegian parliamentary debate and associated Soviet-Norwegian tension, may be seen to reflect on the abiding nature of the concern; it should be noted that the disputed system is merely a navigational aid and therefore very much peripheral to basic Soviet anxieties.

23. NATO-aligned communications and early warning systems, NATO maneuvers as previously conducted and the preparation of bases to permit wartime reinforcement of men and equipment (described by A. Sington in "NATO Defensive Installations in Norway," *NATO Letter,* January 1966) certainly represent cause for Soviet anxiety. But such NATO activity can be and has been tolerated and accepted. It does not infringe on essential Kola security requirements in the way that the described potential radar utilization would. The Lorang controversy of 1977 referred to above falls in this category.

24. See Swedish Ministry of Defense, *Sveriges Säkerhetspolitik*, Stockholm, 1955, or Capt. Araldsen, "The Soviet Union and the Arctic," *U.S. Naval Institute Proceedings,* June 1967.

25. See maps "The Kola Coastline," and "Barents Sea Depths" in *Carte Général Bathymétrique des Oceans,* Carleton University Geography Map Library 9200 Acc. 1487; see also Jan Klenberg's "The Cap and the Straits," *International Affairs,* Occasional Papers no. 17, Harvard University, 1968.

26. Jacobsen, *Soviet Strategy–Soviet Foreign Policy.*

27. T. J. Laforest, "The Strategic Significance of the North Sea Route," *U.S. Naval Institute Proceedings* (December 1967).

28. Jens Evensen, Norwegian Ministry of Foreign Affairs, "Present Military Users of the Seabed: Foreseeable Developments" (Document presented to symposium on the International Regime of the Seabed, Rome, July 1969).

29. See, for example, charts presented in *NATO Letter* (September 1970): 6–11, and chap. 5.

30. Norway, Ministry of Industry, *Oversikt over Oljepolitiske Spoersmaal*, prepared by Jens Evensen (Oslo: Government Release, 1971).

31. See, for example, Norway, Ministry of Finance, *Petroleum Industry in Norwegian Society*, Parliamentary Report no. 25, (Oslo: Government Release, 1973–74).

32. Norwegian Petroleum sources; or see, for example, *Sea Power* (November 1974): "Official Norwegian Reports indicate an opulent future . . . seismic investigation has shown a succession of oil-bearing anticlines as far north as Bear Island, deep in the Arctic Circle, and possessing fields even richer, possibly, than those in the North Sea."

33. Note, for example, Norway, *Oversikt over Oljepolitiske Spoersmaal*.

34. Preliminary negotiations were initiated in September 1970. For Soviet "progress reports," see, for example, *Pravda*, December 8, 1971, March 26, 1974.

35. Moscow's concern is only heightened by reports such as carried by *Aviation Week and Space Technology* November 25, 1974: "Defence of North Sea drilling rigs and future automated production facilities has become a priority item in NATO planning." Norwegian measures to assuage that concern are treated elsewhere in the text; suffice it here to note the insistence with which it returns to the theme in every treatment of continental shelf exploitation problems, as evinced in the Norwegian government sources quoted above as well as in reports such as carried by *Sea Power*.

36. Map, "The Kola Coastline," and see, for example, *Sailing Directions for Northern U.S.S.R.*, Hydrographic Office Publication, vol. 1, no. 47 (Washington, D.C.: Government Printing Office, 1954), and Hydrographic Office Publication, no. 550 (Washington, D.C.: Government Printing Office, 1955).

37. Ibid.

38. For an excellent presentation and analysis of treaty background, participants and clauses, see W. Oestreng, *Oekonomi og Politisk Suverenitet*, (Oslo: Universitetsforlaget, 1974); see also F. Sollie, "Arctic and Antarctic–Current Problems in the Polar Regions," *Cooperation and Conflict*, no. 2 (1969).

39. T. Greve, *Svalbard* (Oslo: Groendahl, 1975).

40. Ibid.

41. Ibid.

42. Ibid. See also *Report No. 39 to the Norwegian Storting* (1974–75), concerning Svalbard, *Pravda/Izvestia*, March 26, 1974, and *Washington Post*, September 20, 1974, Norwegian Ministry of Foreign Affairs, Oslo. (both regarding airfield agreement).

43. As regards the consensus, one might point to the following comment in *Sea Power*; "the Norwegian Sea above 62N to its juncture with the Barents Sea–which Norway shares with the Soviet Union–is Norway's property clear to Spitzbergen."

44. Norway, *Oversikt over Oljepolitiske Spoersmaal*.

45. Norway, *Petroleum Industry in Norwegian Society*.

46. Ibid. One might note that this "fall-back" position is receiving somewhat more prominent treatment in recent Norwegian government documents. See, for example, "Report No. 39," Norwegian Min. of Foreign Affairs, Oslo. (In this, the "hardline" position is implicit in certain sections but never made explicit.)

47. Norwegian Foreign Ministry sources.

48. Traditional Soviet views on the sector principle, as well as the rather unique Soviet definitions of "historic bays," may be found, for example, in Z. Meshera, *Morskoe*

Pravo: Pravovoi Rezhim Morskikh Putei (Maritime Law: Legal Regime of Maritime Routes) (Moscow: Nauka, 1959).

49. See, for example, *The Times Atlas* (London: Times Newspapers, Ltd. 1972), or any of the more detailed bathymetric charts currently available.

50. M. W. Janis and D. C. F. Daniel, "The U.S.S.R.: Ocean Use and Ocean Law," Law of the Sea Institute, Occasional Paper no. 21, (University of Rhode Island, May 1974).

51. Norway, *Oversikt over Oljepolitiske Spoersmaall*; and note the subsequent joint Norwegian-Australian initiative to the Caracas Law of the Sea Conference.

52. It is illustrative to contrast the restrictive U.S. initiative to the August 1970 Geneva Ocean Floor Committee session with the very different Congressional initiatives of 1975.

53. See S. Pavlov in *Pravda*, February 12, 1976; I. Gorev in *Novoye Vremia*, March 12, 1976, and the Soviet Council of Ministers' resolution of February 24, *Pravda*, February 24, 1977.

54. Note above comments on the geologically similar northern Norwegian continental shelf, (footnote 32); see also *Ocean Oil Weekly Report* 9, no. 10 (December 1974); and Vinogradov, "Ocean in the Year 2000," *Novosti* (201H4922/B) (from *Vodnii Transport*).

55. See quotations in C. G. Jacobsen, "Notes on Military-Civilian Integration in the U.S.S.R.: A Case Study: The 'Civilian Fleets,'" in *Soviet Oceans Development.*

56. Ibid.

57. See, for example, Arvid Pardo's treatment, in *Foreign Affairs* (October 1968). Note that the difference between the "med line," which the U.N. Convention prescribes, for situations not affected by "special conditions" favoring alternate principles and the "sector principle" long espoused by Moscow and now portrayed as such as a "special condition" common law equivalent, amounts to 155,000 square kilometers.

58. This information was conveyed by Norwegian Foreign Ministry officials to interested allied parties in the spring and summer of 1975.

59. *Aftenposten*, July 2, 1977.

60. Norway has designated that its State Petroleum Directorate be "responsible, together with Statoil (the State Oil Co.), for all activities connected with petroleum operations on the shelf, including those in the Svalbard area" (*Report No. 39*). As of early 1978, Norway continues to limit drilling to areas south of 62 degrees N., and insists that even in these more southerly reaches production must be curbed and carefully controlled (see, for example, *The New York Times*, September 28, 1975.)

61. Note references to scientific-technical cooperation in *Pravda*, December 8, 1971, and *Report No. 39* Norwegian Ministry of Foreign Affairs, Oslo (1974–75), esp. chap. 7, sections 3, 4.

62. The original September 11, 1975 Tass announcement (see *Pravda*, September 12) that missile tests would be conducted in the area, within a radius of 40 nautical miles from a center point at 73 degrees N., 35 degrees E., was clearly a signal of abiding Soviet concern and determination. The test range overlapped with demarcation-disputed territory. The choice of test site was not fortuitous; it was to be chosen again in subsequent years. It appeared that Moscow was regularizing the phenomenon, emphasizing the fundamental nature of its policy commitment. The increasing pace and scale of Soviet naval maneuvers in the northern Norwegian Sea was noted, for example, by *Time*, June 27, 1977.

63. If anything, the evolution towards home water basing of Strategic Submarine Ballistic Nuclear (SSBNs) (which the introduction of the long range SS-N-8 missles appeared to augur) serves to further increase the crucial sensitivity of the area in the eyes of Soviet planners. See also Chapter Two; section on "withholding." And see Jan Ingebrigtsen, "En studie av Norskehavets Strategiske Betydning som funksjon av Sovjetunionens Nordflaates Operasjoner," *NUPI Rapport* (Oslo: N.U.P.I., August 1975).

64. Canadian Minister of National Defence B. Danson to author, June 30, 1978. The letter synopsized work in progress but did not refer to areas of continued ignorance (see be-

low), or U.S. and other challenges to Canadian sovereignty (see footnote 108 below). The theme was prominent in Defence Department information bulletins of 1977 and 1978.

65. Canada, Department of Energy, Mines and Resources, *Maps and Charts*, no. 79 (Ottawa: 1977).

66. The grids covered are: 25 A, E, D, L, N, part of C, part of K, part of M, part of O; 26 H, J, part of I; 35 F, G. H, I, J, K, part of L; 36 part of C; 37 D, E, part of C, part of G; 47 D, part of A, part of H; 48 part of A; 49 G and part of 340 B; 57 part of B; 58 G and part of F; 59 part of A; 67 A, B; 69 (Regnes and Meighen Islands); 89 and 99 parts (Prince Patrick Island); 98 part of B; 107 B, C, D; 117 coastal parts of A, C, D.

67. *Canada Map Index*, no. 30, June 30, 1975.

68. Canada, Department of the Environment, *Canadian Hydrographic Service 1.B.15*, January 1976. Note the poor scale of the charts that do exist; it contrasts vividly with the scale of charts available for more travelled seas; see Canada, Department of the Environment, *Canadian Hydrographic Service 1.B.1* (Queen's Printer, Ottawa), January 1974 (on the "Great Lakes and Adjacent Waterways").

69. Ibid.

70. Information provided by Bob Marshal, of the Bedford Institute of Oceanography's Hydrography Department. Furthermore, no ocean surveys were scheduled for 1977; see Canada, Department of the Environment, *Canadian Hydrogrphic Service 1976* (Queen's Printer, Ottawa).

71. From the *1977 Chemical Oceanography Arctic Cruise Outline* (Bedford Institute of Oceanography: 1977).

72. Conversation with Dr. Peter Jones of the Bedford Institute's Chemical Oceanography Department and scheduled participant in the expedition, Dartmouth, Nova Scotia, May 27, 1977, and ibid.

73. Conversation with Dr. Jones.

74. Ibid.

75. Conversation with Dr. Robin Falconer of the Bedford Institute's Marine Geoscience Division, May 27, 1977.

76. Canada, Department of the Environment, *Status of Canadian Hydrographic Service Bathymetric and Geological Maps* (Queen's Printer, Ottawa), August 1, 1976.

77. Telephone conversation with G. D. Hobson, Director, Polar Continental Shelf Project, February 17, 1977.

78. G. D. Hobson, P.C.S.P., to author, April 26, 1977. Out of 112 Arctic ventures supported by the Polar Continental Shelf Project in 1977, not one concerned itself with minerals on or under the ocean floor.

79. Information provided by Dr. Stu Smith of the Bedford Institute's Physical Oceanography Department, May 27, 1977.

80. One might point to the U.S. submersible operation north of Alert in September 1976.

81. *Tektonicheskaya Karta Arktiki i Subarktiki*. (Institute for the Study of the Arctic and Antarctic), (Leningrad, USSR, 1967).

82. Ibid. The general maps have a scale of 1:500,000.

83. See, for example, "Changing Pattern in World's Supply of Minerals" (a review of known supplies of strategic minerals), *Minerals Science and Engineering*, July 3, 1974, (hereafter referred to as *MSE*), and "The Recovery of Deep-Sea Minerals: Problems and Prospects," *MSE*, July 3, 1975.

84. Conversation with Dr. Doug Loring of the Bedford Institute's Marine Geochemistry Department (Dr. Loring had visited the impressive Institute of Arctic Geology in Leningrad), Dartmouth, Nova Scotia, May 27, 1977.

85. "Deep Sea Manganese Nodules: A Review of the Literature," *MSE*, January 1, 1975; see, also, *MSE*, July 3, 1975.

86. Conversation with Dr. Loring.

87. Meeting with Dr. Smith.

88. By Professor Langleben of McGill University, under the auspices of AIJEX.

89. *Canadian Hydrographic Service 1.B.1.* provides this information.

90. See, for example, the *National Atlas of Canada*, MacMillan Co. of Canada Ltd. in association with the Department of Energy, Mines, and Resources and Information, Canada, (Ottawa, 1974), and the *Atlas of Canada*, Department of Mines and Technical Surveys, (Ottawa, Canada, 1957 and 1974); reference charts are available from the author.

91. *National Atlas of Canada*; for Soviet charts, see footnote 81, above.

92. *National Atlas of Canada.*

93. Norway's very different traditional posture is that with which this author is most familiar. But Norway's vigorous pursuit of an Arctic presence, while motivated in part by unique rationales, is nevertheless more representative of "Arctic powers" than is Canada's apparent equanimity.

94. Superpower capabilities will be discussed later, but trends are indicated by the fact that even Norway has completed designs of a submarine Arctic tanker.

95. See, for example, Ørvik, "Security and Politics in 'The Northern Rim.'"

96. H. C. Bach *Problemer Omkring Dansk Sikkerhedspolitik* (Danish Security Problems), Danish Ministry of Defence, Copenhagen, 1970; see also H. C. Bach and J. Taagholt, *Grønland og Polaromraadet* (Greenland and the Arctic), (Copenhagen, Danish Ministry of Defence, December 1976), section 2.14.

97. Mel Watkins, ed. *The Dene Nation; The Colony Within* (Toronto: 1977). Note also the indirect but persuasive testimony to this effect in T. R. Berger, *Northern Frontier, Northern Homeland; Report of the Mackenzie Valley Pipeline Inquiry* (Ottawa: Queen's Printer, 1977).

98. Berger, *Northern Frontier, Northern Homeland.*

99. Note the testimony in ibid.

100. P. C. Newman, *Renegade in Power: The Diefenbaker Years* (Toronto: McClelland and Stewart, 1973).

101. Ibid.

102. J. L. Granatstein and P. Stevens, *Canada Since 1867. A Bibliographical Guide* (Toronto: Hakkert, 1974).

103. *Journal of Canadian Studies*, "The True North Strong and Fettered," in Review Section, February 1972.

104. So much so that they even shy away from use of the name "Canadian Basin." See *The New York Times Atlas of the World* (Times Newspapers Limited, 1972).

105. Canada, Department of Defence, Defence Information Service, "News Release," Ottawa, April 22, 1977.

106. Information on Backfire runway requirements supplied by a U.S. Air Force analyst, May 1977.

107. See Professor D. Pharand, *The Law of the Sea of the Arctic* (Ottawa: Ottawa University Press, 1973).

108. The Prime Minister's initiatives of 1969–70 were illustrative. According to *Canadian News Facts 1969* (Toronto); "Trudeau reasserted Canada's sovereignty over its Arctic regions . . . (but did it in such an ambiguous fashion that he) drew an Opposition charge of a weakened Canadian claim over Arctic waters" (p. 262). Trudeau noted (euphemistically?) that all countries do not recognize absolute Canadian sovereignty over the water between the islands of the Arctic archipelago. *Canadian News Facts 1970* reports, "Prime Minister Trudeau said Canada would exercise sovereignty 'over all the Canadian Arctic' but he refused to define the Arctic" (p. 409). The same source went on to note that "a public notice issued in Washington, February 12, by Elliot Richardson, acting State Secretary in

the absence of William Rodgers said the U.S. does not 'acquiesce in or recognize the validity' of permits issued by Canada to explore for natural resources in the area." See also Dosman, *The Arctic in Question* (Oxford: Oxford University Press, 1976); and the critical review by E. B. Wang, "Canadian Sovereignty in the Arctic: A Comment on the Arctic in Question," in *Canadian Yearbook of International Law*, 14, (June 1976), p. 307.

109. Ibid.

110. In the words of a Department of External Affairs spokesman, to the author, spring 1977.

111. According to sources within the Bedford Institute of Oceanography, there have been U.S. government-sponsored research endeavors within the three-mile limit in the Arctic for which Canadian permission was not sought.

7

SOVIET ARCTIC AND
DISTANT OCEAN WEALTH EXTRACTION:
MILITARY AND
CIVILIAN INTERESTS

From its inception, the Soviet regime has evinced on extraordinary appreciation of the military-economic potential of the Arctic.[1] Today that appreciation has grown into a truly vital interest. The early focus was on the "Barents Sea Exit" and the "Northern Sea Route" and on the economic development and exploitation of northern lands and immediately adjacent waters. By 1940, there were over 100 navigational aids just in the Kara Sea section of Soviet Arctic waters (whereas Canada had deployed a sum total of two or three weather stations throughout its Arctic reaches); the second quarter of the century saw the Soviet population in the north grow from 1.8 to about 4.5 million; by the early 1950s, northern fisheries accounted for approximately 20 percent of the Soviet catch.[2] Soviet northern presence grew exponentially through the subsequent decades. By the mid-1970s, its Arctic endeavors had acquired essential importance for the viability of its military-strategic posture and also for the economic underpinning of its standard-of-living aspirations. Soviet military-economic interests in the Arctic had in the process burst their erstwhile geographic bounds and become pan-Arctic.

The uniquely comprehensive labyrinth of Soviet Arctic interests will be analyzed below. Special emphasis will be placed on the demonstrable or potential relevance that current and evolving Soviet capabilities may have for North American and NATO Arctic concerns. To this end, the general composition and function of the purportedly (and to some extent genuinely) "civilian" fleets and associated research facilities will first be sketched with a view to determining both their civilian-economic and their military-associated role in the Arctic. This will be followed by a focus on more purely military potentials, problems, and prospects.

Soviet civilian fleets and maritime research organs are defined by Moscow as integral components of Soviet "naval might."[3] Moscow's establishment and expansion of a worldwide maritime presence through the 1950s and 1960s encompassed the outward movement and growth not only of its navy proper but also of the civilian elements.[4] The latter's thrust was in fact the forerunner of the former's.[5]

The fact that the civilian thrust preceded the navel emergence was in part due to the military-associated tasks of these fleet components. The civilian elements were the navy's intelligence tentacles, performing such tasks as would facilitate the navy's ability to meet the technology-inspired strategic requirement for more forward, distant deployment. Civilian vessels were entrusted with target location data collection tasks and with substantive command and control communications responsibilities.[6] They

> are responsible for installing the required navigational equipment in a naval theatre and also for carrying out diverse other tasks . . . (including) equipping a theatre with navigational devices for enabling aircraft and ships, as the need arises, to determine with great accuracy their precise location while at sea and located at great distances from their bases.[7]

While the command and control communications responsibilities of the civilian fleets lessened somewhat over the years, with increasing reliance being placed on satellite means and potentials, they nevertheless clearly continue to shoulder considerable responsibility for collating surface and subsurface intelligence data and for distributing underwater intelligence devices. Concomitant with the performance of their other tasks the Soviet civilian fleets continue to play an inestimable role in the assembly of information on the deployment patterns and capabilities of Western vessels, both naval and non-naval.[8] In conjunction with their other duties they also provide the navy with crucial reserve logistics and transportation capacity. Still, while Soviet civilian vessels have designed-in wartime capabilities and while some of these capabilities are clearly drawn upon even in peacetime conditions, it does appear that the routine utilization of their military-related potential is calibrated so as to cause minimum disruption to their nominal assignments.[9]

It is, in fact, clear that their nominal assignments are now far from nominal, and perhaps never were. Thus, the case for the proposition that the outward reach of Soviet civilian fleets owed a debt to naval requirements can be countered by a formidable case for the obverse, namely that the expansion of the navy owed a substantive debt to the time-honored requirement for defense of ever more vital distant ocean commercial interests.

The Soviet fishing fleet has grown at an annual rate of 18 percent for the last 25 years. Its catch grew from 1.8 million tons in 1950, to 10 million tons in 1975, and is now the highest in the world.[10] Its produce has become a vital supplement to that of the still problem-plagued agriculture, a vital ingredient in the nation's protein intake and dietary needs.[11] Its exportable surplus is furthermore valued at a premium due to the nonconvertible status of the ruble and Moscow's consequent need to finance imports and credit status through hard currency sales.

The Soviet Merchant Marine grew from 400 ships totaling two million deadweight tons in 1946, to 2,352 ships totaling fifteen million tons by 1975; it is projected to increase to 18.4 million deadweight tons by 1980.[12] While Soviet export growth had outdistanced domestic carrying capacity through the 1950s, with the result that only 37 percent of exports could be accommodated by 1962, the remainder of the 1960s saw a closing of the gap. Today, nearly 60 percent of Soviet trade is transported on Soviet bottoms (as opposed to a mere 5 percent domestic carrying rate for the United States).[13] Aside from the obvious security and flexibility of operations implications attendant upon such capacity, it also, of course, has very consequential economic impact as a hard currency saver and earner.

The oceanographic research fleet of the Soviet Union showed an even more awesome rate of expansion through the late 1950s and 1960s. By 1968, its numbers already exceeded the combined total of vessels performing analagous missions for all other nations of the world.[14] Ocean floor bathymetric depth and relief charts have been drawn up ("the Soviet chart of the Pacific Ocean caused a sensation in the scientific world"), as have "top quality and precision magnetic charts," current, salinity, oxidation tables, and the like.[15] The biological and chemical composition of ocean waters and the geological structures and characteristics of ocean floors have been surveyed and analyzed. Surface vessel activities are supplemented by satellites and automatic buoys:

> The establishment . . . of a system of artificial satellites for ocean exploration would mean an annual gain for all countries ranging into between 900 and 2000 million dollars . . . a widely ramified network of oceanographic buoys [many of the processes in the ocean can be investigated only by continuous stationary observations[16]] and satellites will require high frequency radiometers capable of operating in conditions of outer space, more sophisticated transmitting and receiving devices, larger capacities for recording devices carried, more sensitive sensors, the fuller processing of information aboard the satellite itself and also the faster relaying of the information accumulated to those who need it. . . . By 1975 most of our oceanographic observations including measurement of water temperature, currents, shore erosion, ice movement, etc., will be effected wholly by artificial satellites.[17]

Soviet oceanographic research agencies, furthermore, can call on the help of military aircraft; as indicated above, the degree of military-civilian integration effected by the Soviet Union does have two-way implications.[18] In addition, they can call on a growing fleet of undersea vehicles.[19] The fishing fleet evidently acts as the custodian of the civilian submersible fleet.[20] This is a new branch of the Soviet maritime endeavor and one in which the Soviet Union still lags behind the United States and France. But, once again, the trends are startling; the 1976 total was at least double and perhaps as much as four times higher than that of 1975.[21] The Soviet Union has reached a level of some innovation. Thus, one of the newly developed vehicles, the Triton, intended for construction and support activities in the continental shelf zone, is a true amphibian capable of operating and navigating underwater, on the surface, and on land.[22] The Soviet Union is also pioneering some types of robot vehicles, automated vessels with multi-sensor perception and preprogrammed computer technology and control; these craft have been described as similar in operation to the Lunakhod moon vehicles.[23] Soviet undersea vessels have been used

> to hover over a school of fish and transmit data on the extent, location and speed of movement of the school . . . (for) taking core samples from the ocean bottom for later analysis by petroleum scientists . . . (for) oceanographic and biological research on illuminescence and bioluminescence . . . (for, in general) looking for schools of fish, studying the sea bottom, and selecting areas for trawl fishing.[24]

"Soviet scientists are also working on designs for further underwater bulldozers, graders, excavators and ore carriers for offshore mining operations and undersea harvesters for seaweed farms."[25] The Soviet Union believes that "the seas are storehouses of all useful elements, with resources many times those of dry land. They are food factories producing thousands of millions of tons of protein annually."[26] Soviet appreciation of ocean wealth prospects and determination to take a leading role in their exploitation is shown in the following quotations.

> The seas and the oceans are inhabited by more than 150,000 species of animals. There are about a thousand million tons of fish alone. The total biological mass of the oceans has an estimated weight of 25 thousand million tons.[27]

> The position of schools of fish and other denizens of the ocean is ascertained, first, by the heat regimen and the plankton.[28]

> Fish can be concentrated with the aid of such stimulators as light, sound, electric current, smell, and other physical and chemical factors. . . . Experiments show that the future of fishing belongs to artificially created concentrations of fish, which can be called stimulated fishing. . . . It is important to study the biological bases of fish concentration . . . how concentration depends on the power of stimulators, the effective range of various stimulators, the pro-

cedures for setting up various fields (electric, light, etc.) of certain strength and directivity . . . great significance will have to be attached to selective catching . . . by differentially stimulating fish of various sizes and ages and by varying the selectivity of the fishing tackle. . . . One of the pieces of new fishing equipment will be a type of floating fish pump with selectivity devices . . . (and) floating and stationary storm-proof catchers-collectors, set up in various parts of the seas.[29]

The volume of the hydrosphere depths producing biological products is at least a thousand times greater than the volume of the globe's soil producing the green plant mass. For instance, just the annual "crop" of the sea weed amounts to 500,000 million tons.[30]

One can envisage underwater "trolley buses" harvesting ocean floor "pastures."[31]

The world ocean can provide food for 30,000 million people.[32]

The Soviet Union is equally appreciative of ocean and ocean floor chemical and geological wealth prospects—and equally determined to lead in their extraction:

Each cubic mile of ocean water (the world oceans have 350 million such miles) contains in dissolved form 165 million tons of solid matter representing almost the entire table of chemical elements.[33]

Ultra-basic rock . . . under the (ocean floor) crust substance . . . contains concentrated ores of valuable metals, such as chromites. . . . Valuable ores lie . . . also on the (ocean floor) surface. In many places the bed is literally covered, like cobblestones, with so-called ferro-manganese nodules, which have a higher content not only of iron and manganese, but also nickel, cobalt, copper, molybdenum, and some other minerals . . . the total reserves of ferro-manganese nodules on the surface of the Pacific Ocean's bottom alone amounts to more than 100,000 million tons, but they also lie deeper. To get a graphic idea . . . all the world's cobalt reserves on land amount to approximately a million tons, while there is more than 1,000 million tons in the nodules lying on the bottom's surface alone. . . . The development of ferro-manganese nodules at great ocean depths will be technically fully feasible and economically profitable.[34]

Drilling to (deep) sea bottom will be of great importance. . . . Mineral salts, bromide, magnesium, uranium, gold and platinum are contained in water and can be extracted: automatic mining and concentration factories (will) ply the seas and oceans . . . exploit underwater rocks . . . (and) extract offshore petroleum even from under the Arctic ice.[35]

In 1968 Russia began using a "super-powerful" dredge which not only extracted ilmenite-rutile-zircon sands from the Baltic seabed but was used experimentally to dress minerals aboard the ship. A description of one phase of Baltic subsea mining has been provided by the Russian magazine NTO-USSR, published by the Soviet Union's Council of Scientific-Technical Societies. It told of "experimental-commercial" extraction of ilmenite sands. First the seabed's target area was carefully inspected by aqualung divers. Then a suction dredge was brought to the location and, proceeding at a speed of 2–2.5 m.p.h., removed a layer of sand about 30 centimeters (11.8 in.) thick. Dredging continued even in very rough seas. The sand was delivered to an onshore concentrating installation. Cost of concentrate derived from the subsea sands was 2 to 2.5 times less than from concentrate obtained from onshore deposits. The experimental operation confirmed the expediency and economy of this type of offshore mining.[36]

Soviet engineers are looking forward to the time when they can use an atomic-powered installation on the "floating mine." They point out that an atomic-powered floating unit could be kept in the isolated Arctic region for as long as two years at a stretch and could work during the long winters without refuelling. In addition such an installation could, theoretically, sharply reduce mining costs . . . possibly by two-thirds.[37]

The ocean floor has turned out to be an underwater Klondyke, and it awaits a zealous master.[38]

The references to offshore petroleum extraction "even from under the Arctic ice" and to "atomic-powered floating" mines extracting offshore Arctic minerals are not coincidental. An ever expanding pan-Arctic research effort over the last decades has produced ever more promising data on the existence, location, and peculiarities of northern energy, mineral, chemical, and biological prospects. Existing and developing technologies promise access and cost-effective exploitation. The investment in knowledge has been as impressive as expectations are astounding. Air, surface, and subsurface research endeavors have been continuous and extensive. Military organs have collaborated closely with civilian endeavors.[39]

The older of the two recently operating Soviet Arctic ice research stations, NP-22, (it was abandoned early 1979, leaving the field to NP-23) is typical. After over a year of drifting in Canadian waters it was visited by a Canadian Broadcasting Corporation television crew in the spring of 1977. At that time it was declared to measure 3.5 by 2.5 miles, to be staffed by a complement of up to 100, to have a runway of 5,000 feet (as noted above, this may well accommodate the supersonic bomber Backfire, and is certainly a good bit longer than northern land runways currently being constructed by the Canadian government), nine aircraft, helicopters, and a number of silo-like dry wells (while their size could accommodate missiles, reality was said to be more innocuous: they were said to owe their shape to melting for drinking water and were currently used as natural refrigerators).[40] A June 1977 report from Paris quoted NATO sources to the effect that NP-22 personnel numbered 160, that the station was used for intelligence gathering, and that one of its hypothesized functions lay in guiding Soviet submarines to U.S. waters.[41]

Apart from its suggested extensive military role or potential, NP-22 and its sister research platforms have always been engaged in metereological and ice dynamics research.[42] It is presumed that they also collect data on "water observation, salinity, temperature, plankton, air-ice-water interaction, seismicity, gravity, magnetics, heat flow, acoustics, current meters, bottom geological sampling, etc., etc."[43]

The ice drift stations operate under the auspices of the Institute for the Arctic and Antarctica in Leningrad. The institute now employs over 1800 researchers(!). Among its other facilities it also disposes of a number of Arctic oceanographic research vessels. They currently have vessels on permanent station in each of the Soviet "Arctic seas" and off the northeast coast of Greenland.[44] Their vessels have also operated in the Beaufort Sea and Baffin Bay.

Some geological sampling of ocean floors is, as indicated, probably conducted from Arctic and Antarctica Institute platforms. One presumes that they also conduct bottom photography (Soviet underwater photography is of a high standard).[45] But the main conduit for geological charting of Arctic ocean floors is the Institute of Arctic Geology, which employs at least 600 and perhaps 800 researchers.[46]

The extent of their activity is indicated by the fact that it is now ten years since the publication of Soviet tectonic/metalogic maps detailing the geological structure of pan-Arctic ocean floors, going right up to northern Canadian islands. As was noted before, these old Soviet maps of the offshore bottom have a discrimination ten times better than do later Canadian charts of Canadian Arctic island land areas.[47] In view of the course vagaries of ice islands and their consequent inability to provide comprehensive coverage, it is furthermore clear that much of the Soviet mapping must have utilized underwater vessels, submarines, and submersibles.

Submersibles were and are employed also by the Ministry of Fisheries to chart more general biological potentials. The traditional fish intake has not provided the only focus, even though, as will be seen, Arctic fishery prospects appear slated to become even more important than they have been. Other polar ocean protein sources are also found alluring: scientists have discovered Arctic ocean "pastures" of mollusks and algae "half a kilogram per square meter at shallow depths . . . marine agronomists (will) cultivate plants."[48]

The described institutions are not the only ones involved in Soviet research of Arctic surface and subsurface expanses. Among the others are the Hydro-Meteorological Service with its separate research fleet and facilities; the Main Geodesical and Cartographic Administration of the USSR Ministry of Geology; the Academy of Sciences' Geographic Society, its Oceanographic Committee, Interdepartmental Geophysics Committee, Oceanological Institute (which operates some of the finer polar research ships, including the Admiral Kurcha-tov), School for Investigating the Coastal Areas of the Oceans, and even a num-ber of the Academy's regional inland branches.[49] During the late 1960s, for example, scientists at the Academy's Kievan branch "developed a new and un-usual installation for the extracting from sea water of boron, manganese and other so-called trace elements needed for plant life. Introduction of these ele-ments into the soil considerably raises crop yields."[50]

Even the impressive (both in terms of personnel and of equipment) De-partmental, Academy, and specialized Institute facilities on Arctic research and development do not exhaust the list. Universities are also becoming involved. Thus, by the spring of 1971, Odessa State University's Department of Geology and Geography alone graduated two classes (the first one of which was com-posed of 24 budding scientists) of "marine geological exploration specialists."[51]

It might be natural to query the rationale underlying the unique and in-deed immense Soviet research effort into offshore wealth potentials in general and Arctic in particular. The biological and fisheries programs are perhaps easy to fathom and explain in view of Soviet inability to meet human and husbandry protein requirements from land soil cultivation. But the Soviet Union is an oil and gas exporter, with claimed sizable land reserves to cover future needs.[52] It is unusually favored in the abundance of minerals within its natural borders. Whereas "the U.S. is . . . self-sufficient in only 10 of the 36 key industrial raw materials . . . the Soviet Union . . . fully meets its requirements in 29 of these 36 raw materials."[53] Furthermore,

> The extraction of many minerals in the Soviet Union is doubling ap-proximately every 8 to 10 years. Soviet exports of mineral com-modities include aluminium, antimony, cadmium, chromium, cop-per, iron, lead, magnesium, manganese, titanium, vanadium, zinc, abrasives, asbestos, cement, clays, fertilizer minerals, cryolite, graphite, gypsum, salt, sodium and potassium compounds, sulfur and pyrites, talk, carbon black, coal, coke, natural gas and petroleum. . . . Self-sufficiency is not the entire goal of Soviet mineral develop-ment policy. Export of minerals produce foreign exchange to help pay for imports. . . . Fuels, minerals and metals made up about 40 percent of the total declared Soviet exports in 1974.[54]

Part of the reason behind Moscow's determination to expand its natural raw materials control and export potential base is found obviously in the financial requirements of ambitious importation and investment designs alluded to above. The price implications of a dominant supply position with attendant manipulation possibilities is also not irrelevant to this context, and one should perhaps not forget that economic bargaining leverage has been shown to be translatable into political power, a point keenly appreciated in Moscow.[55]

Another reason lies in the increasing distance, inaccessibility, permafrost-burdened and generally climatologically inhospitable character of many land reserve locations. In view of emerging technologies (see below), the relative cost of exploiting offshore resources versus the cost of extracting and transporting residual land reserves, is shifting in favor of the former. The improved relative cost picture associated with offshore resources is further enhanced by the sheer abundance of some offshore prospects and finds:

> Official . . . reports indicate an opulent future . . . seismic investigation has shown a succession of oil-bearing anticlines . . . deep in the Arctic circle, and possessing fields even richer, possibly, than those in the North Sea.[56]

> In the Barents Sea, seismic surveys have determined the presence of all the basic requirements for an oil and gas bearing complex. . . . Soviet geologists (claim) that commercial hydrocarbons will be found along an extensive area of the Barents Sea shelf.[57]

> Russian geologists estimate that the Kara Sea has 388 trillion cubic feet of gas reserves.[58]

> The "rich deposits" of cassiterite in the Laptev Sea was the first placer (ore concentration) deposit to be exploited; the first extracting venture, in 1970, drilled "40 meters (131 ft.) into this unique ore body without finding its limit."[59]

Technological extraction problems are being overcome rapidly. While an early pioneer in the field of offshore oil production (offshore oil extraction in the Caspian Sea goes back to the 1920s),[60] Moscow lagged through the last decade's revolutionizing of offshore drilling technologies' potential and cost-effectiveness: but it is catching up fast, in part by intensifying domestic development,[61] "Soviet mining technology development is advancing at a rapid pace," in part through judicious and large-scale purchases.[62] ("A sophisticated geological survey ship, with dynamic positioning to allow core drilling in 600 meters of water . . . has been supplied to the USSR by France. Other countries, including the United States, are also selling the Soviet Union advanced drilling rigs and equipment, pipe laying barges, and other offshore oil and gas drilling and production equipment.") The Soviets feel they are now capable of providing the technology for offshore petroleum production even under the most rigorous Arctic conditions."[63]

Concurrent with their perfecting of traditional-type offshore drilling capability, it appears the Soviet Union may also have developed a different "seemingly exotic method of offshore oil production,"[64] a method that may be "especially applicable . . . to development of certain new fields . . . in such hostile environments as offshore Alaska and the Arctic Islands."[65] Since the late 1960s the Soviet Union has pioneered the concept of mining for petroleum and has achieved extraordinary improvements in recovery coefficients, consequent production volumes, and per-barrel production costs. With reference to offshore prospects, two variants of this technology have now been developed, one for areas proximate to land (or islands) and one for areas distant from shores.[66]

The Soviet Union has also developed an unorthodox but promising countermeasure with respect to possible oil well blowouts in Arctic waters. They have "employed PNE's (peaceful nuclear explosions) for the successful control of gas well blowouts" on land.[67] The technique apparently has equal applicability to offshore prospects and has stirred interest in Canadian quarters concerned about Beaufort Sea dangers:

> One can conceive of situations where it may be necessary to use nuclear explosions to control a bad well blowout. . . . It is plausible that the brute force approach could be necessary to control a blowout in a high pressure, thick pay, high permeability reservoir on which control cannot be regained by previously proven industry techniques.[68]

As concerns geological prospects and their exploitation (with the use of both suction and mining methods),

> Soviet mining technology developments . . . is advancing at a rapid pace. The USSR is currently exploiting placer deposits (e.g. tin and titanium-bearing sands) and extracting bromine and magnesium from sea water . . . it is in the process of acquiring . . . manganese mining technology.[69]

> The first generation . . . of a specialized Soviet fleet of ocean-going dredges of various types, ships equipped with ocean mining machinery and floating concentration facilities . . . is . . . now in operation. . . . The first winter's activities of a mining complex in the Arctic Ocean (saw the use of) Malyutka . . . a submarine hydraulic dredger.[70]

Yet Soviet knowledge of and ability to extract and exploit Arctic ocean and ocean floor potentials, geological, biological, and chemical, leaves open the question as to why it need look beyond its own Arctic continental shelf. Discoveries publicized so far lie on this shelf and its size. (Said to equal "almost one-third" of the world's coastal shelf, it covers between 2.5 million and 3.1 million square miles at depths of less than 200 meters.[71]) They indicate that it still contains sizable relatively virginal reserve acreage. The logic flowing from the accessibility implications of the Soviet shelf's shallow depths would also indicate a concentration on home waters. And it is a fact that the recent Soviet declaration of a 200-mile economic exploitation zone was explicitly justified through reference to past similar unilateral rights extensions on the part of Western and Third World nations; the closing of more distant venues was said to necessitate the compensatory protection of adjacent resources.[72]

But the implied resignation may be less important than the implied reluctance and the light this reluctance casts on underlying Soviet perceptions, ambition, and determination. There is evidence that Moscow continues to see a special role for itself in the exploitation of more distant oceans and ocean floors, and there is some indication that Moscow interprets current trends as putting a special premium on distant exploitation prospects in the Arctic, including Beaufort Sea and "Canadian Basin" regions.

The Soviet position on sea/ocean floor issues in general, and the confidence of which it bespeaks is perhaps best illustrated in its stance at Law of the Sea forums. Moscow has consistently championed free passage, steadfastedly sought to limit the exclusivity of coastal states' rights to adjacent waters and beds, and throughout insisted that any possible rules covering distant ocean and ocean floor exploitation must be government-negotiated, government-supervised, and government-implemented. Its stance can only be explained as reflecting ambitious plans for ocean mining beyond its own continental shelves, as reflecting the conviction that distant ocean wealth potentials outweigh the political cost of opposing proposed international supervisory organs that might funnel at least part of their profits to Third World development schemes, and as reflecting confidence both that its technology will be competitive and that its investments can be protected against challengers.[73]

> (Only Maoists) argue against such fundamental, generally accepted legal policies of the oceans as freedom of navigation, free passage of all vessels and overflight through or over international straits, and freedom of fisheries and scientific research in the open sea.[74]

> (Chinese and other) extremist claims (against the limiting of territorial waters *per se* to 12 miles) mean that about 40% of the area of the world's oceans would come under the control of (certain) governments and that their use by all countries would be denied; furthermore, such seas as the North, Mediterranean, Caribbean and others would be divided up between a few coastal states. . . . The Soviet Union . . . acknowledge(s) the right to establish economic zones up to a width of 200 miles, in which the coastal states would have

sovereign rights over living and mineral resources. . . . (But) . . . the key to this is the establishment in the international convention of the principles of complete utilization of the living resources of the economic zones, and primarily, of the principle according to which, if a coastal state harvests only a portion of its fish stocks, then fishermen from other countries should be allowed to harvest the unused portion of these stocks.[75]

(As concerns the proposal that exclusive rights of access to the resources of the larger ocean/ocean floor expanses, the "International region," be given to an "International body"): This clause . . . creates the possibility of depriving sovereign states of their inalienable right of access to the region's resources . . . (and may) be able to prevent countries from prospecting and developing marine mineral resources.[76]

(There is a threat) that the future body may develop from an organization of sovereign states into a supragovernmental corporation of the capitalistic type. It may be run by international monopolies that will be unabled by the system of "joint enterprises" not only to place the body in a dependent position, but also to ensure to themselves monopolistic positions detrimental to the sovereign states in the development of the resources of the sea bed.[77]

Establishment of exclusive rights to conduct research for an international agency, or even giving the agency control over the activities of nations in this sphere, would run contrary to the United Nations charter and other fundamental documents of international law because it would be tantamount to eliminating freedom of research, restriction of the sovereign rights of nations on the high seas, and giving an international agency functions which fall exclusively within the competence of sovereign states.[78]

Acknowledgement of equal rights for prospecting and exploitation of the resources on the sea bed both for government (or, under their control, corresponding physical or legal persons), and for the International body itself could become the basic principle of future policy on the development of the resources on the sea bed in the International region.[79]

Still, while Moscow chafes under the prospect of limitations on distant wealth exploitation, its final accession to the list of states proclaiming 200-mile economic zones does indicate that it accepts the inevitability of at least some limitations, and this acceptance does have consequences for Arctic prospects. In general, limitations on shallower continental shelf areas meant that the residual depths of most oceans, the depths to which an exploiter must now seek, were technologically more awesome than those of Arctic regions. With increasing modern technological ability to operate through or under ice, and in view of the unique Soviet knowledge and experience of these reaches, this may prove a decisive stimulant for some additional priority to more northern development— at least as concerns some resource potentials (i.e., placer deposits that can be sucked or dredged with underwater barges and vehicles).

But there is one resource area for which Arctic prospects may have been made especially alluring by the current evolution of international law: fishing. Fishing is the one distant ocean wealth extraction branch most affected by continental shelf limitations, by more restricted and enforced quotas in shallower waters. A large portion of its present catch comes from just these waters.

Yet there is no indication that Moscow has resigned itself to lower catch rates. On the contrary, there is every indication of expectancies of continued growth, and it appears that this expectation is not related to the fishing industry's embracing of aquaculture. This comment is necessitated by the fact that in recent years the Soviet Union has committed extensive research and developmental funds to this concept and clearly associated it with major potential: "Soviet specialists believe that the future belongs to aquaculture."[80] But that view is long-term; for the immediate and shorter-term perspective, aquaculture's potential in the field of ocean protein supply is clearly seen as supplemental and no more. Current developments will presumably spur additional investments in the perfecting and furthering of aquaculture techniques and production. The main route out of the fishing industry's present dilemma, however, lies elsewhere.

The Soviet Union has pursued a two-pronged policy. On the one hand, the limitations associated with coastal rights' extensions have been sought ameliorated or circumvented through bilateral treaties. Following the example of Japan, Moscow has busied herself negotiating cooperative ventures, treaties that permit the Soviet Union to perpetuate past catch rates in return for technological and other assistance to the development of Third World fishing industries.[81] In a sense, this policy can only be a short-term palliative or reprieve, since presumably the fledgling industries will be able one day and in fact have to demand a larger share of the local catch. Still, the good will entailed may be translatable into lessened damage, a cushioning of the eventuality.

The other and perhaps, in the longer term, more potent Soviet initiative may be seen in its focus on deep sea fishing capability, in its development of vessels capable of sustained distant ocean deep water operations.[82] It seems clear that the Soviet Union hopes to offset near-shore losses with increases further out, in deeper and less easily accessible waters. This is where the Beaufort Sea might well become more important to Soviet fishing designs. Apart from the potential of its deeper reaches, it has the world's one "foreign" continental shelf of undiluted continued promise—in the context of the Soviet (and international law?) position previously discussed on continental shelf access regulations. Its harsh climactic conditions will probably continue to rule out substantive Canadian or U.S. fishing efforts. There is, thus, little prospect of Soviet potentials being cut into by coastal state requirements. At the same time, Soviet familiarity with and experience in analagous conditions may make the prospect for Soviet fisheries in the area look considerably more cost-effective in Moscow than it would in Ottawa or Washington.[83]

Whatever the fate of this prognosis, however, the one inescapable conclusion from any contemplation of the past amalgam and current trends of Soviet Arctic efforts must surely be that pan-Arctic reaches have already acquired vital military-political importance to Soviet planners and that there is every indication that this importance will grow rather than diminish in the future.

It is this overall military-political context to which one must finally return. For it is overall; the two are coordinated and mutually supportive and perhaps dependent. The process of increasing Soviet economic penetration of "pan-Arctica" has been and is paralleled and complemented by increasing military penetration. Soviet nuclear submarines can and do traverse under Arctic ice.[84] Older submarines still equipped with more limited range missiles can now approach North American firing ranges from the north rather than the east or west, and there is every indication that at least some do just that. Soviet hunter-killer and anti-shipping submarines similarly now may choose to traverse polar regions from which they can position themselves closely enough to defy the time requirements of Canadian island chokepoint challenges. The scope of mutually supportive Soviet military and economic endeavors in the Arctic are such as to make the polar regions for them a favorable environment.[85]

The nuclear icebreaker Arktika's pioneering 1977 passage through the ice to the North Pole symbolized the Soviet conquest of the final surface sphere of the Arctic.[86] The Arktika's accomplishment was followed up in 1978, when her sister ship Sibir' extended the northern sailing season by two months and established the northern shortcut. "The route from the Barents Sea to the Chukotka Peninsula through higher latitudes is more than 1000 miles shorter than the usual route along the country's Arctic coast . . . the time is near when convoys will take the shortest road . . . through the centre of the Arctic basin."[87] A "radically new stage" in Arctic development had begun.[88]

NOTES

1. An interesting early Canadian analysis of this is found in R.A.J. Phillips, *Canada and Russia in the Arctic*, (Toronto, Ontario, Canadian Institute of International Affairs, October 1956). The booklet laments the extreme difference between Soviet and Canadian interest and ambition in their respective Arctic regions.

2. Ibid. See also C. J. Webster, "The Growth of the Soviet Arctic and Sub-Arctic," *Arctic*, May 1951.

3. Admiral Gorshkov, *Pravda*, July 25, 1976.

4. *NATO Letter*, September 1970, provides illustrative charts; see also chapter on "The Development of the Navy" in C. G. Jacobsen, *Soviet Strategy—Soviet Foreign Policy* (Glasgow: The University Press, 1972), pp. 123–141.

5. See M. A. Kravanja, "The Soviet Fishing Industry: A Review," in *Soviet Oceans Development* edited by Dr. John Hardt, (Washington, D.C.: Government Printing Office, 1976); see also Sysoev, *Economics of the Soviet Fishing Industry* (Moscow: Pishchevaya Promyshlennost', 1970).

6. See C. G. Jacobsen, "The Civilian Fleets: Notes on Military-Civilian Integration in the USSR," in *Soviet Oceans Development*.

7. V. D. Yakovlev, *Sovetskii Flot* DOSAAF, (Moscow: DOSAAF, 1971).

8. See, for example, *Defence Policy* (NATO Information Service: 1969); Capt. Raoust, "L'Expansion Maritime de l'URSS," *Revue de Défence Nationale* (Paris: 1969), and C. G. Jacobsen and others in *Soviet Oceans Development*.

9. C. G. Jacobsen, in *Soviet Oceans Development*; testimony by M. MccGwire in *Soviet Naval Policy: Objectives and Constraints* (New York: Praeger, 1974) (for further references see references cited therein).

10. M. A. Kravanja, "The Soviet Fishing Industry." See also H. T. Franssen, "A Comparison of the Strengths and Weaknesses of the United States and the Soviet Union in Ocean Capabilities," in *Soviet Oceans Development*.

11. Kravanja, "The Soviet Fishing Industry."

12. Franssen, "U.S. and Soviet Ocean Capabilities." In the period from 1953 to 1973, the Soviet merchant fleet increased by 443 percnet, while the U.S. merchant fleet decreased by 66 percent.

13. Ibid.

14. Raoust, "L'Expansion Maritime de l'URSS."

15. *Krasnaya Zvezda*, February 25, 1969.

16. L. Zenkevich and S. Osokin, *Vodnii Transport*, May 31, 1969.

17. *Krasnaya Zvezda*, May 21, 1969.

18. Conversation with Deputy Director Fedoseev of Leningrad's Institute of the Arctic and Antarctica, June 13, 1977.

19. U.S., Department of Commerce, *International Status and Utilization of Undersea Vehicles*, prepared by J. R. Vadus (10 76-242/01); see also S. Snegov, in *Sovetskaya Litva*, September 1975.

20. Vadus, *Undersea Vehicles*.

21. Vadus, ibid.; and Snegov, in *Sovetskaya Litva*, September 1975. The former gives the 1976 figure as twice that of 1975, while the latter gives a late 1975 figure, which is already twice as high again.

22. Vadus, *Undersea Vehicles*.

23. Ibid. See also D. R. Bakke, "Russia Determined to Lead in Oceans," *Offshore* (April 1973); S. Snegov, "International Report Offshore Technology: USSR" (unidentified copy received from Canada's Department of Energy, Mines and Resources, April 1977); Snegov in *Sovetskaya Litva*, September 1975; and V. S. Yastrebov, in *Reports on the Theory, Principles of Construction and Use of Robots and Manipulators* (Leningard: 1974).

24. Vadus, *Undersea Vehicles*.

25. C. H. Dodge, "Soviet Undersea Research and Technology," in *Soviet Oceans Development*; and see Bakke, "Russia Determined to Lead in Oceans."

26. Professor A. Monin, Director of the USSR Academy of Sciences Oceanological Institute, interviewed by D. R. Bakke, quoted in Bakke, "Russia Determined to Lead in Oceans."

27. *Krasnaya Zvezda*, May 21, 1969.

28. Ibid.

29. "Scientific Fish-Catching Methods in the USSR," *APN* (Soviet News Agency) release (unnumbered).

30. L. Zenkevich, in *Vodnii Transport*, May 31, 1969.

31. A. Vinogradov, "Ocean in the Year 2000," *Novosti* 20 1H4922B (from *Vodnii Transport*).

32. Lobanov, "Soviet Fish Industry," *Novosti* 107E189/K.

33. I. Pavlov, "Harvesting Ocean Wealth," *Novosti* 202E14563/K.

34. Zenkevich, *Vodnii Transport*, May 31, 1969.

35. Vinogradov, "Ocean in the Year 2000."

36. D. R. Bakke, "Russia Strengthens Its Mining Program," *Offshore* (November 1971).

37. Ibid.

38. Soviet scientist, quoted in "Opposing an International Agency to Control Deep Ocean Recourses Seems to Indicate that Russia Has Plans of Its Own," *Offshore* (October 1975).

39. In an interview with the author, June 13, 1977, the Deputy Director of the (Soviet) Institute of the Arctic and Antarctica acknowledged the military's role in supplying and aiding the ice-drift stations operated by his institute; see also references in earlier chapters.

40. *C.B.C. Newsmagazine*, April 3, 1977, 10 p.m. Atlantic time.

41. *International Herald Tribune* (Paris), June 27, 1977.

42. Information provided by Fedoseev, Conversation.

43. G. D. Hobsen, Director of Canada's Polar Continental Shelf Project, to author, April 26, 1977.

44. Conversation with Fedoseev.

45. "Soviet Underwater Photography is Good," in *Offshore* (August 1974).

46. The Leningrad Institute of Arctic Geology employed about 600 researchers when visited a few years ago by Dr. D. Loring of the Bedford Institute of Oceanography, Dartmount (Conversation with author, May 27, 1977); the 800 figure postulated as applying today is arrived at by presuming the institute has witnessed a similar growth over the past years to that of analagous Soviet institutes—and in view of the general Soviet stress on Arctic prospects and developments this would indeed appear if anything to be an underestimation.

47. *Tektonicheskaya Karta Arktiki i Subarktiki*, The Institute for the Study of the Arctic and Antarctica, Leningrad, 1967; the general maps have a scale of 1:500,000; compare with the *National Atlas of Canada*, 1974, for Canadian maps of the surface and geology of Canadian Arctic island areas (these were the best discrimination on such general maps that the author could find; see Chapter Two).

48. Vinogradov, "Ocean in the Year 2000."

49. See section on "The Organizational Aspects of the Soviet 'Civilian' Fleets," in C. G. Jacobsen's chapter on "The 'Civilian' Fleets," in *Soviet Oceans Development*.

50. I. Pavlov, "Harvesting Ocean Wealth."

51. *Pravda* report, cited in Bakke, "Russia Strengthens Its Mining Program."

52. See statements quoted in "Opposing an International . . . Its Own," and in J. P. Riva's chapter on "Soviet Offshore Oil and Gas," in *Soviet Oceans Development*.

53. J. E. Mielke, "Soviet Exploitation of Ocean Mineral Resources," in *Soviet Oceans Development*.

54. Ibid.

55. C. G. Jacobsen, "Japanese Security in a Changing World; the Crucible of the Washington-Moscow-Peking 'Triangle?'", *Pacific Community* (April 1975).

56. *Sea Power* (November 1976). The description refers to the Norwegian side of the dividing line but is presumed equally applicable on the other side; see also other quotes below. The presumption is accepted by Norwegian petroleum sources.

57. Riva, "Soviet Offshore Oil and Gas."

58. "Russia Will Explore Gas Field North of the Arctic Circle," *Offshore* (December 1974).

59. Bakke, "Russia Strengthens Its Mining Program."

60. Snegov, "International Report Offshore Technology: USSR."

61. Franssen, "U.S. and Soviet Ocean Capabilities."

62. Ibid.

63. Riva, "Soviet Offshore Oil and Gas." See also "Russia Will Explore Gas Field."

64. W. J. Ciezlewicz, "Russia May Resort to Undersea Mining," *Offshore* (September 1976); see also Buriakovskii and Gadzhiev, *O Podzemnom i Podvodnom Metode Razrabotki Morskikh Neftianikh Mestorozhdenii* (Baku: 1965); Alizade et al., *K Voprosu o Ratsional' noi Razrabotke Neftianikh Mestorozhdenii Pod Bol'shimi Vodnimi Basseinami* (Baku: Azerbaidzhanskoe Neftianoe Khoziaistvo, 1975). *Pravda*, May 26, 1976; *Sotsialisticheskaya Industria*, January 14, 1976; and other sources cited in Ciezlewich, "Russia May Resort to Undersea Mining."

65. Ciezlewich, "Russia May Resort to Undersea Mining."

66. Ibid.

67. D. A. Grant, "A Counter-Measure with Respect to Possible Oil Well Blowouts in Arctic Waters," *DND Staff Note* (May 1976); see also O. L. Kedrovesky, *Application of Underground Nuclear Explosions to the Liquidation of Uncontrolled Oil and Gas Wells* (Report to International Atomic Energy Agency Panel, January 1970).

68. Grant, "Counter-Measure to Possible Oil Well Blowouts."

69. Franssen, "U.S. and Soviet Ocean Capabilities."

70. Mielke, "Soviet Exploitation of Ocean Mineral Resources." See also *Pravda*, April 4, 1975.

71. Bakke, "Russia Strengthens Its Mining Program."

72. Resolution, Soviet *Council of Ministers, Pravda*, February 24, 1977.

73. "Opposing an International . . . Its Own."

74. I. Gorev, "The Oceans of the World—A State for Cooperation," *Novoye Vremya*, March 12, 1976.

75. S. Pavlov, "Detente and the Oceans of the World," *Pravda*, February 12, 1976.

76. Gorev, "The Oceans of the World."

77. Ibid.

78. "Opposing an International . . . Its Own."

79. Gorev, "The Oceans of the World."

80. Snegov, "International Report Offshore Technology: USSR." See also *Development*.

81. Kravanja, "The Soviet Fishing Industry."

82. Ibid.

83. Note: V. I. Kiselev ed., *Zakonodatelstva Kanadi Predotvrashchenia Zagriaznenia Prilegaiushchikh Arkticheskikh Morei* (Canadian Legislation on the Question of Preventing Pollution in Adjacent Arctic Seas) (Moscow: Moskva Transport Publishers, 1976). Note the title's careful noncommittal wording. Note also that the foreword describes the book as intended for "captains, first officers and engine chiefs." It has an initial print run of 4,000.

84. Of related interest, the general Soviet stress on subsurface capabilities and potential is vividly illustrated by the statistic that it devotes twice as high a proportion of its navy budget to submarine development as does the United States, 40 percent versus 20 percent (the U.S. carrier predilection is perhaps mainly responsible: 50 percent of U.S. funds go

to support the carrier element); see "Ocean Science and Technology" section of Franssen, "U.S. and Soviet Ocean Capabilities.

85. H. C. Bach and J. Taagholt, *Grønland og Polaromraadet—sikkerhedspolitisk set*, (Copenhagen: Forsvarskommandoen, 1976); also, by the same authors, see *Udviklingstendenser for Grønland*, (Copenhagen: Nyt Nordisk Forlag, 1976), and their more cursory *Greenland and the Arctic Region—in the Light of Defence Policies* (Copenhagen: Information and Welfare Service of the Danish Defence, 1977). And see W. Østreng, "The Strategic Balance and the Arctic Ocean," *Co-operation and Conflict*, no. 12 (1977).

86. *Soviet Union*, no. 11 (1977).

87. Ibid. The quote is from a commentary written by Timofei Guzhenko, Soviet Minister of the Merchant Marine.

88. Ibid.

8

MOSCOW AND THE SOUTHERN FLANK: NEW POSTURE, NEW CAPABILITIES

The second half of the 1970s saw Western consciousness jarred awake to substantial Soviet interest and action potential in "southern flank" areas, notably Africa. Soviet involvement in Africa rested on long antecedents, but its potency had been circumscribed by the strategically peripheral nature of its interests and the acknowledged paucity of its means. By the mid-1970s, however, it was becoming clear that both conditions had changed. As described elsewhere in this volume, Moscow was developing economic and political ties sufficiently weighty to compel or lure it to explicit commitment, protection, and pursuit and was also procuring the credibility prerequisite of demonstrable power projection capabilities.[1] The following will treat the first physical expression of the new constellation—Angola—as well as the more awesome subsequent demonstration of its potential—Ethiopia. The focus will then shift to a treatment of the latest incidents of Soviet distant crises involvements, tracing trends and consequences.

Previous sections have alluded to the history and extent of the Soviet role during the Angolan crisis and have dealt with some of the peculiarities of that involvement: that the Soviet Union's strategic adversaries were maneuvered into a situation in which they could oppose Soviet policies only through support of tribal groupings unable to attract recognition from a single African regime; that its adversaries allowed themselves to be perceived in the politically disastrous role of quasi-allies of Pretoria; that neither was able to back declaratory policies with the requisite action policy—deterred by political constraints in the one case, physical inadequacies in the other. But then all political crises are unique, involving their own amalgams of political and moral contradictions, temptations, restraints, and dangers. This section will look at the physical capability exhibited by the Soviets in their Angolan initiative. It will attempt to survey the quantity and quality of Soviet aid to the MPLA. The period covered will be that of post-independence 1975, especially the latter months of the year, when the conflict escalated, and the first months of 1976, when the issue was decided.

An early 1976 source of some repute listed Soviet aid thus:

21 MIG 21's and 3 MIG 15's (the MPLA already possessed 3 FIAT G91's left by the Portuguese);

Combat vehicles delivered included at least 30 T54 battletanks, about 80 older T34 battletanks, 68 PT76 amphibious light tanks, 92 BTR-50 amphibious tracked APC's, 74 BTR-60PA amphibious wheeled APC's, 20 BRDM armoured cars with heavy machine guns, 32 old BRT-40 light armoured vehicles, 877 unspecified reconnaissance vehicles;

Over 100 BM21 40 tubed 122 mm. mounted rocket launchers (described as the single item of possibly greatest effect);

384 GAZ51 trucks, 55 one and a half ton trucks, 80 quarter ton trucks, 160 heavy trailers, and thirty medium trailers;

10,000 AK-47 rifles, 10,000 AKM rifles, 10,000 SKS rifles, 2,000 Toakarev pistols, 80,000 hand grenades, 40,000 anti-tank and anti-personnel mines, 290 belt-fed heavy machine guns, unknown numbers of AT-3 Sagger anti-tank missiles, unknown numbers of SA7hr SAM's, 1,100 RPG-2 anti-tank rocket launchers, 1,700 B-10 82 mm. recoiless anti-tank guns, 1,000 82 mm. mortars, and 240 tactical communication sets.[2]

Other sources testified to the delivery of bridge-building equipment,[3] be and to the fact that it appeared to be effectively used.[4] Yet other sources reported on the delivery and conflict utilization of helicopter gunships.[5]

It is clear that most of these data had been supplied by U.S. intelligence sources. Indeed, the stories were usually explicitly attributed to such; hence also the fact that similar figures were given credence by a wide variety of Western publications.[6] One, therefore, might suspect an inherent politically biased tendency towards exaggeration. Yet, there were no reports from the field, be they from Western, neutral, or Eastern journalists or commentators, that ever actually challenged the basic accuracy of the presented data. In view of Moscow's own stress on the value, quantity, and quality of its support,[7] it therefore appears fair to conclude that the figures are at least "in the ball park."

By the last months of 1975, the rocket luanchers had come to dominate action on the ground. As one observer noted,

The armies now seldom meet within rifle range, or even mortar range. Instead the 122 millimeter rockets are set up in batteries of 24 on the backs of jeeps, and fired at National Front or UNITA positions some nine miles away . . . (with) Popular Front soldiers moving up behind the rocket barrage. In this way the Popular Movement has captured territory in nine-mile chunks.[8]

By mid-January 1976, helicopter gunships also had became prominent, especially in the MPLA/Cuban drive southward against the now more rapidly retreating UNITA/South African forces in that region.[9] In the rural campaign the gunships controlled the air and rendered vital ground support.[10] Against urban centers, such as Huambo and Novo Redondo, the MIGs and FIATs were also brought to bear.[11]

By mid-February came reports of offshore naval bombardments and amphibious operations against coastal centers still controlled by UNITA/South African forces. One source testified to a well-executed amphibious landing operation against Mocamedes; Soviet vessels were said to have bombarded the city with armor piercing and fragmentation shells from a distance of approximately seven miles, before landing "several hundred Cuban troops, amphibious armoured cars, tanks and personnel carriers."[12]

The turning of the tide towards the end of 1975 reflected the post-October arrival of increasing numbers of Cuban officers and men and stepped up deliveries of Soviet arms. According to Secretary of State Kissinger's January 29, 1976 testimony, Moscow had to that date flown 46 cargo flights into Luanda or Congo Brazzaville loaded with military equipment, "while a steady stream of Soviet and Cuban aircraft has continued to bring Cuban troops across the Atlantic."[13]

Another late January 1976 source noted that after U.S. diplomatic pressure temporarily denied Cuba refuelling privileges in Barbados, Guyana, and the Azores, the Soviet Union countered by flying the Cubans in IL-62s direct from Cuba to Conakry.[14] The same source placed the January 7-21, 1976 arrival rate at 200 Cubans per day, with another 1,000 expected to arrive on a concurrent sealift of 6-8 cargo vessels.[15]

A third outlined Soviet naval involvement in this way:

> The Soviet Union maintained a steady stream of cargo ships between the Soviet Union/Cuba and Angola, delivering both military equipment and Cuban troops. The Soviet sealift was also complemented by the presence of several Soviet warships. In mid-January it was reported that a Kresta II class guided missile destroyer, a Kotlin class guided missile destroyer, an amphibious vessel and four naval tankers were positioned just north of Angola.[16]

It appears it was elements of this force that were involved, for example, in the shelling and landing at Mocamedes.[17]

Before proceeding with a discussion of arms utilization, however, one comment must be made concerning the arms themselves; while by no means outdated, they were not of the newest vintage.[18] Some had already been phased out within the Soviet Armed Forces. Most was standard inventory of the Cuban forces, including the T-34, T-54, and PT-76 tanks and the MIG-21s. It appears clear that at least a considerable part of the weaponry used by Cuban personnel in Angola came from Cuban stocks. The MPLA itself and its African allies, however, were supplied from elsewhere. Black Sea or other Warsaw Pact ports appear to have seen the dispatching of most of the equipment. But some, such as older vintage tanks, originated in Iraq, Algeria, and probably Somalia.[19] The confusion regarding points of origin of MPLA arms serves to underline the problems that would be encountered in attempting to add up Moscow's "bill." Which nations, if any, donated without Soviet assurances of recompense? What was the nature and extent of solicited or promised recompense?

Analagous problems encumber the question of arms utilization or, rather, arms operators. It may be assumed that the Cubans operated their own arms. They may also have provided the relevant expertise to their African hosts and allies. Certainly the MPLA itself did not possess a sufficiently large pool of appropriately qualified personnel to absorb fully the large infusion of comparatively sophisticated weaponry. The question that remains concerns the possible combat role of Soviet advisers, technicians, engineers, flyers, and the like.

Available data does not suffice to give an adequate answer. But the limited numbers of Soviet personnel present does indicate that actual Soviet combat involvement must have been minimal. Thus, most sources spoke of something like 200 Soviet "military advisers" in Angola at the start of 1976.[20] This figure compared to a total of 3,000 Soviet military advisers in Africa as a whole, including, according to one source, 33 in Mali, 600 in Algeria, 300 in Libya, 80 in Sudan, 300 in Uganda, 200 in Egypt, 1,000 in Somalia, 25 in Mozambique, 50 in Nigeria, and 110 plus in Guinea.[21] (The same source provided a 1971-75 overall Soviet military aid cost estimate of 2 billion dollars and juxtaposed this to 765 million dollars worth of nonmilitary economic aid).[22] There was no absolute concensus concerning personnel numbers, and it is of course self-evident that numbers would fluctuate.[23] Yet they do indicate a range.

To the suggested level of Soviet presence on land must be added those involved offshore, but here the figure defies computation. Should one include the total complement on board Soviet ships in or near Angolan waters? Or does one count merely those participating in actions such as the shelling of Mocamedes? As concerns this particular action, how could one estimate the role, if any, played by Soviet personnel in the actual landing operation?

The official U.S. view of Angolan events and consequences was summarized by Secretary of State Kissinger. He claimed that the Soviet involvement in Angola marked the "first time since the aftermath of World War II that the Soviets have moved militarily at long distances to impose a regime of their choice. It is the first time that the U.S. has failed to respond to Soviet military moves outside their immediate orbit."[24] At a later press conference, he elaborated on the cost, claiming that Soviet financial aid to the MPLA totalled "nearly

200 million dollars," on top of which Moscow was said to have provided "nearly 300 million dollars in Soviet equipment."[25] Deputy Secretary of Defense R. Ellsworth pursued the primary theme: "If the Soviets are successful in either establishing military bases or obtaining operating rights in Angola, their strategic and tactical capabilities would be greatly enhanced. . . . Moscow's ability to project naval power would be materially enhanced by gaining access to Angolan refuelling and berthing facilities."[26]

But such conclusions or fears appeared exaggerated, even at the time. The scale of Soviet assistance was novel. Yet it could also be seen as but a natural extension of Moscow's increasing and more general involvement in African affairs. While the scale in the Angolan context might be seen by some to represent a quantum leap, it could on the other hand be seen as the minimum response needed to insure defeat of the South Africa-supported factions.[27] The very fact that the scale and purposefulness of assistance might be seen merely as extensions of an already established trend was, of course, itself noteworthy. But it was noteworthy as evidence of changing power perceptions and power coordinates on a more general plane and not one exclusive to the Angolan scenario. There were considerably larger Soviet "military adviser" contingents in a number of other African states. While Cuban personnel figures in Angola may have been more startling, the fact of Cuban presence in an African nation also had so many precedents as to be anything but startling.

There was, furthermore, reason to doubt the claim that port facilities made available to Soviet ships in Angola could upset the strategic equilibrium. True, Angola possesses numerous fine deep water anchorages. But African coastal facilities already secured by Moscow through the early 1970s had long sufficed to make the specter of a Soviet potential against the West's "oil lifeline" a reality rather than merely a prospect.[28] Possible Soviet access to Angolan ports constituted a convenience or insurance but did not in itself entail major strategic significance.

Soviet success in Angola was important for different reasons, three of which deserve enumeration. First, the image of will, resoluteness, and capability conjured up by Moscow's original involvement was dramatically reinforced by its response when South Africa and other FNL/UNITA allies upped the ante. The demonstration of steadfastness and ability to follow through was important both to quell mutterings that such had not always been evident in the past and to highlight the contrast between Soviet potential and Chinese impotence.

The second and to Moscow perhaps most important advantage accruing from Angolan events also relates to the competition with the PRC. Not only was the practical superiority of Soviet aid exhibited, so also was its ideological superiority. The contrast between Soviet ideological steadfastness in resolutely supporting the socialist-oriented MPLA and China's heretical support of anti-socialist, C.I.A.-associated groupings was a significant factor in weaning the Tanzanian and Mozambiquan leaders from too close an association with Peking.

Finally, one must note the sophistication inherent in Moscow's not making the demands it might have made in return for its investment. Moscow did not demur when the MPLA propagated the writings of Franz Fanon rather than (if not to the exclusion of) Lenin in the villages.[29] Nor did Moscow demur when the MPLA favored a continued level of economic and trade ties with the West rather than immediate nationalization and confiscation,[30] or when the MPLA denied that Moscow had requested or would be given bases.[31] Moscow acquiesced in the purge of a purportedly more pro-Soviet faction of the MPLA which had initiated an abortive coup on May 27, 1977.[32] The Soviet Union appeared to have absorbed the awkward lesson that dependence does not mean acquiescence, that dependence-generated pressure usually spawns defiance rather than compliance. Moscow's low-key approach might, in fact, be seen as a better guarantor of Angola's future good will and cooperation than could have been effected through more heavyhanded policies. Of perhaps even greater import, though, was the anticipated impact on other African capitals. It served to lessen the credibility of Western doomsayers, and thus create a climate more favorable to future Soviet interests.

The next instance of major Soviet interventionary activity in Africa, in Ethiopia, was protected by an equally fortuitous environment.[33] Whereas Soviet actions in Angola had been anointed by the moral absolutes of anti-colonialism and anti-racism, the decisive support provided to Addis Ababa's early-1978 campaign to repel the Somali invasion of Ogaden was sanctified by the Organization of African Unity's principle of the nonviolability of established borders. The imperative of self-preservation compelled even African allies of the West to condone, if not support, a Soviet-Cuban intervention defined as defending Ethiopia's territorial integrity. This made overt U.S. countering action politically impossible in a situation for which covert action was to prove inadequate. This time the quantity and quality of Soviet aid was far more awesome than witnessed in Angola. It reflected on the more formidable capacities of the new adversary. But it also provided telling testimony of the pace of improvement of Soviet interventionary potentials.

Early January 1978 saw the employment of up to 225 Soviet transports (planes) and the arrival of "several hundred" Soviet personnel and 2000 Cubans.[34] February saw U.S. estimates of 1000 to 1500 Russians, 2000 to 4000 Cubans, "several hundred" to 1000 South Yemenis, as well as "several hundred" to 2000 East Europeans (mostly from the GDR, but also some Bulgarians and others)—together with 40 Israelis—with a suggested total as high as 6000.[35] About one-third of the number appeared to be combat troops.[36] By March there was a peak report of 12,000 Cubans and of the directing presence of top-ranking Soviet and Cuban generals.[37] European estimates, especially those ascribed to French "intelligence," tended towards somewhat lower numbers yet not so much lower as to seriously dilute the concensus perception of scale.[38]

January saw Soviet naval shelling of rebel-infiltrated Massawa.[39] By mid-February, the contingent of Soviet naval vessels in the Red Sea numbered "more than twenty"; the following week brought a figure of 25.[40] As concerns land-related equipment, Western reports asserted the February presence of MIG-17s and MIG-21s; March listings included PT-76 and T-62 tanks, MIG-21s and 23s and the very large MI-6 helicopters (capable of lifting tanks).[41] The value of Soviet aid was said to have reached 850 million dollars by early February, and to approach one billion dollars by early March.[42]

The scale of the Soviet and allied involvement is perhaps best portrayed by this description of the final "combined operations" battle for Jigjiga, in mid-March:

> Led by veteran Soviet generals and spearheaded by a powerful Cuban shock force of tanks, planes, artillery and paratroopers, the Ethiopian Army stormed the Somali stronghold of Jigjiga. Five Somali brigades held out for three days; on the fourth, they broke and ran. . . . The Somalis were routed from Jigjiga in a textbook-perfect assault that employed massive airlifts and bombing raids along with pinpoint barrages of artillery to clear the way for columns of tanks backed by battalions of Cuban troops in armoured personnel carriers. "It was over almost before it started," said an awed Arab military attache in Mogadishu, the Somali capital, "it was the kind of maneuver that up to now has been done only on paper maps in staff colleges." . . . After a billion-dollar transfusion of arms to Ethiopia—including hundreds of lightweight PT-76 and medium T-62 tanks, at least 50 MIG-21 and MIG-23 jets, and a flotilla of giant MI-6 helicopters—the Soviet-Cuban juggernaut began to move. . . . Apparently under the overall command of Gen. Vasily Ivanovich Petrov, a combat-hardened veteran who is first deputy of Soviet ground forces, the Cubans launched a series of short, sharp thrusts against the main Somali lines near the key Ethiopian centres of Harar and Dire Dawa. The object was to clear the area for the concentration of Petrov's attack forces and to suck more Somali troops into Jigjiga so that they could be destroyed in one, decisive engagement. The Somalis fell neatly into the trap: they were still sending reinforcements to Jigjiga when the final assault began. Instead of trying to dislodge the main Somali force in the Ahmar range west of Jigjiga, Petrov chose to flank it with an impressive end run around—and over—the mountains. . . . Petrov sent a full Cuban armoured brigade looping around the northeastern end of the range. . . . Petrov used his MI-6s, which can carry men, enormous stockpiles of fuel and ammunitions—and, by some accounts, 14-ton PT-76 tanks—to a staging area on a plateau northwest of Jigjiga. When the two forces linked up late in February, the stage was set for the final assault. . . . The task force struck towards Jigjiga behind massive artillery barrages and, by Somali count, 130 separate air strikes. Simultaneously, a second Cuban armoured brigade knifed straight up the main road into the Kara Marda pass . . . resistance . . . collapsed. . . . The Cuban tanks rumbled into Jigjiga and rumbled out

again as quickly, heading east and south in pursuit of the broken Somali forces.[43]

In justifying their involvement, the Soviets hammered at the theme of Somali aggression and Somali unwillingness to negotiate.[44] Somali aggression and Somali intransigence purportedly made Soviet aid to the victim a moral imperative, an imperative transcending the bonds of erstwhile alliances: "When Somali troops invaded the territory of Ethiopia, the U.S.S.R. sided with the victim of aggression, proceeding from the fundamental principles of its foreign policy, and at the request of Ethiopia is giving the country the appropriate material and technical assistance.[45]

The awkward fact that the aggressor had been a self-proclaimed socialist state, until then militarily and politically alligned with Moscow, was explained as being due to the perverting perfidy of U.S. subversion, to the fact that through moral and physical means Washington had fuelled Somali chauvinism and hence driven a wedge between Moscow and Mogadishu:

No "explanations" by the U.S. State Department can refute the fact that last spring Washington began working hard to worsen Somalia's relations with the Soviet Union. A group of U.S. newspaper editors, invited to the White House at that time, were frankly told that the United States "would challenge the Russians in Somali" by covert encouragement of Somalia's territorial claims on Ethiopia. Those who took this road and prodded Somalia this way were well aware of the Soviet Union's principled stand in condemning the seizure and annexation of land anywhere in the world. The Soviet Union did everything in its power to prevent the Somali-Ethiopian conflict even though this could lead and actually did lead to unfriendly steps by the Somali leadership in relation to the Soviet Union. The matter is not whether or not the United States began to supply arms to Somalia in the aggravated situation in that part of Africa, but that promises were given to make such deliveries . . . they caused bloodshed.[46]

It was way back in the spring of 1977 that President Carter told journalists about the U.S. intention to "challenge the Russians." . . . It was then that Washington promised aid to Somalia. Tempted by the promise, the Somali leaders started the policy of rapprochement with the U.S. allies. At the same time Siad Barre set forth his territorial claims to Ethiopia and shortly thereafter launched military operations against that country. The source of the aggressive flood coming in from Mogadishu is to be sought, above all, in the West.[47]

Having supposedly enticed Mogadishu away from Moscow and on to the road to aggression, Washington was also portrayed as responsible for the scale of the Somalian effort and, hence, indirectly, for the resulting exaggerated scale of the required Soviet counter. Washington was said to be prevailing on allies to supply Somalia with cash and hardware. West Germany, Egypt, Iran, Saudi Arabia, and Sudan were singled out in particular as conscious and willing conduits, with Britain, France, and Italy noted as playing peripheral roles.[48]

Soviet assertions received a good amount of confirmation from establishment-linked Western publications. *Time* magazine acknowledged that Somalia received "nonmilitary" financial assistance from West Germany.[49] *Newsweek* spoke of assistance provided by Saudi Arabia, Iran, Egypt, and the Sudan and the fact that "Siad Barre's government had managed to buy European arms and reportedly received 30 old American tanks from Oman, which in turn had borrowed them from Iran."[50] It also reported:

> Somalia . . . enlisted a European consortium to supply it with arms and pilots. Siad Barre ordered his ambassador in Paris to seek help from France, and secret meetings were held in London, Paris, Rome and Madrid. Soon, 43 Cobra helicopters were ordered from a Bell Augusta plant in Italy for shipment to Somalia via Madrid. The deal, financed by Saudi Arabia, also covered millions of rounds of ammunition, 300 cannon turrets and anti-aircraft missiles. Shipments were arranged by a Madrid firm, F. Internacional, which performs topographical work for the Spanish Government but also acts as an arms-sales agent. . . . A British firm named Secrun, Ltd. . . . was approached to supply 183 Americans with Vietnam experience to fly and maintain the helicopters at salaries of $500 to $1000 a week. By last week, an advance party of four Americans was standing by in the Persian sheikdom of Dubai.[51]

The arresting point about current Soviet African policies is not just that they are asserted to be righteous, selfless, and moral, that interventionary aid is said to be given only to internationally sanctioned governments and movements that expressly ask for it,[52] or that international acceptance of such aid has hitherto been oiled by the justifying principles of anti-colonialism, anti-racism, and anti-aggrandisement.[53] Rather, as elaborated upon elsewhere, it is the increasing tendency to elasticize the moral imperative, by incorporating anti-neo-colonial and anti-"feudal" dictas.[54] The United States is said to be working "through the hands of internal African reactionaries, through the hands of those forces which are waging a subversive fight against the progressive regimes."[55] Thus, the United States allegedly established "an alliance of reactionary Arab regimes, backed financially by Saudi Arabia, to liquidate the revolutionary-democratic regime in Ethiopia."[56] Imperialist and reactionary forces, treated increasingly as synonymous, are ranged against "progressive regimes" and "national liberation movements," which perforce in effect themselves have to become synonymous for purposes of self-preservation.[57]

This stance was starkly evident in the Soviet reaction to the May 1978 invasion of Shaba (Katanga) province in Zaire by Katangan refugee forces and the subsequent intervention of French and Belgain troops:

> As Western propaganda still continues to blame the death of Europeans in Shaba on the National Liberation Front of the Congo, this organization has published a statement in which it stresses the falsity of those contentions. The statement says that troops of the Front have behaved all the time correctly, this being evidenced by Europeans who left Shaba and confirm that whites were killed by the Zairean army. The Western countries must realize the lawfulness of the struggle conducted by the Congolese people under the guidance of the Front, the statement notes.
>
> The statement refutes concoctions by Western propaganda that the Front is supported by Cuba, the GDR and the Soviet Union and emphasizes that the aim of these concoctions is to divert the attention of the broad public from the true causes of the uprising in Zaire against the existing regime.
>
> The actions by France and other Western powers in Zaire are of a clearly expressed neo-colonialist, imperialist nature and are directed against the freedom and independence of the African peoples, it was stated by the Secretary of Libya's Supreme People's Committee for Foreign Affairs, Ali Abdel Salam al-Treiki. The imperialists, he stressed, have proved again that they treat Africans as people of a lower race.[58]

This propaganda statement is interesting for a number of reasons. First is the categorical denial of Soviet or Soviet-allied involvement. Since even sources within the U.S. administration leaked scepticism about the evidence on which some of their superiors rested contrary assertions, it is perhaps reasonable to let the point pass.[59] More important for the future is the implied case made for the conclusion that Soviet or Soviet-allied intervention would in fact have been warranted morally.

Again, the Soviet posture was to receive considerable support from Western publications of repute. The (Manchester and London) *Guardian* wrote: "The capture of Kolwezi by the French signals the end of . . . formal obeisance to the notion of African independence. . . . Politically as well as economically Africa is being recolonized."[60] The French *Le Monde* made the statement: "The real question will sooner or·later be asked: Must we in order to defend the 'friends' of France (or economic interests) in Shaba or Chad, maintain leaders rejected by a large part of their people?"[61] The German *General-Anzeiger* paper put it thus: "For the West, the real dilemma lies in its need to support 'moderate' pro-Western regimes (such as Zaire's) which probably cannot be maintained. Corruption, economic mismanagement and oppression are the deeper causes of this situation."[62] The *Daily Nation* of Kenya mused, "it would appear that

France is eager to take on the role of policeman of the world, or at least of Africa."[63] Conservative and "liberal" papers of Europe pursued the theme, in stories illustratively headlined, "But How Much of Africa Can Giscard Embrace?"; "West's Policeman in Africa"; "France as the Gendarme of Africa"; "French Bluff Called"; "Should the West Prop up Africa's Men of Straw?"[64]

On the other hand, whereas France has been the most extensively involved Western military actor in Africa and has drawn the most notice, it has not been the only such actor, nor the only one whose role is acknowledged by Western media. Moscow, for example, has been able to note:

> The world press also carried reports saying that West German companies had built a launching site in Zaire to test prototypes of ballistic and cruise missiles. It is furthermore highly significant that West German Ambassador to Ethiopia Hans Lankes who was recently expelled from Ethiopia had been expelled from Guinea a few years earlier for conspiring in a plot organized by the Portuguese colonialists against that country.[65]

In Africa the emotionally repugnant specter of returning colonialism was joined to memories of aggrandizing militarism. When wedded also to pervasive prejudices against past colonialism and racism, the composite did indeed conjure up a more alluring and compelling rallying cry than promised by trumpetings of anti-communism. Moscow was returning to the harder-line ideological posture that Khrushchev had had to abandon. But conditions had changed dramatically since those days. At that time the option of effective Soviet protection or alliance was plainly not credible due to the recognized paucity of Soviet power projection capabilities. Also, much of Africa was experiencing the optimism of recently granted or imminent independence; the environment pictured colonialism as a relic of the past rather than a threat for the future. Then, too, residual Cold War polarization minimized West European and others' receptiveness to Soviet propaganda themes. By the late 1970s, however, Soviet means clearly did allow for credible alliance alternatives. Furthermore, a decade or two of all too often frustrating independence had persuaded a number of African countries that independence really was ephemeral in conditions of multinational trade and development dominance and increasing north-south disparities.[66] Finally, through *Ost-politik* and other manifestations of West Europe's evolution from the era of polarization, "moral" attitudes previously viewed as corrupted by association with Moscow now increasingly came to be seen in a more secular hue and to be accepted as inherently humane and just—and hence to warrant support from liberals and even small "c" conservatives. As exemplified in the above list of respected institutions supporting at least some elements of Moscow's African policy posture, the days were gone when such (limited) support could be dismissed as the delusions of "fellow travellers" or the treachery of a "fifth column."

The straight jacket that limited Washington's counter-potential to actions through proxy and covert C.I.A. activities in Angola and elsewhere was not solely the product of Vietnam and Watergate-inspired defeatism, apathy, or isolationism.[67] To a very large extent it was due rather to the above-described constellation. In the carefully chosen instances of blatant Soviet involvement, Washington had to be deterred by the knowledge that overt U.S. action could no longer count on even Western sanction and that it entailed a negative political and economic fall-out potential that was new in principle. Ironically, the perceived necessity to resort and restrict oneself to subversive activities might itself perpetuate the emasculation of more substantive ambitions. As the noted African specialist Colin Legum put it, the West can no longer continue to "directly meddle in the internal politics of those States through shipments of arms and direct subversion, and yet expect support for sanction against 'communist' interventions."[68] Greater Western potency appears to demand either the elimination of the hypocrisy now drowning assertions of morality, or else the discarding of the morality that presently sabotages the aspirations at the core of the hyprocrisy.

By the late 1970s, Moscow had succeeded in transforming the allegiance map of Africa, securing at least a measure of access and influence in every major region of that continent. The Soviet Union had suffered some dramatic reversals in the process, most particularly the alienation of Egypt and Somalia. On the other hand, these losses had been partly offset by closer alignments with neighbors (Libya and Ethiopia), and for the longer term Moscow might draw some expectation from the fact of continued support from potent opposition groupings within each of the estranged allies. Still, the aura of strength that it now projected did emanate from success stories based on judicious and cautious choices of settings. Aside from Rhodesia, Namibia, and South Africa, there appeared few other settings promising similar amalgams of conducive morals.[69] The fact that Moscow did not intervene in Zaire in 1978 may be as important as the fact that it suggested such intervention might have been warranted: in the absence of clearer-cut colonialist and racist issues, the issue of feudalism or reaction did not by itself promise sufficient sanction.

In conclusion it might be appropriate to supplement Chapter Three's presentation of the evolving Soviet theoretical justification for interventionary designs with some more "secular" quotations.

Two articles by I. Shavrov on local wars are worthy of mention. He argued that local wars, of which there were 470 between 1945 and 1975, had become the typical form of post-World War II conflict. This was ascribed to the emergence of "two opposed groups of states" in the world "that seek by means of local military engagements to improve their strategic position" in anticipation of "a greater collision." "The rise of the national-liberation battles of peoples" had brought imperialist efforts to suppress them, and thus prevent a collapse of the colonial system. Meanwhile, the "catastrophic consequences of a world nuclear-missile war for the existence of the capitalist system itself forced its political leaders to review many strategic conceptions of using military force." Strivings to improve international positions through force were hence channelled; "local wars became considered to be one of the most effective forms of achieving this goal." Reviewing the history of such conflicts, Shavrov asserts, first, that still "a product of imperialism, one of the forms of its reactionary, aggressive policies," local wars remain highly significant, proving that imperialist attitudes to small countries remain unchanged and that it is only the form of the struggle against "world revolutionary and national liberation movements" that has changed. Second, after World War II, the struggle against these movements and socialism became part of the imperialists' global strategy, and local wars, tied to maintaining military bases abroad and other factors, were seen as an effective way to combat the anti-imperialist struggle while avoiding a catastrophic confrontation with the socialist states. Third, in conditions of international detente and the general crisis of capitalism the balance of forces between socialism and capitalism has seen "a sharp change." With the continuing "rise of revolutionary and national-liberation movements" this has forced imperialism to use local wars in "efforts to find a way out of the crisis." Fourth, the "lessons of local wars and military conflicts" teach that such aggressive acts by imperialism's "militaristic circles" carry "in themselves a threat to peace and entail the danger of their transformation into a world war. The experience of local wars is widely employed in preparing armies and improving their organization and technological outfitting. But this experience also has significance for the forces of national liberation" and can lead to new forms of battle on their part.[70]

The general Soviet posture is of course that—notwithstanding bourgeois propaganda to the contrary—one must be careful to distinguish militaristic and imperialistic adventures from the fact that "revolutionary and national-liberation wars, and wars in defence of the conquests of socialism, are deeply just."[71] All the more arresting, then, to note Shavrov's initial identification of pragmatic power considerations distinct from moral cloakings.

Finally, Soviet support for southern African liberation struggles invites a consideration of Soviet official attitudes towards "partisan warfare":

> In the majority of them (post-1945 conflicts and local wars) partisan activity was the chief form of armed struggle for one of the sides for a long period. . . . In civil and national-liberation wars, as long as the progressive forces still have not created their own regular army, partisan actions remained not only one but the only form of armed struggle.
>
> It must be underlined that in the battle for national and social liberation many of the armed clashes which see the wide application of partisan operations are distinguished by the great results and the finality of the victory of the oppressed peoples. The successes of the progressive forces that have used partisan forms of struggle have led

to a weakening of the political, military and economic positions of imperialism in particular regions of the world. . . . (Continued use of these methods is mandatory, since) reactionary imperialist circles try in every way to oppose the efforts of people for freedom from nationalist and social oppression. . . . Partisan operations are taking an ever increasing place in military strategy . . . (in World War II it) was a new strategic factor . . . (more recently) where partisan actions were for one side the only form of armed struggle, in essence they comprised the basic content of military strategy.

(On the other hand, where partisans supplement the operations of regular armed forces, one speaks) of the strategic use of partisan forces in the interests of the operations and campaigns carried out by the regular army . . . strategy (must be) unified. . . . (The military "art" of the regular and partisan struggles are also interconnected as) often in national-liberation and civil wars the partisans' military organization becomes transformed into a regular cadre army . . . the presence of unified political leadership on the part of Communist Party and other progressive forces (is necessary for optimum use of partisans as part of the more general struggle). . . . (Soviet moral, political and material help to struggling peoples . . . is an expression of fraternal solidarity and a fulfilling of internationalist duty to the oppressed masses.[72]

One might mention that the Republic of South Africa is the one African nation with a long-established traditional Communist Party. Furthermore, while the various black liberation groupings in the republic are multi-hued politically and ought not to be dumped automatically under any "Communist" rubric, their early-twentieth-century roots and legends do have important Marxist imprints.

NOTES

1. See Chapters Two through Five.

2. *International Defence Review*, February 1976, pp. 19–20.

3. *The Washington Post*, January 26, 1976.

4. *The (London) Times*, January 20, 1976.

5. *The New York Times*, February 10, 1976.

6. One might point to the *Christian Science Monitor* of January 23, 1976, which quoted intelligence sources to the effect that the MPLA had received 36,000 pistols, rifles, and machine guns, a figure which tallies nicely with that presented by the first source cited.

7. See, for example, V. Kirsanov, in *Voenno-Istoricheskii Zhurnal*, no. 3 (1977): 71–79 (hereafter referred to as *V-IZ*); and M. Filimoshin, *V-IZ*, no. 10 (1977): 82–89.

8. M. T. Kaufman, "Suddenly Angola." *New York Times Magazine*, January 4, 1976.

9. AP/Reuter report in the *Toronto Globe and Mail*, January 16, 1976.

10. *The Washington Post*, January 18, 1976.

11. *The New York Times*, February 10, 1976, reported MPLA employment of 6 MIG and FIAT jet fighter bombers plus 20 helicopter gunships against Huambo; *The New York*

Times, January 28, 1976, had reported on MIG-21s and FIAT-91s active in the battle for Novo Redondo.

12. *The New York Times*, February 15, 1976.

13. Testimony of H. Kissinger, in U.S., Senate, Foreign Relations Committee Subcommittee on Africa, Congressional Record, January 29, 1976.

14. *The Washington Post*, January 22, 1976.

15. Ibid.

16. W. Inglee (Library of Congress Research Service) *Soviet Policy Towards Angola* (research paper for this author, April 1976).

17. *The New York Times*, February 15, 1976, report Soviet involvement in a shelling and landing operation at Mocamedes.

18. *The Military Balance 1975-76* (London: 1975) International Institute of Strategic Studies, p. 64.

19. Inglee, *Soviet Policy Towards Angola*.

20. *The Washington Post*, February 18, 1976. Note that *The (London) Times*, November 15, 1975, had reported the presence of approximately 400 Soviet advisers in Angola in August. Assuming both figures to reflect the best available Western intelligence of the moment, one might be tempted to conclude that the late autumn decline in Soviet numbers reflected the arrival of sufficient numbers of Cuban experts.

21. *The Washington Post*, February 18, 1976.

22. Ibid.

23. Note, for example, the different estimate of *The (London Times*, November 15, 1976, and the fact that the suggested reason is speculative.

24. H. Kissinger's Senate testimony.

25. U.S., *State Department News Conference NYT*, February 13, 1976.

26. Testimony of R. Ellsworth, in U.S., Senate, Foreign Relations Committee, Subcommittee on Africa, Congressional Record, February 3, 1976.

27. A. Ivanov and L. Mogila, *V-IZ*, no. 12 (1976): 87–93; see also G. J. Bender, "Angola, the Cubans, and American Anxieties," *Foreign Policy*, no. 31 (Summer 1978): 3–30; *Guardian*, February 26, 1978; and sources cited in Chapter Two.

28. P. F. Nugent, "The Soviet Navy in the Indian Ocean,"(M.A. thesis, School of International Affairs, Carleton University, Ottawa, Spring 1976).

29. See Kaufman, *The New York Times Magazine*, January 4, 1976.

30. See interview with Angolan Prime Minister Lopo do Nascimento in *The New York Times*, February 1, 1976, or comments by Dr. Almeida, MPLA Director of Information, as quoted by the Canadian press, in the *Ottawa Citizen*, January 31, 1976.

31. Ibid.

32. Bender, "Angola, the Cubans, and American Anxieties."

33. Chapter Two discusses this.

34. *Guardian* (weekly), January 22, 1978.

35. Figures from *Newsweek*, February 13, 20, 1978, and *Time*, February 20, 27, 1978.

36. See Secretary of State Vance's estimate, in *Newsweek*, February 20, 1978.

37. *Newsweek*, March 13, 20, 1978.

38. *Le Monde* report, reprinted in the *Guardian* (weekly), February 19, 1978; see also chart of "The Cuban Role in Africa," in the *Guardian*, May 21, 1978.

39. The *Guardian* (weekly), January 29, 1978.

40. *Newsweek*, February 13, 1978, and *Time*, February 20, 1978.

41. *Time*, February 20, 1978; and *Newsweek*, March 13, 20, 1978.

42. *Time*, February 6, 20, 1978 (the latter talks of $900 million); and *Newsweek*, March 13, 1978. Jijiiga, in original, corrected to Jigjiga; Harer, in original, corrected to Harar.

43. *Newsweek*, March 20, 1978; see also "Victory in the Ogaden," *Pravda*, March 16, 1978.

44. *Pravda*, January 16, 18, 19, 1978; *Tass*, January 20, 1978.

45. *Pravda*, January 22, 1978.

46. *Izvestia*, January 23, 1978.

47. *APN* Commentary, January 23, 1978; see also *Izvestia*, March 18, 1978.

48. Ibid. See also *Izvestia*, January 25, 1978; *Komsomol'skaya Pravda*, January 27, 1978; *New Times*, February 2, 1978.

49. *Time*, February 6, 1978.

50. *Newsweek*, February 13, 1978.

51. *Newsweek*, February 20, 1978.

52. *Izvestia*, March 1, 1978; and see *APN* Commentary, January 18, 1978, and *Pravda*, March 17, 1978 (they make similar point concerning Cuban "assistance").

53. Ibid. See also, for example, *APN* Commentary, April 19, 1978, and *Pravda*, May 21, 1978.

54. See Chapter Three.

55. *Izvestia*, March 18, 1978.

56. *New Times*, February 2, 1978.

57. *Pravda*, February 4, 1978.

58. *Pravda*, May 31, 1978.

59. Note, for example, reports in the *Washington Post*, June 4, 1978.

60. The *Guardian* (daily), May 22, 1978; and see *Atlas*, July 1978.

61. *Le Monde*, May 23, 1978.

62. *General Anzeiger* (Bonn), May 20, 1978.

63. *Daily Nation* (Nairobi), May 22, 1978.

64. Respectively, *The Economist*, May 27, 1978, the *Guardian* (weekly), January 9, May 21, and June 11, (two last article titles) 1978.

65. *Komosomol'skaya Pravda*, January 27, 1978 (concerning Western reports on West German missile testing in Zaire, note especially article by Tad Szulc, "Germany Rearms," *Penthouse* (March 1978): 76–82.

66. See, for example, *Pravda*, March 10, 1978.

67. Bender, "Angola, The Cubans, and American Anxieties," and sources cited therein; see also, for example, *Newsweek*, May 15, 1978 ("New Book of Revelations," review of ex-C.I.A. officer John Stockwell's *In Search of Enemies: A C.I.A. Story*.)

68. "The Stakes in Africa: A European Expert Calls for Sensitive Diplomacy," Atlas Dialogue, *Atlas* (July 1978).

69. See *Pravda*, March 21, 1978; and *Komsomol'skaya Pravda*, January 27, 1978, for report on West German nuclear and other aid to Praetoria (!); see also V. Khalipov, in *Vestnik Protivovozdushnoi Oborony*, no. 6 (1977): 6–11 (hereafter referred to as *VPO*).

70. I. Shavrov, in *V-IZ*, no. 3 (1975): 57–66, and *V-IZ*, no. 4 (1975): 90–97.

71. N. Shumikhin, *VPO*, no. 1 (1977): 17–22.

72. V. Adrianov, *V-IZ*, no. 7 (1975): 29–38.

CONCLUSION:
WHITHER SOVIET ASSERTIVENESS?

Moscow had succeeded in establishing a credible "second strike" force of consequence by about 1965. Through the remainder of the 1960s and early 1970s, it proceeded to match also the wider panoply of U.S. strategic power, thus providing itself with sufficient excess capacity to allow for the contemplation of luxury options such as "withholding" and "selective targeting." The remainder of the 1970s have been devoted in good part to a pursuit of global power projection capabilities. Having become a regional superpower (in the true sense of the word) during the 1960s, the Soviet Union was now emerging as a global power able to initiate and sustain a wide spectrum of assertive military-political actions in regions distant from the homeland. The military impunity once associated with Western aspirations in the Third World was being challenged.

In the approach to the 1980s, Moscow clearly strove to circumvent the restrictions that residual and, in some cases, growing Western military prowess nevertheless continued to place on Moscow's freedom of maneuver. As concerns the strategic arena, the emergence of a naval "withholding" doctrine and the move to end-run NATO anti-submarine designs by establishing Arctic operating capabilities stood out as two notable avenues of endeavor. As concerns the more conventional theater of confrontation, in Europe, improved air mobility and increased stress on a "combined arms" approach stood in the forefront of Soviet efforts. Yet, expectations remained limited. Moscow appeared to view these measures as vehicles for marginal advantage, vehicles whose ultimate import would rest as much on the political perceptions that they generated as their inherent military utility. While Moscow was highly appreciative of the manipulative potential of perceptions of advantage, there was evidence that its greater hopes lay elsewhere.

One area of greater hope was evidenced by the extraordinary preserverance, in years and levels of funding, of the Soviet search for a viable means of ballistic missile defense. The increasing pace of Soviet activities in this field through the later 1970s, Soviet innovative research into high energy laser, particle beam, and other technologies of promise clearly reflect a rather considerable determination and expectation. Moscow appears intent on insuring a continued advantage against the offensive potentials of third powers (especially China). It would seem that Moscow has not despaired of the possibilities of off-setting even the more awesome penetration capabilities of the other superpower. Although scientists differ widely in their assessments of either superpower's defense prospects, Moscow's continued distaste for Mutual Assured Destruction's (MAD) essence,

134

namely, that your survival is hostaged to the rationality of your opponent, together with the relatively high priority accorded to Soviet defense aspirations, do serve to undermine complacent projections of today's balance-of-power parameters. Yet, most analysts saw this as a question mark for the 1990s or beyond, not the 1980s.

A more immediate venue for consequential and perhaps decisive change in its favor lay in the Soviet Union's mentioned pursuit and acquisition of distant interventionary capabilities. By the end of the 1970s, the United States retained greater aggregate interventionary power through its carriers as well as its air transport means. But the dramatic difference between scarcely any distant Soviet projection capabilities at the start of the decade and the challenging vigor of Soviet theory and ability towards its end signified a far more potent relative shift of capabilities than could be effected, say, by Soviet improvements in Europe. Soviet protection of new clients had previously been associated with minimal credibility and hence scant allure. The realizability of Soviet presence and protection of consequence in distant arenas has entailed a startling change in the spectrum of options available to Third World governments.

The Soviet Union's establishment of a multifaceted strategic, military, and civil presence on the ultimate flanks of pan-Arctica and the southern hemisphere made the traditional Western balance-of-power preoccupation with Europe look parochial and possibly lulling. Moscow had established the kind of global financial stakes that had in earlier eras justified other powers' procurement of the protective shield of global military capacities. Still, while Moscow was by no means as autarchically independent as some analysts thought it to be, there could conversely be little doubt that the basic Western dependence on overseas markets and raw materials remained greater and that the Soviet Union was deeply conscious of this fact. Moscow's move to the outer flanks did entail immediate military benefit of dispersal and mobility, more absolute to the north, more relative to the south. Beyond the narrow military benefits, however, there is little doubt that the wider strategic-economic benefits and potentials were of major consequence.

The assertiveness and confidence of Moscow's late-1970s involvement in distant conflicts mirrored the nature of its newly acquired means. Yet Moscow chose its ground astutely, cautiously; clearly it respected the continued capacities of its adversaries. The Soviet modus operandi testified to acute awareness of the difference between power and license. The muscle flexing testing grounds chosen were areas where it could associate herself with the motherhood issues of international politics. Extensive publicly acknowledged military involvement in distant arenas was only hazarded where such could be presented as defending the causes of anti-racism and anti-colonialism, or as defending the territorial integrity of internationally sanctioned entities. At least initially, the Soviet Union chose to exercise and thus demonstrate its emerging capabilities only in conflict constellations where adversarial counters would be constrained by the world sanction accorded to her prima facie motives. In Angola, resolute U.S. opposition was constrained by the alliance of Moscow's opponents with the apartheid regime of South Africa and their consequent inability to secure recognition from a single African regime. In Ethiopia, the fact that Somalia was the aggressor against a territorial status quo previously defended by every Western government again guaranteed that even most of Washington's African allies would feel compelled to condone the Soviet presence. Anti-racism and anti-colonialism are today greater moral imperatives than anti-communism. United Nations votes and World Church attitudes testify that this perception is a fact of contemporary world opinion and, hence, contemporary world politics. Moscow has an advantage in a theater of conflict like southern 'Africa, Rhodesia, Namibia, and the Republic of South Africa itself. There is also evidence that the Soviet Union is striving to enlarge the sphere of relative sanction by associating "anti-feudalism" and "anti-neocolonialism" with this category of moral imperatives. This effort, if successful, might also give Moscow disproportionate sanction to intervene against regimes such as Mobuto's in the Congo, but it has been wary so far. Even if Moscow does prove less restrained in the future, even if it succeeds in widening the definition of preeminent moral sanction, the theaters of applicability still remain limited. There is the additional point that the greater its success in widening the area of moral sanction, the greater its own danger of appearing to transgress (mutterings of "Soviet colonialism" take a back seat at present, but they could become more potent).

Historically, established world powers have always found it difficult to adjust to the emergence of new actors on the international stage. The potency had limitations of challengers tend to be alternately exaggerated and denigrated. Bewilderingly, the logically exclusive extremes of reaction have often even co-existed simultaneously. The frequent inability to assess novel threats realistically, the tendency towards either paranoia or complacency, or irrational vacillations between the two, are byproducts of governments' inevitable preoccupation with familiar problems and themes.

The emergence of the Western powers as we know them today each in turn sparked, spurred, and ultimately confirmed or denied the immediate prejudices of more established capitals. Today it is Moscow's turn. In the 1990s or sometime in the next century it may or may not be China's turn.

The emergence of the Soviet Union as an actor able effectively to match the power potential of the most potent established player(s) has followed the pattern with a vengeance. Complacency was generated in some quarters by the espoused idealism of the leaders of the 1917 revolution, and it was later maintained, in some minds, by subsequent Soviet regimes' asserted continued commitment to the utopian dreams of Karl Marx. Others less enamored of the ideals of Marxism nevertheless found cause for complacency in the evident problems and bottlenecks of the Soviet economy, in the obsolescence or convoluted nature of so many Soviet products and institutions.

The other extreme, primitive hysteria, is often associated with the Cold War and "McCarthyism," but ought more properly to be traced back to the London *Times'* strident vituperations against Lenin in 1917, and even beyond. In a visceral way, it took the revolutionaries' claim that the fight for truly equal opportunity and protection was incompatible with capitalism literally and accepted that the confrontation now set was one of life and death in which no quarter was possible. The survival and advance of the Soviet economy and of Soviet power, because it was indeed viewed as a mortal threat, cast a shadow of fear which tended to suffocate appreciations of problems and weaknesses.

The mirror image of this prejudice nurtured the paranoia of the revolutionaries. Their ideological preconceptions, that capitalist interests would feel compelled to try to squash their espousal of wider democracies, were seen to have been proven by the Allied, British, U.S., Japanese, French, and other interventionary attempts of 1918–24. Soviet leaders were fully aware of the fact that these attempts only petered out because the eruption and extent of Allied domestic opposition and war weariness (expressed through Army mutinies in France, street demonstrations in Britain, and the like) precluded continued prosecution. Prosecution of capitalist interventionary designs had to await resolution first of World War I's legacy of social turmoil and second, of the devastation of economic Depression. The first capitalist phoenix, Nazi Germany, duly "proved" that it could not be deflected, and that anti-Bolshevism remained the one absolute policy aim of capitalism's citadels. The post-World War II, rhetoric from capitalism's new bastion, in conjunction with the threatening appearance of encirclement that was suggested by a Moscow view of world bases and deployment charts, again conformed to socialized expectations; it provided the latest confirmation of and step on the confrontational ladder.

There were moderates on both sides who feared the mutually reinforcing logic of the opposing paranoias. There were others who found the paranoia logic useful, and open to manipulation.

There were many ironies. One lay in the Western governments' acceptance of Moscow's self-association with "communism." Stalin and later Soviet leaders claimed themselves champions of communism, much as Franco, of Spain, felt compelled to present himself as a guardian of democracy. Yet the governing institutions and traditions of the former bore as little resemblance to the dicta of Karl Marx as the petty tyrannies of the latter had to the spirit of Plato. Lenin had himself been rather "creative" in his interpretation of Marxism's operational requirements, not least in his espousal of a conspiratorial vanguard party to direct events. But he had seen his liberties as the expedients or requirements of *real-politik*, dictated first by the facts and consequences of a tsarist secret policy apparatus, later by the contingencies of civil war and interventions. One does not know what might have happened had Lenin's early debilitating heart attacks not intervened. One does know that his last enfeebled years (during much of which the Father of Revolution found himself in something akin to house arrest) were spent futilely battling against the Stalinist bureaucracy, against the weakening of the "democratic" half of the party's doctrine of "democratic centralism," and against the usurpation of power from the "Soviet" chain of elected councils.

The chauvinism attendant upon the Stalinist definition of "socialism in one country" was to be partly responsible for the never ending debate of later decades, whether the heirs of the Revolution and of Russia were more "revolutionaries" or more "Russian." The problem is that Stalin and his successors defined their revolutionary creed in such a way as to make it nearly indistinguishable from the tenets of Russian nationalism. The postwar establishment of Soviet hegemony in Eastern Europe was viewed as "communist aggrandizement" by Western ideologues. Yet, Russian nationalists going back to Catherine the Great (that other eminent "Russifier" of non-Russian origins), had always viewed control over this territory as a defense requirement dictated by Russia's geopolitical circumstances. In fact, all perceived manifestations of "communist" intrigue, in both foreign and domestic affairs, could be interpreted as having tsarist roots. Stalin's policy towards Korea or Greece could be seen to echo tsarist aspirations. Stalin's purges resurrected memories of Ivan the Fourth's *oprichnina*. Stalin's insistence that Moscow alone had the right to interpret Marxist canon sparked memories of earlier regimes' perception of Moscow as the third and last "Rome" (after the fall of Rome and Constantinople) and of themselves as the chosen interpreters of the faith.

Ironically, the intermeshing of "communist" and "Russian" interests may have served to retard rather than expand the scope for Soviet/Russian aggrandizement. The sometimes blatant injection of chauvinist considerations has soured the internationalist idealism and hence attraction of the ideology. Catalonia in the late 1930s, Hungary in 1956, and Czechoslovakia in 1968 all engendered disillusionment and self-doubt in the minds of many who had previously favored Soviet designs. Conversely, the need to pay at least *pro forma* obeisance to the idealism of the ideology may well have blunted more brutal expressions of national interests. In England, France, Germany, and the United States, rapid industrialization was in every case accompanied by extremes of chauvinism and by self-righteous crusades and aggrandizements abroad. There would have been ample precedent for expecting a "bourgeois" Russian government presiding over an industrial revolution similar to that effected under Stalin to be both ruthless and assertive in its pursuit of foreign interests. The fact that such a government would not have had to concede the territorial losses forced upon the Bolsheviks and that it would have emerged from World War I in possession of Constantinople (the realization of this centuries-old Russian dream had been promised by the Allies as the price for continued war participation), would of course have given it a far more advantageous base from which to proceed.

Still, even if one postulates a continuing relevance for and of ideology, there remain problems. One is epitomized by the fact that one of the most feared elements of Soviet ideology lies in its purported universality, in the described inevitability of the demise of capitalism. Yet, it may not be too facetious to suggest that there might be a parallel to our own conviction that slavery, feudalism, and various forms of dictatorship are ultimately doomed by their vulgarly nondemocratic distribution of riches and privileges. There is also the point that, as pure "communism" has never been implemented, so also with pure "capitalism." John D. Rockefeller's eventual eminence owed much to the quality of his hired guns. In today's world, which has seen a Republican president (Nixon) introduce a version of that "communist" leveller, national medical care, and which has seen Soviet governments introduce profit bonuses to their citizens and a variety of investment inducements to multinational corporations, one might well question the relevance of the "isms."

The point is that that Soviet arrogance should be viewed as merely a modern relfection of the "manifest destiny" of another time, another continent. It may be more benevolent, or more vicious. But any overconcentration on ideological labels does tend to be blinkered, if not superficial.

The lesson of history, to those who feel threatened by the new global reach of Soviet power, calls for pragmatism and *real-politik*. Power does entail the ability to demand privileges. But power is limited. Pursuit of the paranoia can be afforded by neither side. Unilateral abdications of interests can be equally unfortunate in that they are likely to reflect and spur untenable assumptions fraught with future danger. There is no need for Washington and Moscow to "like" each other. There is a desperate requirement that emotionalism be exorcized.

APPENDIX: A

PARTY-MILITARY RELATIONS IN
THE SOVIET UNION:
SOVIET STRATEGIC POLICY COUNCILS—
MYTH AND REALITY

Western studies of party-military relations in the Soviet Union have long suffered from the general acceptance of myths of dubious value. We cannot hope to advance the state of knowledge in the field without expressly acknowledging the character and raison d'être of these fallacies. Since studies of the Soviet military have been especially prone to founder on the shoals of mistaken assumptions and unwarranted projections, these should perhaps be addressed first.

One might start by looking at two articles by Albert Wohlstetter, in *Foreign Policy*, nos. 15 and 16, which attempted to debunk prevailing notions about the arms race. Unfortunately the data appeared to be rather selectively chosen. He plotted a number of 1962 to 1972 U.S. projections of Soviet strategic arsenals in an attempt to demonstrate that since these had consistently underestimated Soviet progress, they could in no way be portrayed as having contributed to a fuelling of the arms race. But he hurt his case by the unnecessary claim that "the prediction made in 1965 is quite typical,"[1] when other evidence indicated that 1965 is the year in which the least accurate (most grossly underestimated) predictions were made."[2] Furthermore, he ignored the relative weight, if not the existence of, predictions that countered prevailing notions.[3]

This vulnerable use of data was unfortunate for two reasons. First, it perversely reinvigorated withering arms races theories. As regards the U.S. side of the equation, most analysts had already come to accept that research, de-

Paper originally printed as *Current Comment*, no. 10, by the School of International Affairs, Carleton University, Ottawa, May 1976. It had been presented previously to a U.S.A.F.-sponsored conference on party-military relations in communist societies, held at Maxwell Air Force Base, October 1975.

velopment, and procurement policies reflected less on the Soviet threat itself and more on the tempting implications of advancing technology and the politics of competing bureaucracies. As regards Soviet policies, a number of Western analysts had come to recognize that the lower estimates of the 1960s had at best reflected an insufficient awareness of Soviet literature and, at worst, U.S. domestic political considerations. This relates to the second reason for disappointment with Wohlstetter's initiative. Its focus was unfortunate. By attacking arms race propagandists it only served to perpetuate neglect for the real cause for concern, namely, the persisting disregard by many of Soviet publications.

Access to Soviet writings was all too limited. Available snippets were too often ambiguous when divorced from their proper context and therefore all too amenable to interpretations that owed a greater debt to the Western analyst's personal biases and inclinations than to those of the Soviets.

These expectations on the part of some U.S. analysts in the early 1960s that Moscow might rest content with minimal deterrence just could not have been derived from then contemporary Soviet sources,[4] and must as a consequence be seen as motivated by domestic U.S. considerations. So also with the selectively chosen quotes of the same era which purported to show Soviet support for flexible response and limited war scenarios and Soviet interest in conventional rather than nuclear concepts.[5] These quotes were as a rule not only taken out of the context of Soviet writings as a whole; they usually jarred even with the immediate context of the article or book from which they were drawn.

Since the early 1960s Soviet works have been unambiguous in their demand for parity (if not superiority). Since the early 1960s they have been unambiguous in their scepticism vis-à-vis flexible response and limited war concepts. They insist on the incompatibility between such theories and realistic conflict contingencies, repeatedly resurrecting and emphasizing the caveats to that effect of writers like Kissinger and Brodie! Since the early 1960s they have furthermore been equally unambiguous in their expectation that any war between the superpowers would be nuclear, "a decisive armed conflict between two opposing systems." The fact that conventional arms would be used "as well," or "under certain circumstances" reflects on the perceived totality of the eventuality; they would supplement but by no means replace nuclear potentials.[6]

Most students in the field owe more than they realize to the prodigious efforts of Tom Wolfe. If only for this reason, it is incumbent to note that he was partially responsible for the acceptance accorded at least some of the mistaken inferences treated above.

Similar motivations make it incumbent to single out Roman Kolkowicz for having provided unfortunate encouragement to analyses that purport to dissect the conflicting ambitions of cliques or groups within the Soviet military establishment. His work on the so-called Stalingrad Group stands as the best of the genre. The Stalingrad Group of commanders were thought to have coalesced on that front around Khrushchev and to have followed the former First Secretary to Moscow and hence up the ladder of power. Others have challenged the concept of "group," pointing to the disparate experiences and tendencies of the individuals involved. This author has previously noted that even if one allows the concept of group, its antecedents should be pursued further to the schools and academies that originally brought the individuals together.[7] The point is not so much that Kolkowicz was mistaken; like Wolfe, he must in general be credited with having inserted all the right caveats. It is rather that the caveats were insufficiently obtrusive and tended to be overlooked by less sophisticated students.

The contention here is not that cliques may not exist. Human nature being what it is there must of course be individual ties of import, empathies derived from shared experiences, and the like. But most past "group"-oriented analyses have been too facile, based on too superficial a selection of evidence, and too prone to challenge. Some have begged to be dismissed as projections and to be interpreted as searches for challenging groups based on nothing more substantive than the Western analyst's personal distaste for prevailing "group" orthodoxy.

A disparagement of group analyses leads inevitably to a consideration of Soviet military "debates," if only because group designations are often inferred from apparent differences or contradictions among various authors' articles. One must not forget the obvious fact of censorship and the fact that published Soviet articles are usually commissioned. Apparent differences of tenor or emphasis can usually be explained by differing journal audiences, differing journal roles, peculiarities of the prevailing domestic or international political scene, and/or a host of more subtle establishment-related perceptions.

One must be exceedingly leery of such labels as "dogmatists," "moderates," "conservative," and "flexible," not because analogous inclinations do not exist, but because they usually defy identification. Former Politburo member Piotr Shelest was noted primarily as the deliverer of harsh condemnations of the insidious and invidious enticements of bourgeois culture and as a staunch opponent of detente; yet he is reported to have given the most conciliatory of speeches at the Soviet Politburo's showdown meeting with their Czechoslovak colleagues at Cierna Nad Tissou in 1968. Alexander Shelepin was noted for his uncompromising initiatives vis-à-vis Peking, yet appeared a model of moderation in many of his references to the Federal Republic of Germany. The same man had earlier gained notoriety as Chairman of the KGB (State Security Committee), yet should be given credit for having shaken up the less than imaginative *apparatchik* core of that organization through the infusion of more sophisticated, more flexible, less "dogmatic" recruits. M. A. Suslov, long regarded as the hard-line defender of ideological orthodoxy, was to be associated with the opponents of the Czechoslovak intervention, and later with an ideologically highly unorthodox equanimity with regard to Willy Brandt's Socialist party. N. V. Podgorny, on the other hand, once thought of as a champion of moderation, has increasingly come to be identified as a promotor of orthodoxy. It might well be that all these apparently contradictory stances are genuine, reflecting merely the greater complexity of character of the individuals involved. But this explanation is too glib.

To approach the problem from a different vantage point, one might note the fact so often acknowledged and referred to by Soviets that Brezhnev's speeches are always read from prepared texts, never delivered spontaneously. The answer is not to be found in the manipulations of some mythical behind-the-scenes mastermind. Rather, it lies in the fact of collective leadership, in the fact that even the general secretary must at least to some extent defer to his colleagues, and in the fact that the collegium does on occasion assign to any one member the task of delivering any one address that the collective might deem to be opportune. The person assigned to deliver a specific speech might or might not agree with its particulars. As a longstanding member of a relatively homogenous decision-making body (note the impressive tenure of most present members of the Politburo), one would presume an underlying consensus as regards basic strands of policy. But there must necessarily be differences of emphases, different conceptions of priorities, of implementation procedures, and so on. Nevertheless, there is no automatic connection between an individual's personal biases and those of speeches or articles ostensibly associated with that individual. The exigencies and requirements of the position take precedence over those of the individual.

It is not that genuine debates never surface. In some fields and at some times it is clear that such debates are in fact actively encouraged and promoted. The Lieberman proposals for economic reforms and associated debates through especially the mid-1960s spring to mind. One might also point to the various debates that have surfaced at one time or another about municipal organizations; the relative power, authority, and role of local Soviets, and various cultural matters. Yet it is clear that even these debates are controlled, however minimally, within parameters of discussion decreed from above. It is also clear that the restrictive character of this control is directly related to the sensitivity of the topic at hand. Suffice it to note here that no topic is more sensitive to Moscow than that of security.

It might be illustrative to turn to the academic-governmental "think tanks" for other relevant examples.[8] A good bit of recent debate-oriented speculation in the West has focused on inferences of discord in articles by General Milshtein and G. A. Trofimenko, two of the better known strategic thinkers associated with the Institute for the USA and Canada. Again, it must be emphasized that there is no way of distinguishing between views of individuals and differences decreed by higher authority. It must be reiterated and emphasized that most Western "debate" studies have been fraught with mistaken premises, inferences, and conclusions for the simple reason that they ignored this dictum.

Real strategic debates do occur, but they are in-house and as a rule not reflected in outward appearances. Even if they should sometimes be so reflected, there would be no way of knowing. The data for satisfactory comment is just not available.

It is this author's personal knowledge that the "think tanks," or institutes, do employ a few dissenters in the true sense of the word; individuals who not only have inclinations or preferences differing from those of the establishment but whose very fundamental philosophical outlook is alien to the guardians of that establishment. These are individuals who would probably not survive as professionals outside the confines of the institutes. Their presence testifies to the degree of establishment concern that the widest possible gamut of views be aired, if only to limit the potentials of the unknown.

Yet it should be noted that these individuals are not allowed to publish, except the most functionally oriented of treatises. They do not appear as "debate participants." Their function is in-house and in-house alone. They are not free to meet with Westerners. Their unofficial contact with Westerners is minimal and severely limited.

As regards the Soviet institutes' in-house debates, there is no acceptable data on their character, intensity, or frequency. Since the same comment is applicable to Politburo debates, it is obviously impossible to attempt any kind of remotely scientific correlation of the respective debates. One knows of individual tie-ins of import, such as the apparently easy access of Arbatov, director of the Institute for the USA and Canada, to Brezhnev's private staff. Certain institute associates are clearly privy to establishment discussions and involved in policy debates of consequence. But the involvement is individual, behind closed doors, and undefinable.

There remains yet another pitfall awaiting the Western analyst. Not only does one not know whether an individual's speech or article is consonant with his own inclinations, or whether it may rather reflect the establishment's perceptions of that individual's role and possibly be contrary to personal predilections; not only is it impossible to divine the nature of internal debates and the possible nature of individual inputs to such debates; but even if one hypothesized acquaintance with any one individual's input as regards one or other internal debate, one would still not be able to relate that input to its proper institutional setting, if any. Apart from the near impossibility associated with assigning particular functionally derived preferences and inclinations to whatever institution with which an individual might once have been attached, there is the very real problem of deciding just which institution might once have commanded the loyalty of the individual. There is the problematical but standard question as to whether any one Foreign Service or Armed Forces Branch Officer, for example, might actually be on the payroll of other interested organizations. Then there is the more vexatious problem epitomized by Milshtein: we know he was once associated with the Soviet Military Intelligence (GRU), but we do not know in what capacity or for how long. We know he came to the Institute for the USA and Canada from the General Staff, but we do not know whether he was still involved with the GRU at that time, whether he might still be on GRU's payroll, whether he might have transferred to a different General Staff organ, whether he might still have ties to that organ, whatever it might be, and so forth. In other words, even if one hypothesized institutional loyalties, never mind split loyalties, it would be well nigh impossible to determine the "who," "how," or "to what extent." Are Milshtein's General Staff ties formal or informal? Are they in fact General Staff ties as such, or are they GRU ties? Conflicting elite loyalties cannot be satisfactorily documented. There are too many unknowns.

To draw full circle on the question of debate relevance and the siren-like temptations of subjective inferences, some attention must finally be paid to the persisting specter of "Red Hawks." As often as not sparked by Victor Zorza's analyses of articles by Colonels Rybkin and Bondarenko, the Western press has periodically succumbed to temptingly dramatic speculations about military-party friction in the Soviet Union. Yet these two favorite "Red Hawks" are political officers. Both are instructors at the Lenin Military-Political Academy and therefore speak for the party. Indeed their most uncompromising articles, published in the journal "Communist of the Armed Forces," have been accompanied by small-print announcements that they form part of special party lecture series![9] In fact, the journal itself is the bi-weekly organ of the Main Political Administration of the Soviet Army and Navy, the party's ideological watchdog over the Soviet Armed Forces.[10]

As indicated in preceding sections, it is futile to speculate about hidden motivations and conjectured split loyalties. What is crystal clear in the case of Rybkin and Bondarenko is that their public initiatives reflect their institutional roles as agents of the party. Their speeches and articles are commissioned, structured, and nuanced in accordance with party requirements.

We must rid outselves of our fascination for possible group antagonisms, personalized jealousies and the like. It is not that such may not exist, but the data is too tenuous, too amorphous, and therefore too prone to subjectivist and projectionist interpretations. The past history of studies of perceived discord is not one of scholarly renown. Its main import has lain in its unfortunate diversion of interest from less glamorous investigations of Soviet doctrine and of Soviet literature.

Rather than focusing on discord, the past history of which is strewn with fallacious or futile inferences, it is time to focus on the extraordinary wealth of evidence of unity of basic conceptual outlooks.

While there is but the most tenuous of evidence for those who postulate profound organizational or conceptual divergencies as between the party and the armed forces, there is a wealth of evidence for those who see the two as intertwined, complementary, and mutually supportive.

From the time of Lenin to today, party leaders have given utmost priority to the defense of the socialist motherland. Present party leaders remember the Civil War, they were active at the time of Allied interventions against the struggling Bolshevik regime,[11] they donned uniforms again during World War II, and they sat on military councils and other security-related organs after the termination of that war. As William Odom put it recently, CPSU (Communist Party of the Soviet Union) leaders have never considered the question of guns versus butter in Western terms; rather, "It is a question of how much butter must be produced in order to obtain the highest rate of military growth."[12] CPSU leaders' personal experiences have long since confirmed and "proved" the inculcated ideological tenet that capitalist interests were bound to combat Bolshevism with every means at their disposal.

Thus, there is no documented evidence of military aspirations for improved combat potentials ever being thwarted by party barons. Rather, as previously documented by this author and others, there is considerable evidence that CPSU leaders have occasionally forced a sometimes staid and bureaucratic military leadership to adopt newer technological potentials. The constant concern of the party has combatted occasional tendencies towards stagnation and fuelled modernization drives. The party has always been in the forefront of efforts to upgrade the armed forces, for the simple reason that the most effective military establishment was always conceived of as being essential to the defense and furtherance of party ambitions. The raison d'être of the party has always required priority attention to military needs.

The extraordinarily high rate of party and Komsomol memberships among armed forces personnel should occasion no surprise; nor should the very considerable military representation on the higher elected organs of party and state. When a minister of defense is elected to the Politburo, as in the case of Grechko, it should not be seen as reflecting on the relative power of a functional military. It should rather be seen as in accordance with the dominant post-1917 tradition and in accordance with the Politburo's interest in a wide gamut of functional representation. Grechko is in the Politburo because of the Soviet leadership's integrated view of strategic requirements as emanating from the necessary interdependence of military, economic, societal, cultural, and other concerns. He sits in the Politburo for the same reason that leads party leaders to sponsor the inclusion of economic specialists on military organs and the inclusion of military experts on state economic organs.

The increasing militarization of society that we have witnessed in recent years may be seen to serve both the military and "civilian" components of the strategic leadership. The extension of para-military training of the civilian populace and the 1967 law that saw previously voluntary programs made obligatory may be seen on the one hand as a mutually agreeable offset to the then agreed reduction of military service from three to two years (a reduction spurred by economic requirements and fully supported by military officers steeped in the theory of the interdependence of military, economic, and other factors and thus expressly cognizant of the corollary that improved economic potential is a sine qua non for improved military potential). On the other hand, the civil defense increment entailed by the new programs may be seen as a natural reflection of continuing Soviet stress on war survival requirements at a time when current missile defense technology was proving unequal to the task of countering developing offensive arsenals. (In fact, evidence suggests that the new programs should not be seen as having emasculated missile defense protagonists but rather as allowing for a minimal supplement to their efforts while more promising concepts are researched.) The para-military training of the populace serves both to reduce the effects of shorter formal training periods and to improve mobilization prospects. The indirect effect of the possible improvement of discipline on the workshop floor is as much appreciated by the civilian as it is by the military leadership.

There is, in fact, congruence on all major matters of policy. The Bolshevik predilection for a command economy is clearly optimal from a military viewpoint. It follows that the military supports such economic contacts with the West as may enhance the competitiveness of the command economy structure and minimize the needs for its reform. One might interject that positive interest in selective economic ties with the West on the part of the military-civilian strategic leadership in Moscow should not be seen as indicative of desperation. The interest is relative and based on appreciation of the comparative cost-effectiveness of such ties. As long as they are perceived to promise a minimal cost increment to the otherwise expected growth rates, then they will be supported. Should they be enmeshed in too high a cost, whether financial or in the form of unpalatable Western "conditions," they will be shunned by civilian as well as military cadres.[13]

As there is congruence on economic policy, so there is congruence on most other aspects of domestic policy, such as relates to ethnic minorities and cultural dissidence. The military must value the CPSU for its centrist, unifying, and therefore morale and discipline-facilitating character. These are mutually reinforcing and complementary aims of both party and armed forces. If the two are equally leery of minority ethnic and centrifugal aspirations, so for similar reasons are they equally leery of more narrowly cultural and political dissidence. They place equal premium on the need for societal cohesiveness, morale, and discipline.

Similar comments apply to foreign policy. As concerns the immediate environment, one must surely concede that interests are almost completely complementary regarding Eastern Europe. Even concerning a question such as SALT, a similar contention would appear a lot more defensible than the obverse. The military leadership would seem to have at least as much cause to express measured support for strategic arms stabilization schemes as would their more politically oriented colleagues. They know they have achieved effective parity. They know that today's conflux of existing and foreseeable technologies and deployed and deployable arsenals is such that neither side can realistically expect to effect militarily significant superiority. The unremitting pursuit of all technological potentials in today's military-strategic arena would be unnecessary with regard to third powers, while being of highly dubious worth in the superpower context. In view of its resource-draining potential, it would therefore not appear to be cost-effective. In fact, it might be argued that the quantitative superiority of today's Soviet arsenal has not been dictated by military calculations (which would see the numerical advantage as militarily insignificant in view of the sophisticated nature of the overall balance). It is the political leadership that would be inclined to authorize the requisite program in accordance with its traditional emphasis on the political role of military force, and the consequent appreciation of the fact that the military insignificance of a few extra missiles is more than compensated by the political fallout from resultant appearances.

The list of complementary attitudes is endless. One might point to the political officer phenomenon which, if we rid ourselves of preconceived ideas of military-party antagonism, can be viewed in terms highly favorable to military concerns. As Odom put it, "The party's control apparatus within the military provides an alternative information channel to the top, and it thus serves to raise the uncertainty level of subordinates and make collusion among them risky. It follows quite logically that the system of party control may well enhance rather than reduce Soviet military power . . . it is *edinonachalie* (unity of command) that allows military subordinates to feed the high command selective information that distorts the top's perception and thwarts rational corrective action."[14] Another aspect is indicated by noting that the political complement on board Soviet ships is about equal numerically to the religious complement on U.S. vessels; like the chaplain in the West, so the Soviet commissar serves a variety of positive counseling and morale-supporting functions.

Projecting from their own view of the military as a societal and economic parasite, many Westerners have bemoaned the waste perceived to be inherent in Soviet priorities. Yet relative trade-offs and, hence, relative waste are subjective. Perceptions are changed when you view the military component as the Soviets do, not as a parasite, but as the prerequisite to societal survival. Furthermore there is little doubt that Moscow's integrated view of the body politic and its express appreciation of mutual interdependence between military, economic, and other concerns do have corollaries that tend to ameliorate the *pro forma* cost. Thus Brezhnev's testimony to the 24th CPSU Congress in 1971, that 42 percent of its (the defense industry's) output is used for civilian purposes,"[15] while reflecting on the past low priorities and remaining inadequacies of the civilian sector, does at the same time reflect on a somewhat more extensive interrelationship between the two sectors than is normally conceded by Western analysts, and it does point up the Soviet view that they are part of the same totality. Not only does the military economy supply sophisticated items beyond the present capacities of its civilian counterpart; it also provides services and cheap manpower. The list of civilian structures erected by the armed forces, from buildings to bridges, is astonishing. Moscow State University is but one example.

As a less concrete but psychologically important indication of the party's view of the armed forces as a societally vital adjunct, one might finally point to the party's sponsorship of a plethora of children's books that glorify military service.[16] The Soviet child is inculcated with the notion that military service is not a necessary sacrifice; rather, it is a glorious opportunity to serve society as a whole, to serve the nation and its ideals, and thus to serve oneself. It is not a patriotic duty but a patriotic privilege.

CONCLUSION

The intent of this paper is perhaps best summed up by looking at one glaring disparity between the situation of 15 years ago and the situation today. At that time a proliferation of strategic writing in the West contrasted with a relative dearth of available literature in Moscow. Today the field appears stagnant in the West, with few if any books of note, whereas Soviet literature in the field abounds in both quantity and quality.

Fifteen years ago few authors had access to what was available of Soviet literature; little was translated, and even less was well translated. In those heady days of prolific Western writing and debate it was perhaps natural that the jarring and often dour notes of Soviet doctrinal promulgations were drowned by the arrogance of apparently pioneering dynamism. Discordant tunes from Moscow were dismissed as reflecting lack of sophistication. Where a Soviet paragraph appeared ambiguous, the more tedious scholarly route of clarification through cross-references and additional research was discarded in favor of whatever interpretation appeared more consonant with prevailing Western thinking. Full play was given the all too human tendency to assume one's own premises and logic to be optimal and therefore to discard contrary analyses as inherently inferior and "lacking in sophistication."

Western works of this era were, however, available in Moscow. Most of them were translated at an early date. Soviet specialists had access to current Western thinking. Yet Soviet preferences remained essentially unchanged. Indeed, it was a perturbing phenomenon if faced explicitly. Still, to avoid discomforting challenge through arrogant *a priori* dismissal, as was the wont of some Western analysts at the time, must surely be seen to have been unfortunate.

Today there is even less excuse, what with more numerous and much improved translations coming onto the market. More important, ignoring Soviet precepts might even be becoming dangerous, what with today's situation of dramatically improved Soviet capabilities. Perhaps 15 years ago one could afford disdain towards Soviet thinking. In today's much-changed strategic environment, however, it is essential that one appreciate the ever expanding volume of Soviet strategic literature. It is essential to appreciate the astounding continuity of basic precepts that has characterized this literature over the past decade or two: it is essential to appreciate its topicality.

As W. F. Scott recently put it, "There is no excuse today for mere speculation. . . . We have readily available a vast amount of Soviet military and political-military writings. . . . There is a strange reluctance in the West to examine these Soviet writings in their totality. It is much easier to sit on the fence and speculate about what course the Soviets might take. A thorough analysis of Soviet publications on military matters, combined with known facts about Soviet weaponry, could present explanations of Soviet behavior that would be uncomfortable to study. Thus, in the marketplace, the myths still have a ready sale."[17]

NOTES

1. Albert Wohlstetter, *Foreign Policy*, no. 15 (1974).

2. Michael Nacht, *Foreign Policy*, no. 18 (1975).

3. One might point to the work of Harriet Fast Scott, whose unique contribution to the field has long lain in a singular aversion to inferential analysis joined to uniquely compensive presentations of Soviet source materials.

4. See W. F. Scott, "Soviet Military Doctrine and Strategy: Realities and Misunderstandings," *Strategic Review* (Summer 1975); or see Soviet Sources referenced in C. G. Jacobsen, *Soviet Strategy—Soviet Foreign Policy*, 2nd ed. (Glasgow: The University Press, 1974).

5. Those who postulated Soviet acceptance of flexible response type tenets rested their case on highly misleading and selective quotes, especially from Generals Shtemenko and Lomov (as in T. Wolfe's *Soviet Power and Europe 1965-1969*, pp. 279, 280); not only was one typical quote from Lomov actually extracted from the General's discussion of U.S. attitudes(!), but it was presented, with a misleading suggestion of continuity, together with a snippet taken out of context six pages further down in the original text. For a complete translation of the articles referred to here, see H. F. Scott and W. Kitner, *The Nuclear Revolution in Soviet Military Affairs*,(Norman, Oklahoma: Oklahoma Press, 1968).

6. Most Western analysts who postulated a Soviet reversion from nuclear-oriented thinking based their case on the Dnepr maneuver of 1967, which they thought "appeared to be primarily a test of Soviet conventional warfare capabilities" (Wolfe, *Soviet Power and Europe*, p. 285). For an elaboration of very different intentions and inferences, see the official Soviet report on the maneuver, in *The Great Manouvers*, esp. pp. 7, 16, 34. Note also "XXX's" article "The Adoption of Soviet Ground Forces to Nuclear War," *Military Review* (September 1966) (from *Revue De Defense Nationale*, Paris, February 1966).

7. C. G. Jacobsen, *Soviet Strategy—Soviet Foreign Policy*, p. 174; for Kokowicz's treatment, see *The Soviet Military and the Communist Party*, (Princeton: Princeton University Press, 1967), pp. 224-55, 279, 281.

8. See C. G. Jacobsen "The Soviet 'Think-Tanks,'" *1975 Soviet Military Annual*, (Gulf Breeze, Fla.: Academic International, Winter 1976), for elaboration of the roles and functions of Soviet "academic" institutes (including an analysis of their security-related work).

9. *Communist of the Armed Forces*, esp. no. 17 (1966), no. 24 (1968), and nos. 7, 8 (April 1969). For alarmist Western misinterpretations, see V. Zorza in *Washington Post*, January 8, 1969, and J. Alsop, *Washington Post*, January 10, 1969.

10. As noted by Scott, "Soviet Military Doctrine and Strategy."

11. It might be of interest to note this author's observation from a 1968 Moscow stage performance of the play "Intention." British, U.S., French, and Japanese flags were unfurled on stage; the action had a distinct contemporary, as opposed to historical, ring.

12. W. E. Odom, *Foreign Policy*, no. 18 (1975). This does not of course mean that the Soviet Union is immune from the guns vs. butter quandry, but it does mean that its preferred approach to the resolution of that quandry has been qualitatively different from the approach of most Western academics.

One might remember that although the financial squeeze was immeasurably more severe in earlier decades, it was nevertheless ignored or tolerated to the extent that it was never allowed to sabotage perceived strategic requirements. If that squeeze could be tolerated, there can be little doubt about the Soviet will and ability today to sustain any military expenditures that might be deemed necessary.

13. Two recent events are illustrative. 1) Moscow's refusal to accept the late 1974 United States Congressional attempt to attach one-sided political conditions to the previously negotiated US-Soviet Trade Agreement of 1972. 2) Moscow's similarly predictable refusal to countenance the October 1975 United States Administration's demand that discounted Soviet oil be made available in return for market price United States grain (see the *New York Times*, October 12, 1975).

The USSR shows continued interest in Soviet-American trade, as evinced in the fact that she kept up her 1972 negotiated Lend-Lease repayments even after the formal demise of the Pact. But she continues to insist on principled reciprocity, and clearly does not feel compelled to accept unbalanced demands.

The Soviet economy is not stagnant. The desire for Western inputs is indicative not of crisis but rather of a determination to explore every venue that promises low cost incremental improvements of Soviet growth rates. Note also above footnote.

14. W. E. Odom, "The Soviet Military; Party Ties," *Problems of Communism* (September–October 1973).

15. From his *Report to the Central Committee, the 24th CPSU Congress* (Moscow: Novosti, 1971), p. 72.

16. S. Barusdin's *Soldier Striding on the Street*, is typical; its first (Moscow, 1970) edition ran to 600,000 copies.

17. Scott, "Soviet Military Doctrine and Strategy."

APPENDIX: B
SINO-SOVIET CRISIS IN PERSPECTIVE

The Sino-Soviet crisis that erupted with China's February 1979 war against Vietnam will be addressed at length below. This was one of the unique wars of history where each belligerent, China, Vietnam, and Vietnam's ally, the Soviet Union, could be argued to have emerged victorious. Ironically, this state of affairs was to prove de-stabilizing rather than stabilizing. Before delving into the battlefield details and the subsequent course of events, however, it is necessary to place them in a longer-term perspective. An introductory review of Sino-Soviet relations is essential.

BACKGROUND

The years since about 1972 have seen Soviet Eastern policy in transition. Mao's final years and the subsequent era of succession uncertainties re-opened the question of a possible normalizing of Sino-Soviet relations. It should be noted that the "Gang of Four" had espoused Mao's anti-Sovietism at its most vitriolic. Deng Xiaoping's past administrative record, on the other hand, encouraged cautious optimism in Moscow (as it did in Washington). Yet the Hua Guofeng-Deng Xiaoping compromise regime was to retain assertively nationalistic anti-Sovietism as one of its prime public policy planks. By late 1978-early

Working paper originally requested for *Soviet Armed Forces Review Annual (SAFRA) III*, Academic International, Gulf Breeze, Fl. 1979. For follow-on analysis, see this author's contribution to *Current History*, October 1979. For background, see surveys of Soviet China-policy in *SAFRA I* and *SAFRA II*, and this author, "Strategic Considerations Affecting Soviet Policy Towards China and Japan," *Orbis*, Winter 1974.

1979, though still focusing most of its anti-Chinese propaganda on the person of Hua, Moscow had clearly resigned itself to a period of high tension gamesmanship.

Two events typified Moscow's increasing disinclination to negotiate. When China rejected a Soviet offer to discuss improved relations, in March 1978 (due to Moscow's refusal even to consider the suggested goodwill gesture of a border pull-back), there followed highly publicized Far Eastern "inspection" trips by Secretary General L. I. Brezhnev and Minister of Defense D. F. Ustinov. Then, within a fortnight of the late April resumption of border negotiations, Peking found cause to accuse Moscow of a border violation involving the purported abduction of Chinese citizens. Moscow merely said the violation had been a "mistake," resulting from the "pursuit of a dangerous criminal." When Peking declared the explanation incongruous and unacceptable, it was ignored.

Soviet policy increasingly concentrated on containing China. One prong of this policy focused on the ideological rivalry for leadership of Third World revolutionary movements. Until the mid-1970s Soviet verbal and physical caution had given the advantage to the vigorous rhetoric of Maoism. The Soviet demonstration of new-found distant power projection means, in Angola in 1975 and in Ethiopia in early 1978, changed the situation. The new Soviet ability and willingness to intervene in distant arenas highlighted China's (logistical) inability to compete. China's frantic scrambling to counter the impression of impotence merely added to the damage by suggesting that its ideological commitment might be as hollow as her military capability. Certainly China's alliance with the American-supported and rather reactionary FNL movement in Angola began the process of disillusionment that was to split many Western Maoist parties and groupings.

The de facto anti-Mao campaign of the Hua-Teng leadership further alienated many Western Maoists. More importantly, in the Third World it seriously undermined the "idealistic" memory and connotation of Mao and Mao's China. Once Moscow had shown off its ability and willingness to more actively promote distant interests, Peking's one remaining advantage lay in the fact that its ideological stance appeared purer, less self-serving. That advantage was being lost. Peking's staunchest African allies prior to 1975, Mozambique and Tanzania, became pragmatic supporters of Soviet (and Cuban) African policies. China's only European ally, Albania, denounced its new policies as betrayal.

The other element to Soviet containment efforts was more direct. The Soviet Union strove to undermine any movement to formalize the complementarity between China's new policy stance and NATO interests. Moscow reacted with outrage when prominent Western security representatives (such as UK Air Marshal Neil Cameron or U.S. Presidential Adviser Brzezinsky) suggested the commonality of anti-Sovietism, and it warned repeatedly against the sale of Western arms to China (proposed British Harrier jet sales drew the most ire through 1978). A purported hardening of Moscow's arms control negotiating stance was said to be at least partly due to Western receptivity to Chinese courting. Conversely, China's one attempt to supplement its NATO contacts with an undermining of the Soviet Union's position in Eastern Europe, an attempt symbolized by Chairman Hua's visits to Bucharest and Belgrade, was countered by hints that Moscow and Tirana might once again find a communion of interests.

Moscow strove to ward off the prospect of a Sino-Japanese friendship treaty. Soviet concern about this treaty was heightened by the surge of nationalistic pro-military sentiment in Japan. Nevertheless, there was little indication of the kind of willingness to compromise that one might have thought would have been induced by this specter. Moscow proved unwilling to countenance the sacrifices on the disputed islands issue that its purpose would have required (see below). Similarly, the late 1978 normalizing of Sino-U.S. relations did reflect at least to a degree Moscow's refusal to contemplate such strategic arms (SALT) and other concessions as might have stayed Washington's decision to "play the China card."

Moscow's preferred policy options lay elsewhere. On the northern flank, along the Chinese border, Moscow still appeared content with the basic force size that had emerged from the buildup that followed the border squirmishes of 1969. But the pace of its qualitative upgrading efforts was stepped up. The Far Eastern region was accorded priority in the early delivery of mobile SS-20 intermediate-range ballistic missiles. It also received the latest generation combat aircraft, including the newest MIG-23 and 27 variants (the Soviet air force inventory facing China was numbered at 1,800 by mid-1978). The sixth Airborne Division, stationed at Khabarovsk, was brought up to full strength, 7,200 men. Although clearly targeted primarily against Manchuria and Peking, the division made the politically telling point of parachute maneuvers on one of the Japanese-claimed islands opposite Hokkaido (Japanese sources furthermore asserted that 5,000 troops were now stationed on these islands and that permanent bases were being constructed on two of them). A fourth major naval port was also reportedly being constructed, at Korsakov, on southern Sakhalin island.

But the most noteworthy news of 1978 came late in the fall, with Japanese reports that Moscow was assigning modern Delta-class strategic submarines to the Pacific Fleet (they had previously only been assigned to the Northern Fleet), and that it was also intending to transfer at least one of its new VTOL aircraft carriers. The latter in particular would obviously substantially enhance her interventionary potential off China's coast. Finally, there was one other news report of possible consequence for this theater of confrontation, namely, the November 1978 Warsaw Pact (minus Romania) decision to increase defense budgets. The public rationale referred to rising NATO defense budgets. But it was rumored that a Soviet desire for an increase in the pact's symbolic presence in the East was also involved.

The year 1978 also saw a number of Soviet initiatives on the potential southern flank of a direct conflict. One presumes that China was at least one (if possibly a minor) factor in Moscow's Afghan policy at the time of the April coup that installed a regime friendly to the Soviet Union, and there is some evidence of a "China consideration" at the time of the June coup in South Yemen which installed a pro-Moscow faction of the national liberation front of that country. But whatever the relevance of the "China consideration" on these events, or of the events themselves, there can be no doubt that Peking provided the glue of the crucial Soviet-Vietnamese alliance that was cemented during 1978.

The warming of Moscow-Hanoi ties had been heralded in 1977, when the Soviet Union encouraged and supported strong Vietnamese re-affirmations of its sovereignty claim over the Spartly and Paracel islands (China occupied two of the latter just prior to the American disengagement from Vietnam, and remained entrenched). Through 1978, Moscow steadfastly supported Hanoi in its growing military-political-economic confrontation with China. Leery of too great a reliance on Moscow, Hanoi long strove to settle its differences with Peking. But, as *Newsweek* put it (June 3, 1978), all Hanoi "olive branches" were "utterly rejected": "the Chinese Politburo's line does appear intransigent." Peking's ostentatious championing of the Chinese minority in Vietnam stirred xenophobic memories of earlier Chinese regimes' attempts to vassalize the peninsula. The ghost of past centuries' battles against encroachment from the north enlivened Vietnam's fears of fifth column potentials. The response, which stepped up expulsion of Vietnam's Chinese business community, served in classic fashion to defuse these fears while simultaneously satisfying demands of chauvinist resentment and ambition. The oldest dictum of *real-politik*, seek out your enemy's enemy, made Hanoi increasingly receptive to the blandishments of Moscow.

China's punitive cutting off of all aid to Hanoi, on the 3rd of July, was followed on the 29th by Vietnam's formal accession to Comecon. China's throttling of aid to Hanoi had been heralded by the withdrawal of most of China's nearly 20,000-man construction corps in Laos. An additional spur to Vietnam's Comecon move, the withdrawal had the immediate effect of conceding Hanoi's dominance in the area. Subsequent Thai reports that a missile-tracking and intelligence-gathering Soviet radar facility had been established in the Laotian border town of Suvannakhet served to spotlight the reason for Peking's displeasure and discomfort.

The unravelling of China's southern flank position continued. Public Chinese commitments to the anti-Vietnamese Pol Pot regime of "Democratic Kampuchea" (Cambodia) were followed by the November signing of a Soviet-Vietnamese friendship treaty. The announcement of Peking-Washington ties in December was followed within a fortnight by the Vietnam-sponsored "uprising" (cum invasion) that swept Cambodia in January 1979.

The latter coincidence of timing was of course just that, coincidental. The organizing and planning of Pol Pot's overthrow clearly dated back at least to that regime's suicidally provocative incursions into southern Vietnam in January

1978 (the southern Vietnamese province had once been controlled by the Khmer Cambodians). Yet the appearance of sequence was arresting. With the media still in full stride eulogizing the mutual benefit of China's rapprochement with Washington, Peking suddenly found itself more penned in by Soviet initiatives than ever before. Amidst speculation that the nebulous Chinese-U.S. alliance might give both leverage against Moscow, Peking found it had to swallow the abject humiliation of a neighboring Soviet ally overturning the one south Asian regime to which it had committed herself, and doing so in utter defiance of a Chinese military buildup on their border.

By its encouragement to and alliance with Vietnam, Moscow changed East Asian power calculations. Earlier, China could rest relatively secure that Soviet options for pressure were limited to border incidents, which could be tolerated, or else all-out nuclear assault, an eventuality that few analysts thought Moscow would contemplate except as a last resort. Since few if any could conceive of a Moscow thus persuaded, at least not within a limited time frame, the military disequilibrium remained of scant value as a political deterrent. The fact that Soviet opprobrium could only be expressed physically by too little or too much entailed considerable license for defiant action on China's part. Now, however, Moscow was acquiring a range of options for a medium-level power response. It was in a position where it might, for example, give decisive support to a yet more assertive Vietnamese presence on or around the Spratlies and Paracels (especially in the event that seismic data on oil abundance is confirmed). Moscow might itself under certain circumstances acquire "facilities" on one of the islands. Its superior naval capabilities would be eminently suitable should it decide to extend it protection of the Vietnamese homeland seaward. Or one might speculate on Soviet-Vietnamese initiatives vis-à-vis the hitherto Peking-oriented rebels of Thailand's hinterland. The power increment that the shadow of Moscow's presence gives Hanoi is of course complemented by the very real military advantage of Moscow of a large, tough, and well-equipped ally on China's southern border.

One of China's greatest advantages has derived from its geographical location and its implicit positing to Soviet planners of the dread of two-front war. The mutually advantageous *real-politik* alliance of Moscow and Hanoi meant that a similar threat for the first time became a fact of life for Chinese planners. There was little chance that Peking could finesse the finesse, for example by perpetuating anti-Vietnamese Khmer guerrilla activities. Geography and other power determinants (the state of logistics, power projection means, and so on), favoured Hanoi—and Moscow—, at least in the longer term.

China's new predicament was placed in sharp relief during and immediately after Deng Xiaoping's historic early 1979 visit to the United States. Again and again the point was made that China could not accept Vietnam's "brazen interference" in Cambodia. Japanese sources described a further influx of Chinese land and air units to staging areas near Vietnam's border. Washington shied away from explicit support, and Thailand ducked repeated Chinese requests to allow arms transits to forces opposed to the new masters of Phnom Penh. But Vietnam's Navy appeared finally to have succeeded in choking off Chinese gunrunning to Cambodia's coast and islands. This meant that action that was to have a chance of success could not long be postponed. Moscow tried to ward it off. A Soviet naval squadron sailed into the Gulf of Tonkin. In Moscow, Prime Minister Kosygin described China's "outrageous charges" against Vietnam and the Soviet Union as being akin to "a declaration of war," and Kremlin leaders (in the established guise of an "Alexandrov" commentary in *Pravda*) warned that China must end its "unconcealed military pressure" on Hanoi. More intensive air patrols and fighter sorties along the border underlined the Soviet stance. Yet, the momentum of China's commitment and buildup, said to have reached between 330,000 and 360,000 men, was not immediately deflected.

THE WAR

On the morning of February 17, tank-led assaults crossed along the length of the border. Peking claimed the intent was to "punish" Vietnam, not to occupy permanently or annex territory. But its forces soon funneled into what looked like two Hanoi-directed prongs, aiming through Lang Son and Lao Cai. Hanoi's defenses, down to about 50,000 men (many of the best divisions remained in the south, supporting the new Cambodian regime's pacification efforts) deployed in an arc north of the capital. On day one, the Chinese forces reportedly gained ten kilometers. Although claiming limited success (200–250 Chinese troops killed; an undisclosed number of tanks disabled), Hanoi lost no time calling for Soviet and world support. Moscow reacted with a sharp initial condemnation of the invasion. By day two, with Chinese forces 16 kilometers into Vietnamese territory, Moscow followed up with a sharper warning to withdraw while there was yet time. Moscow said categorically that it would if necessary live up to the mutual defense obligations implied by the Soviet-Vietnamese friendship treaty (it asserted considerable faith in Vietnam's own ability to repel the aggressors), and it orchestrated a national outpouring of expectant outrage. The same day saw more confident assertions from Hanoi (a considerable number of Chinese units were delcared to have been destroyed or to be surrounded) and the first reports of Vietnamese bombing inside China. The third day saw Hanoi claims that 3,500 Chinese troops had been killed and over 80 tanks destroyed. Chinese forces were now said to be only ten kilometers from the border. There was speculation that the strength of resistance and outside pressure might be forcing re-evaluation and withdrawal. Vietnam signed a defiant concordat with its Phnom Penh allies, as Washington "intelligence" told of evidence that Moscow was considering its own mini-invasion of China; in Peking Deng Xiaoping hastened to stress the limited (though still ill-defined) nature of China's intent. The question of Chinese withdrawal then became uncertain; Washington sources talked of lack of clear evidence. Soviet spokesmen announced that their forces had been put on alert.

The next day brought news of increased fighting, some new Chinese advances (especially around Lao Cai), and further Chinese troop reinforcements. Hanoi countered by recalling some of its Cambodian-based forces. Soviet Foreign Minister Gromyko repeated Moscow's blunt warnings. Chinese evaculation of Manchurian and Sinkiang border regions was announced, as was an alert of troops in these areas. The following day, the fifth, saw China pressing an attack against Lang Son. But Hanoi asserted that this attack had been beaten back, thus offsetting the psychological effect of apparent Chinese success against Lao Cai. Hanoi took time out to celebrate their new treaty-defined status in Cambodia (the treaty specified that Vietnam had the right to station "advisors" in Cambodia to "preserve the territorial integrity" of that nation—the same language as had earlier formalized the Vietnamese presence in Laos). Soviet planes repeated earlier overflights over the battle zone and, according to Japanese evidence, began overflights over sectors of China's Pacific coast; the Soviet naval detachments in the South China Sea and off Vietnam were beefed up.

Peking appeared to be battling for the kind of symbolic field victory that would allow withdrawal to be accompanied by a 'mission accomplished' claim, gambling that this could be effected before and without precipitating major Soviet initiatives. Moscow, on the other hand, clearly hoped that their force demonstrations would suffice or that Hanoi would succeed in repelling the invaders by itself. The fact that Hanoi had not yet committed its premier battle-hardened divisions encouraged at least some optimism on this score. The optimism was buttressed by Vietnamese statements that while conducting "a very close exchange of views" with Moscow, "we are prepared [at present] to cope with the worst situation." Such an outcome would leave uncluttered a Soviet public relations advantage of major proportions. India had issued a cautious condemnation of China's action. The PLO (Palestine Liberation Organization) had terminated its 14-year relationship with Peking. Others were following suit. The suggestion of Chinese aggressive tendencies doused the prospect of Western arm sales (posing acute embarrassment for British Industry Minister Varley, en route to Peking to complete a major deal centering on the Harrier fighter). The tarring-by-association of the US (Tass noted that the *New York Times* found grounds "to state that the U.S. was informed about China's forthcoming attack against Vietnam") suggested U.S. complicity but also reinforced allegations that Peking was now a conscious tool of "imperialist" ambition. China was said to be acting as a proxy for U.S. interests bent on revenging their own humiliation at the hands of Hanoi. It was a propaganda theme that found receptive ears. However, appreciation of this fact also acted as a goad to Peking, making it more difficult to withdraw without some achievement of substance.

The sixth day began with a Chinese advance beyond Lao Cai, to about 25 kilometers from the border, and a major Chinese build-up against Lang Son.

Hanoi reinforcements were said for the first time to include some regular front-line troops. Lang Son seemed set for a confrontation of some significance. At this time it was reported that a Soviet troop concentration was in progress along the Sino-Soviet frontier and that troops in Outer Mongolia had mobilized (it is not clear whether this referred to Mongolian forces or only Soviet forces stationed in Mongolia); China meanwhile was said to have extended its mobilization to Inner Mongolia. Moscow also sent a "command destroyer" with "a senior admiral" aboard to join its southern flotilla. This was followed on day seven by still increasing Chinese pressure against Lang Son coupled with a new prong to the southeast which was presumed to be aimed at cutting highway four and encircling Lang Son defenders. Vietnamese forces answered with artillery shelling into China's Quang Tri province.

The second week of fighting opened with a large-scale Soviet sealift of missiles and material beginning to unload at Haiphong. China was said to have launched limited air strikes against inland warehouses supposed to have received some of the supplies, but damage was acknowledged to be limited, and Hanoi apparently did not engage its intercepters. A major Soviet airlift was reported also to be underway. By the next day, a three-front Chinese artillery barrage was said to have become more intense than anything seen during the U.S. engagement in Vietnam. Yet, while Moscow was coordinating steadily mounting pressure and support in aid of its ally, it still apparently had not felt compelled to call up the reserves needed to provide a full complement for all its Far Eastern border divisions.

In fact, Moscow appeared increasingly confident that Vietnam would succeed in thwarting Peking intentions. The Chinese statement later that day, that it (now?) would "not move into the flatlands of the Red River Delta," a de facto concession that Hanoi was immune, might merely have been a belated defining of original modesty; but it would be logical to presume that it also bore a relation to problems on the ground and around the periphery. Still, while Peking apparently found it necessary to specify that it would not (or could not) defy the presumed limit to relative Soviet restraint, it did need that one victory of seeming substance. Japanese officials announced their understanding that "the mauling of at least one Vietnamese division" was the current aim and that a final concerted Chinese buildup and drive to this end was in progress. The massive artillery shelling continued. Hanoi serenely (if perhaps deceptively so) repeated claims of mounting Chinese casualties. If their figure of over 16,000 Chinese killed was thought to be exaggerated, many analysts nevertheless gave credence to assertions that China had suffered disproportionately higher casualty rates. The crawling and indeed halting pace of China's advance, against less than Hanoi's best, gave heart to its antagonist(s). A Chinese hint that its eventual pullback would be to the border as drawn in Peking and not necessarily as drawn on international maps, reinforced scepticism. It suggested a limited-area border occupation as a final fallback aim, in the event that regular Hanoi divisions proved too hardshelled to crack. But Peking had not yet resigned itself to that proposition.

By the tenth day of conflict, the deepest thrust of Chinese advance, in the northwestern sector of the front, reached 40 kilometers into Vietnam. Hanoi announced that engaged Chinese forces now stood at 25 divisions, divided into 5 army corps. The number of Chinese combat troops (as distinct from support and logistics personnel) was said to exceed the highest total assembled by the United States during its involvement in Vietnam. Deng Xiaoping pointedly welcomed a U.S. call for Chinese withdrawal from Vietnam to be coupled with Vietnamese withdrawal from Cambodia. Moscow warned of Chinese designs against Laos.

But the original invasion plans had clearly gone astray. Fighting continued at an intense level through the following day. No further Chinese advances were reported, however. In fact, Peking had to acknowledge the galling news that Vietnam had made two substantial counter-thrusts into China itself. One roving battalion had struck towards Nanning at the end of the first week of fighting and had succeeded in operating inside China for at least three days. Furthermore, it now appeared that reports of Chinese 'strategic' bombing inside Vietnam had been exaggerated and possibly fictitious, and that China continued to shy away from confronting Hanoi's sophisticated air defenses. Chinese media calls for negotiations to end the war were effectively rebuffed. Hanoi said it would not talk with Chinese troops on its soil.

Increasing Chinese pressure focused on Lang Son. Six divisions and over 100 artillery pieces had reportedly been assembled for the assault. The town had been evacuated, but Vietnamese defenders were dug in on heights overlooking the town from the south. Amid constant artillery barrages between the defenders and Chinese concentrations to the north, east, and west, Chinese infantry evidently launched a number of "human wave" assaults on the town below. But while many of the town's facilities, including the hospital, were destroyed by the incessant shelling, physical occupation was thwarted again and again. Vietnam claimed to be inflicting "heavy losses," putting total Chinese dead at 27,000. The Lang Son battle became psychologically important because it saw the involvement of one of Hanoi's finer infantry divisions, the first Vietnamese front-line division to be thrown into the fray.

In the fighting to date Vietnam had employed only militia and regional forces, not main-force army units. The rather astonishing success of the "irregular" forces not only reflected on their mettle; their tenacity had flaunted and acutely embarrassed China's hopes of at least braking some of Hanoi's vaunted front-line troops. The presence of regular Vietnamese troops by Lang Son appeared to act as a magnet for Chinese reinforcements. But although Hanoi evidently felt forced to call back more of its Cambodia-based units (though not enough to undermine seriously its Phnom Penh ally), the next days saw no Chinese breakthrough. The first Chinese claim that it had taken Lang Son came on the final day of the second week of fighting. Even then, Hanoi refuted the claim. It appeared that the most China might have achieved was that its flanking pressure had caused a limited and ordered withdrawal by the defenders. Subsequent "Thai intelligence sources" indicated that the town of Lang Son had not actually been occupied, that Chinese forces had extended their hold on the surrounding highlands, but that Vietnamese defenders remained entrenched on some of the hills to the south and southeast. A U.S. analyst commented that a Chinese platoon might have managed to scurry in and out under cover of darkness; certainly there was no evidence to corroborate further cliams. The fact that a new formal Chinese request for negotiations no longer made any reference to the earlier demand that Vietnam end its role in Cambodia also buttressed Hanoi's credibility.

China's battlefield problems were compounded by an intensification of Soviet pressure. Planted rumors that Moscow would send "volunteers" to the Vietnamese front, a *Pravda* warning that the war "can" expand if China did not withdraw "immediately," a Kosygin affirmation that Vietnam "will not be abandoned in a time of trial" (he also warned against a Chinese invasion of Laos and declared that "the changes which have taken place in Cambodia are irreversible"), and a Brezhenv threat that a Laotian incursion would bring "harsh retribution," together with another notching up of Soviet naval strength and activity in the South China Sea, were squeezing estimates of the time still at China's disposal. At the same time Japanese Foreign Minister Sonoda's statement that China's actions were "unjust" brought home international image ramifications. The Chinese claim at the end of the week that "two or three" Vietnamese divisions had been destroyed was clearly false, since Vietnam had not engaged that many of its regulars. But it was a claim demanded by considerations of 'face' and propaganda, in the event of PRC disengagement. It therefore appeared to augur a Chinese desire to effect withdrawal.

As the third week began, Chinese officials did indeed talk of imminent withdrawal; by day sixteen, Japanese sources claimed that some withdrawal had in fact begun. But the same day saw Hanoi exhibiting Chinese prisoners, the first airlift speeding Vietnamese reinforcements northward, and a declaration of general Vietnamese mobilization—for a "war of resistance." The day also brought "informed" speculation that Moscow would feel impelled sooner or later to administer "punishment" of its own, even if China now extricated itself. Hanoi asserted that the battle for Lang Son was in fact continuing. This was followed by a Chinese statement that it was beginning to withdraw its forces and a call for future friendship. Hanoi, however, declared the statement a sham, a smokescreen for continued assault, and said that it was pressing the fight. The rationale for the conflict had already been overtaken by the morass of the battlefield; it appeared that its termination might be equally confounding to the assumptions of planners—one of history's oldest lessons.

On March 6, with three front-line divisions reportedly readied for attack, Hanoi again said that it would negotiate peace if China withdrew immediately, totally, and unconditionally. The next day brought a Hanoi claim of "splendid victory" (contrasting with Peking assertions that its "aims" had been achieved), a statement that Chinese troops would be allowed to withdraw unmolested, and a caution that any further Chinese combat activity would be "severely punished." Specifically, Hanoi asserted that the molesting of civilians and looting of homes, purportedly engaged in by retreating Chinese, had to stop, or it would rescind its promise to allow unharrassed withdrawal. China claimed 10,000 Vietnamese killed or wounded, 1,000 prisoners; Hanoi said it had "put out of action 45,000 enemy soldiers, 273 tanks and armored personnel carriers and hit hundreds of artillery pieces and mortars." Japan began to act as an intermediary. As the third week ended, Hanoi expressed scepticism, suggesting once more that China's withdrawal was a ruse to gain respite and time to reinforce. Clashes were said to be continuing north of Lang Son and in other frontier areas. But the general ferocity of the fighting seemed to have abated; the war appeared to be winding down.

Still, the military and political problems of Chinese withdrawal defied easy management. More Hanoi charges of atrocities were followed by reports of intensified battle. Hanoi accused China of burning and plundering. Peking accused Vietnam of stepped-up harrassment and attack, including renewed shelling into Chinese territory. New reports of Chinese pressure on the Laotian border heightened the uncertainty generated by the fighting on the main front. Attempts to hurry withdrawal grated against attempts to insure its orderliness. The contradiction kept alive fears of further conflagration. There clearly remained a danger that the apparent end to the conflict might yet prove to be merely the end of its first phase.

At this juncture the immediate score sheet looked as follows: China had not succeeded in changing the course of events in Laos or Cambodia. In spite of reports that it had not expected to succeed, that PLA officers had in fact supported the action on the premise that the expected defeat would be the surest guarantee of future funding commitments of substance, a consideration of Peking's initial propaganda stance nevertheless indicates that there must have been some hope of greater achievement. There may not have been any intention to attack Hanoi itself, although Vietnam had to prepare for the eventuality. The odds on Moscow intervening if required for the defence of Hanoi/Haiphong were too great. On the other hand, it would appear logical to presume that China might have hoped to be able to take and hold a 15–25 kilometer strip south of the border. If such a strip could have been secured, then it might indeed have been able to bargain for "mutual withdrawal." It clearly could not be secured. Still, while one must conclude that China was not able to demonstrate the capabilities that it would have liked, it did demonstrate "will"—and this may in fact have been the sum total of its expectation, and motive. Peking had scorned Washington for not backing up its acknowledged means with the requisite will. It had now demonstrated that while it might fall short as concerns the former, it did not fall short on the latter point. Peking also succeeded in seriously souring Moscow-Washington Relations, at little cost. (The tilt inherent in Washington's "evenhandedness" and the fact that the scheduled exchange of ambassadors went ahead in the midst of the conflict reflected more favorably on China's diplomacy than on that of the Potomac).

Vietnam, on the other hand, seemed once again to have taught a larger nation not to presume on apparent power discrepancies. The conflict had also diverted attention from admittedly serious economic reconstruction problems. It provided the pretext for the re-establishment of a war economy, the type of mobilized command economy to which their experience was suited. The war served as a valuable patriotic unifier and reinforcer.

Finally, through its carefully calibrated escalation of pressure and commitment, Moscow appeared to have succeeded in "proving" that it would not desert an ally in need. It had done enough to retain its own credibility, yet not enough to sully the memory of Chinese "aggression."

THE "PHONY WAR"

The remarkable fact that apparent victors and apparent vanquished could all claim success was not, however, to prove a recipe for stability. Subsequent weeks saw the ensconcement of a "phony war" state of high tension, suspicion and jitteryness, accompanying determined preparations for a possible resumption of military hostilities. After formal Chinese assertions that a full withdrawal had been effected, in mid-March, Chinese officials were invited to an abortive "peace talks" session in Hanoi. A Hanoi suggestion of a demilitarized zone along the border was not followed up. Mutual recriminations made further talks impractical. Hanoi returned to its charges that Chinese withdrawal had not been complete. China insisted it had, and countered with repeated claims of Vietnamese shelling and incursions north of the border. Hanoi, Laos, and Moscow all made new charges of Chinese force demonstrations and intent along the Sino-Laotian border. Laos expelled the final remnants of the Chinese construction corps on its soil, reaffirming its allegiance to Hanoi.

Vietnam remained mobilized. Some of the front line troops thus released were thrown into a concerted campaign to break remaining Khmer Rouge guerrilla concentrations before the onset of the rainy season. By mid April reports were made that the last significant rebel redoubt, against the Thai border, was being over-run. In the meantime, Hanoi had continued its more rapid movement of premier divisions to the northern border regions of both Vietnam and Laos. The scale of the buildup was thought by a number of western analysts to exceed defensive requirements.

Soviet Air Force units were provided to facilitate Vietnamese troop and equipment transport, in Vietnam, Cambodia and Laos. The Soviet Navy began to call on Cam Ranh Bay. Vietnam denied that Moscow had received or would receive permanent base rights. Nevertheless, the extension of limited repair and provisioning facilities had evidently been seen to answer mutual interests, and this was continued. April also saw the movement of the Soviet Union's new VTOL aircraft carrier, the Minsk, around Africa and into the Indian Ocean, evidently on its way to join the Pacific Fleet. The timing of the cruise astounded western naval analysts who had presumed that the Minsk was scheduled for a much longer testing period in its launch area in the Black Sea. The obvious inference was to highlight the premium Moscow attached to the Minsk's presence in the Far East. The military-political impact of its appearance off African and Indian Ocean rim countries, while considerable, was clearly not alone sufficient to hazard extraordinary procedures. The possibility of the Minsk "observing" a Vietnamese "visit" to the two Chinese-occupied Paracel islands suggested itself as a more plausible rationale, especially in view of Chinese April claims that Soviet and Vietnamese naval demonstrations had already taken place in the area.

There remained many uncertainties. For the longer-term future, there was little doubt that Moscow remained desirous of accommodation—if too arrogantly so—and that the aspiration found at least limited echo in Peking. But for the immediate future, power politics remained the name of the game. In view of scepticism as to the ultimate character and steadfastness of U.S. aid to China there was surprising but compelling reason to suggest that it was Moscow that emerged from 1978 and early 1979 with the better hand. Certainly China's action against Vietnam indicated that it feared this to be true and, furthermore, that it considered the consequences to be so detrimental to its interests that a major gamble was required.

The very fact that this balancing of accounts can be suggested with a semblance of logic is important. It is particularly important if juxtaposed to evidence that the 'China consideration' acted as a spur also to assertive Soviet policies in other regions. Washington and other NATO capitals professed to think of the political effect of their China policies as the handicapping of Moscow. It led instead to a greater Soviet willingness to pursue particular interests elsewhere, as indeed appeared to be the case, then the weighting of benefits would become a murkier affair altogether.

INDEX

ABOUT THE AUTHOR

C. G. JACOBSEN completed a doctoral thesis on "Strategic Factors in Soviet Foreign Policy" in 1970 at the Institute of Soviet and East European Studies, Glasgow University, Glasgow, Scotland. He spent 1970-71 in Moscow on a British Council Fellowship. This was followed by appointments with Carleton University's School of International Affairs and Institute of Soviet Studies, in Ottawa, with Columbia University's Russian Institute, in New York, and with Harvard University's Center for International Affairs, in Cambridge. Dr. Jacobsen is presently Professor of Strategic Studies at Acadia University, in Canada. A frequent government consultant, he is the author of the book *Soviet Strategy – Soviet Foreign Policy* and has published many articles on Soviet strategy and doctrine.